Critical Perspectives on the Security and Protection of Human Rights Defenders

Edited by
Karen Bennett, Danna Ingleton, Alice M. Nah and James Savage

Routledge
Taylor & Francis Group
LONDON AND NEW YORK

First published 2016
by Routledge
2 Park Square, Milton Park, Abingdon, Oxon, OX14 4RN, UK

and by Routledge
711 Third Avenue, New York, NY 10017, USA

First issued in papperback 2017

Routledge is an imprint of the Taylor & Francis Group, an informa business

British Library Cataloguing in Publication Data
A catalogue record for this book is available from the British Library

ISBN 13: 978-1-138-10560-7 (pbk)
ISBN 13: 978-1-138-68299-3 (hbk)

Typeset in Times New Roman
by RefineCatch Limited, Bungay, Suffolk

Publisher's Note
The publisher accepts responsibility for any inconsistencies that may have arisen during the conversion of this book from journal articles to book chapters, namely the possible inclusion of journal terminology.

Critical Perspectives on the Security and Protection of Human Rights Defenders

Human rights defenders – who by peaceful means promote and strive for the protection of the rights and freedoms of others and of themselves – are key agents of change in their own societies. They highlight injustices, strive for equality, advocate against discrimination, and call for accountability where human rights are threatened.

While many defenders are able to conduct their work in safety, many are put at risk for challenging those in power and for acting against social, cultural, and religious norms.

Since the United Nations General Assembly's adoption of the Declaration on Human Rights Defenders in 1998, there has been considerable effort to recognise and protect the right of individuals, groups and communities to promote and protect their own rights and the rights of others. Over time, a multi-level, multi-actor international protection regime for the rights of human rights defenders has emerged, which is based on rights, principles and values of the the international human rights regime.

The authors in this book reflect on the positive developments that have emerged over time to strengthen the protection of defenders, as well as the debates, tensions and contestations in such practices. This collection provides a critical appraisal of the construction, function, ethical boundaries, and evolution of this protection regime, as well as its multi-scalar social and political effects. In particular, the authors consider the effectiveness of international and regional protection mechanisms for defenders and examine the relationship between repression, activism, and tactics for managing risks in the face of danger.

This book was originally published as a special issue of *The International Journal of Human Rights.*

Karen Bennett is Senior Research Fellow in Human Rights and Director of the Human Rights and Social Justice Research (HRSJ) Institute at London Metropolitan University, UK. She teaches and conducts research in human rights, including assessing implementation of human rights protection mechanisms that support human rights defenders, and designs human rights capacity building training programmes (primarily in conflict and post-conflict countries).

Danna Ingleton has a feminist and legal human rights background and has worked with numerous international organisations such as the Red Cross, the Organisation for Security and Cooperation in Europe and Amnesty International. She works on issues related to NGO and advocacy ethics, including informed consent, participatory approaches and data management.

Alice M. Nah is a Lecturer at the Centre for Applied Human Rights, University of York, UK. She conducts research on human rights defenders at risk, migration and asylum in Asia and organisational effectiveness in civil society.

James Savage is Program Officer for the Enabling Environment for Human Rights Defenders at the Fund for Global Human Rights. Previously he was Director of the Human Rights Defenders Programme at Amnesty International UK, where his work involved research, policy, advocacy, campaigning, capacity-building, grant-making and direct protection interventions in support of HRDs at risk and their enabling.

Contents

Citation Information

The chapters in this book were originally published in *The International Journal of Human Rights*, volume 19, issue 7 (October 2015). When citing this material, please use the original page numbering for each article, as follows:

Chapter 1
Critical perspectives on the security and protection of human rights defenders
Karen Bennett, Danna Ingleton, Alice M. Nah and James Savage
The International Journal of Human Rights, volume 19, issue 7 (October 2015)
pp. 883–895

Chapter 2
Towards developing a critical and ethical approach for better recognising and protecting human rights defenders
Luis Enrique Eguren Fernández and Champa Patel
The International Journal of Human Rights, volume 19, issue 7 (October 2015)
pp. 896–907

Chapter 3
European Union Guidelines on Human Rights Defenders: a review of policy and practice towards effective implementation
Karen Bennett
The International Journal of Human Rights, volume 19, issue 7 (October 2015)
pp. 908–934

Chapter 4
Protecting human rights defenders at risk: asylum and temporary international relocation
Martin Jones
The International Journal of Human Rights, volume 19, issue 7 (October 2015)
pp. 935–960

Chapter 5
Political opportunities in non-democracies: the case of Chinese weiquan *lawyers*
Elisa Nesossi
The International Journal of Human Rights, volume 19, issue 7 (October 2015)
pp. 961–978

Chapter 6

Violence and human rights in Russia: how human rights defenders develop their tactics in the face of danger, 2005–2013
Freek van der Vet and Laura Lyytikäinen
The International Journal of Human Rights, volume 19, issue 7 (October 2015) pp. 979–998

Notes on Contributors

Karen Bennett is Senior Research Fellow in Human Rights and Director of the Human Rights and Social Justice Research (HRSJ) Institute at London Metropolitan University, UK. She teaches and conducts research in human rights, including assessing implementation of human rights protection mechanisms that support human rights defenders, and designs human rights capacity building training programmes (primarily in conflict and post-conflict countries).

Luis Enrique Eguren Fernández is Guest Lecturer and Researcher at the Human Rights Institute of the University of Deusto (Bilbao, Spain), and Researcher with Protection International (Brussels). He has worked on different aspects of the protection of human rights defenders for the last 25 years.

Danna Ingleton has a feminist and legal human rights background and has worked with numerous international organisations such as the Red Cross, the Organisation for Security and Cooperation in Europe and Amnesty International. She works on issues related to NGO and advocacy ethics, including informed consent, participatory approaches and data management.

Martin Jones is Lecturer in International Human Rights Law at the Centre for Applied Human Rights and the York Law School at the University of York, UK. He conducts research and teaches on the emergence and significance of the human rights defender regime; the refugee protection regime (primarily as manifest in the Middle East and Asia); and the relationship between the two regimes.

Laura Lyytikäinen is a Postdoctoral Researcher in the Department of Social Research, University of Turku, Finland. She has conducted research on civil society, political opposition and youth activism in Russia.

Alice M. Nah is a Lecturer at the Centre for Applied Human Rights, University of York, UK. She conducts research on human rights defenders at risk, migration and asylum in Asia and organisational effectiveness in civil society.

Elisa Nesossi is a Research Fellow at the Australian Centre on China in the World, Australian National University. Her research interests include Chinese law and institutions, human rights law, and practice and comparative criminal justice.

Champa Patel is the Interim Director of Amnesty International Secretariat's South Asia and South East Asia Pacific Regional Office. She previously worked as Head of the Campaigns Programme at Amnesty International UK where she was active in research, campaigning, advocacy, and the management of human rights defender protection actions.

James Savage is Program Officer for the Enabling Environment for Human Rights Defenders at the Fund for Global Human Rights. Previously he was Director of the Human Rights Defenders Programme at Amnesty International UK, where his work involved research, policy, advocacy, campaigning, capacity-building, grant-making and direct protection interventions in support of HRDs at risk and their enabling.

Freek van der Vet is a Postdoctoral Fellow at the Liu Institute for Global Issues at the University of British Columbia, Canada. He conducts research on human rights protection in Russia and the Caucasus, strategic litigation before international courts, and transitional justice after violent conflict.

Critical perspectives on the security and protection of human rights defenders

Karen Bennett[a], Danna Ingleton[b], Alice M. Nah[c] and James Savage[d]

[a]Human Rights and Social Justice Research Institute, London Metropolitan University, UK; [b]Amnesty International Secretariat; [c]Centre for Applied Human Rights, University of York, UK; [d]Amnesty International, UK

Since the United Nations General Assembly's adoption of the Declaration on Human Rights Defenders in 1998, there has been considerable effort to recognise and protect the right of individuals, groups and communities to promote and protect their own rights and the rights of others. Over time, a multi-level, multi-actor international protection regime for the rights of human rights defenders has emerged, derived from the international human rights regime. Actors in this goal-driven regime adopt a human security approach, emphasising the importance of having a holistic, multi-dimensional understanding of 'security'. In this article, we note positive developments in state commitment to the protection of defenders, as well as the debates, tensions and contestation that continue to exist. We emphasise the need for critical appraisal of the construction, function and evolution of this protection regime as well as its multi-scalar social and political effects, both intended and unintended. We highlight three specific areas where critical scholarship is needed to understand the nature of this protection regime, discussing the contributions of authors in this special issue: the definition and use of the term 'human rights defender'; the effectiveness of protection mechanisms; and the complex relationship between repression, activism and risk. In conclusion, we identify key areas for further research related to human rights defenders, stressing the need for the development of theory and practice related to their 'risk', 'security' and 'protection'.

The human rights defender protection regime

The United Nations (UN) General Assembly's adoption of the 1998 Declaration on the Right and Responsibility of Individuals, Groups and Organs of Society to Promote and Protect Universally Recognized Human Rights and Fundamental Freedoms (commonly known as the Declaration on Human Rights Defenders)[1] marked a milestone in the development of a multi-level, multi-actor international protection regime for the rights of human rights defenders. This regime has had a long genesis; the declaration itself was a product of a 'slow and drawn-out drafting process' lasting over 15 years, marked by tension, disagreement and compromise.[2] Since its adoption however, there has been considerable effort to recognise and protect the right of individuals, groups and communities to promote and protect their own rights and the rights of others.

What are the key features of the human rights defender protection regime? First, it derives its 'principles, norms, rules, and decision-making procedures around which actor expectations converge'[3] from the international human rights regime. The declaration itself did not create new rights, but 'reaffirms rights that are instrumental to the defence of human rights'.[4] Over time, a number of key principles have emerged in the operation of this regime. These include: the recognition of local actors as key agents of change; the importance of promoting and protecting 'civil society space'[5]; the need to tailor protection interventions to meet the unique and specific needs of individuals, groups and communities[6]; and the necessity of complementing reactive measures with efforts to build a 'safe and enabling environment' for the defence of human rights.[7]

Second, the regime is goal driven – its aim is to protect and support defenders who operate in their own contexts in the face of threats and risks. Depending on the circumstances and the actors involved, these threats and risks might include surveillance, harassment, verbal and written threats, stigmatisation, criminalisation, restrictions on funding and registration as non-governmental organisations (NGOs), arbitrary arrest and detention, spurious investigations, fabricated charges, unfair trials, kidnapping, torture, ill-treatment and killings.[8] Perpetrators range from state actors to non-state actors – such as government officials, armed forces, police officers, religious fundamentalists, transnational corporations and criminal gangs. In a significant number of cases, defenders do not know the identity of those who attack them.[9]

Third, the regime adopts a human security paradigm, with individuals, groups and communities as subjects of security rather than states. Its goal-driven, practice-oriented, rights-based nature helps actors in this regime sidestep some of the debates that question the usefulness of the human security paradigm for meaningful action, policy and research.[10] Similar to proponents of a 'broad' human security approach (in particular, those who adopt a feminist framework[11]), defenders and practitioners have emphasised the importance of having a holistic, multi-dimensional understanding of 'security'. Women human rights defenders, in particular, emphasise the importance of understanding how discrimination, stereotyping and stigmatisation – rooted in social structures in society, such as patriarchy and the militarisation of society – compromise security.[12]

Jane Barry and Vaida Nainar reflect on how women human rights defenders define security as including: freedom from constant threats, economic security, political security, environmental security and health security, which resonate with definitions of human security that encompass the dimensions of 'freedom from want' and 'freedom from fear'. Drawing upon reflections of women human rights defenders around the world, they introduce the term 'integrated security':

> For us, security has to be integrated, which means employment, social wellbeing, development and national sovereignty in terms of natural resources. Security is not only for the individual, but also for the community.[13]

This concept – especially its emphasis on self-care and personal wellbeing – has resonated deeply with defenders around the world.[14] Organisations that conduct security training (such as Front Line Defenders, Protection International and Tactical Technology Collective) draw attention to the importance of interventions in three interconnected domains – physical security, digital security and self-care. Some defenders and practitioners argue that self-care is both a necessary act of physical and psychological protection as well as a political strategy for sustaining and furthering the work of defenders.[15]

Fourth, it is a multi-level regime – formal protection mechanisms for human rights defenders exist at the national, regional and international levels. In Mexico, for example, defenders are able to seek protection measures from the government through the 2012 Law for the Protection of Human Rights Defenders and Journalists[16]; make urgent appeal to the UN Special Rapporteur on the Situation of Human Rights Defenders to request the government to take all appropriate action on behalf of a human rights defender at risk; gain practical support from European Union (EU) embassies on the basis of the EU Guidelines on Human Rights Defenders; and make petitions to the Inter-American Commission on Human Rights (IACHR) in the hope that it will request Mexico to adopt precautionary measures to prevent 'irreparable harm' to the defender. However, there is geographical unevenness in the availability of protection mechanisms. Many countries have neither enacted laws nor created institutions that recognise and protect the rights of human rights defenders.

Fifth, the regime has many stakeholders – civil society groups, donors, national human rights institutions, states, multilateral bodies and individual defenders – who create and use different types of tools, strategies and tactics to identify, support and protect the rights of human rights defenders. These include the provision of emergency grants, temporary relocation initiatives, security training, advocacy, accompaniment, trial monitoring, networking and capacity building.[17]

In the next section of this article we show how there has been growing commitment by some governments to protect human rights defenders around the world. We then contrast these developments with examples of how other governments continue to challenge the legitimacy of defenders and restrict their rights. We turn to three specific areas where critical scholarship is needed, highlighting the contributions of authors in this special issue: the definition and use of the term 'human rights defender'; the effectiveness of protection mechanisms; and the complex relationship between repression, activism and risk. Emphasising the need for critical appraisal of the construction, function and evolution of this protection regime as well as its multi-scalar social and political effects, intended and unintended, we identify key areas for further research.

Developments in the normative framework

Over the past three years, there have been a number of initiatives that strengthen the normative framework for the protection of human rights defenders. At the national level, Switzerland's Federal Department of Foreign Affairs published guidelines on the protection of human rights defenders in 2013, aimed at making the work of Swiss diplomats and officials in this area of work more coherent, systematic and effective.[18] That same year, the United Kingdom issued its first National Action Plan to implement the UN Guiding Principles on Business and Human Rights, which included strengthening support to defenders engaged in business and human rights problems.[19] In 2014, Côte d'Ivoire adopted the Law on the Promotion and Protection of Human Rights Defenders – the first African state to enact specific legislation to protect human rights defenders.[20]

At the regional level in Europe, both the Council of the EU and the Organization for Security and Cooperation in Europe (OSCE) have strengthened their contribution to this protection regime through recent policy developments. In 2014, the EU marked the 10th anniversary of its European Union Guidelines on Human Rights Defenders by committing better support for vulnerable and marginalised human rights defenders, women human rights defenders and those operating in remote regions; advocating for the creation of a safe and enabling environment for human rights defenders; and strengthening the implementation of an effective and coherent policy on human rights defenders.[21] The OSCE (within its Office of Democratic Institutions and Human Rights) initiated extensive consultations with human rights defenders and other human rights experts across the OSCE geographic regions to develop the OSCE Guidelines on the Protection of Human Rights Defenders, published in June 2014, to harness better protection and support for human rights defenders by member states.[22]

Internationally, in 2013, the Group of Eight (G8) adopted a Declaration on Preventing Sexual Violence in Conflict that acknowledged the vital role of women human rights defenders, committing to provide them with better protection.[23] In 2013, the UN General Assembly passed the first ever resolution on the protection of women human rights defenders.[24] The UN Human Rights Council has also passed a number of important resolutions that signify its commitment to the protection of human rights defenders. This included Resolution 22/6 on Protecting Human Rights Defenders in March 2013, which outlined the gravity of the deteriorating climate for human rights practice around the world. This resolution emphasised that more must be done to address attacks and reprisals against defenders, unjust laws that criminalise defenders, and impunity for actions against defenders.[25]

States have also recognised that some human rights defenders are particularly vulnerable – such as those who work on contested issues (such as sexual and reproductive rights, and rights abuses related to extractive industries, land and the environment) as well as those who hold particular identities and come from specific communities (such as women human rights defenders, LGBTI (lesbian, gay, bisexual, transgender and intersex) defenders and indigenous people).[26] States have also raised concerns about the security of defenders in a number of ways, including through the Universal Periodic Review (UPR) process.

In 2014, the outgoing UN Special Rapporteur on the situation of human rights defenders, Margaret Sekaggya, used her last report to the Human Rights Council to set out a framework for building a 'safe and enabling environment' for defenders.[27] The new Special Rapporteur Michel Forst, in his first report, reemphasised the importance of disseminating the declaration and raising the visibility of the situation of human rights defenders. He committed to addressing national legislative impediments to the work of defenders; challenging impunity for human rights violations against defenders; and tackling reprisals against defenders, in particular those who engage with the UN and other international and regional human rights mechanisms.[28]

Debates, tensions, contestation

While there have been positive developments in the evolution of this regime, some states continue to challenge the recognition, legitimacy and integrity of the work of defenders. Defenders continue to be attacked, even in countries where they have legally enforceable rights to promote and protect human rights. National laws and administrative practices that criminalise defenders have been justified by some states in terms of their measures to protect national sovereignty; counter terrorism and extremism; further economic security and development; and assert particular cultural, traditional and religious norms and practices. In September 2014, for example, the Egyptian government revised Article 78 of its Penal Code introducing severe penalties for those accessing or facilitating access to foreign funding. In India, every NGO receiving funds from 'foreign sources' requires either prior permission or registration under the Foreign Contribution Regulation Act (FCRA) 2010. This legislation has been used to target those dissenting from the economic model pursued by successive governments that violates the human rights of Adivasi tribal peoples and other communities.[29]

In countries where laws are enacted to criminalise human rights defenders' practice, more research is needed to document the immediate impact on defenders, and to consider how such laws may have wider regional influence and multi-sectoral impact. For example, following Russia's clamp down on civil society practice through oppressive legislation (i.e. limits on foreign funding for NGOs), we now see similar laws being debated by legislators in Tajikistan, Kyrgyzstan and Kazakhstan.[30] Such measures are used not only in repressive regimes but also in nominally or fully democratic states.[31] In the United Kingdom, for example, the Transparency of Lobbying, Non-Party Campaigning and Trade Union Administration Act 2014 restricts civil society organisations (CSOs) in the period before an election by setting financial limits on regulated campaigning activities above which there is a legal duty to register. Indeed, the International Centre for Not-for-Profit Law has documented the introduction or enactment of measures to constrain civil society in more than 50 countries between January 2012 and December 2014.[32] Protection-oriented actors who support defenders around the world struggle to respond effectively to this diverse and rapidly changing legal and administrative environment that impacts defenders. While there have been a number of notable initiatives to address these restrictions,[33] more research and analysis is needed to understand, prevent and respond to them effectively.

Another troubling development is the extent to which states conduct surveillance and share intelligence on defenders. In some cases, spurious intelligence reports and statements by public officials purportedly based on intelligence data misrepresent defenders and NGOs as impediments to economic growth and threats to national economic security.[34] States also continue to use anti-terrorism legislation and measures to criminalise defenders and restrict the activities of NGOs. For example, Uzbekistan has consistently used anti-terrorism laws as part of an aggressive campaign against defenders, criminalising – and in some cases torturing – them for purported religious extremism, terrorism and 'wahhabism'.[35] A number of states have also drawn upon Recommendation 8 of the Financial Action Task Force's International Standards on Combating Money Laundering and the Financing of Terrorism and Proliferation to regulate and restrict NGOs under the guise of preventing terrorist financing and money laundering.[36]

Increasingly, human rights defenders find their recognition by and access to the UN under attack. The legitimacy and integrity of their work has been called into question during Human Rights Council sessions and in General Assembly resolutions related to human rights defenders and to civil society space.[37] This has been the case not only by states such as China and Eritrea that see any form of civic protest or challenge to state authority as anathema to social and political stability, but by democratic states with growing geopolitical influence, such as South Africa and India.[38] In addition to direct confrontation with the human rights defender framework within the UN, states hostile to the work of defenders impede defenders' access to the UN by delaying applications for United Nations Economic and Social Council (ECOSOC) status and engaging in reprisals against those who attempt to engage with human rights mechanisms.[39] There have also been cases where human rights defenders experience harassment, intimidation and threats during and following their engagement with the Human Rights Council. Such was the experience of journalist Gnanasiri Kottegoda from Sri Lanka in 2012, who was subjected to a state-sanctioned smear campaign. A pro-government TV channel broadcast images of him and called him a traitor. He was forced into hiding when military intelligence sought him out, and eventually fled the country. Some states have held back from working with the Special Procedures mechanisms, and some states have also demonstrated a lack of engagement with requests made through the UPR process to protect the rights of human rights defenders.

The definition and use of the term 'human rights defender'

Although the Declaration on Human Rights Defenders itself does not use the term 'human rights defender', in practice, the definition is derived from Article 1, which states that:

> Everyone has the right, individually and in association with others, to promote and to strive for the protection and realization of human rights and fundamental freedoms at the national and international levels.

This term has been used to refer to a broad range of individuals and collectives promoting or protecting human rights, including lawyers, journalists, activists, trade unionists, members of community-based organisations, people in social movements and staff of human rights organisations involved in different work in very different contexts. It has been used to refer to those less obviously characterised as rights defenders, including protesters, teachers, students, social workers, health care professionals, community workers, sexual minorities, religious minorities and peace builders, amongst others.[40] The term 'human rights defender' tends to be invoked when those engaged in rights-related work are threatened or put at risk for what they do – it is a way of legitimising, bringing visibility to and reiterating their right to do this type of work.

There are clear reasons and benefits for using this term, not least that it confers on defenders recognition and status within the international human rights framework through which they can access support, protection and redress for violations. Furthermore, many funds, programmes and resources are specifically allocated for work related to human rights defenders, and NGOs and individuals who want to access these funds use this term in their proposals and activities. However, being called a human rights defender is not always advantageous – in some cases, the use of the term can inadvertently raise the level of risk that defenders face and be used to politicise their work. Some aggressors have also started to appropriate this term, referring to themselves as human rights defenders, to the consternation of civil society groups who see them as perpetrators of rights abuses.[41]

Protection-oriented actors are concerned about ensuring that the definition corresponds to the breadth of actors put at risk for defending human rights. Matters are complicated by the fact that, in many cases, human rights defenders do not refer to themselves as 'human rights defenders'. Furthermore, the declaration and associated protection mechanisms do not set out clear decision-making processes to help with status determination.

The Office of the United Nations High Commissioner for Human Rights has tried to provide guidance on who should be referred to as a human rights defender through a factsheet called *Human Rights Defenders: Protecting the Right to Defend Human Rights* (henceforth Fact Sheet 29).[42] Fact Sheet 29 suggests three 'minimum standards' required for a human rights defender: that the person accepts the universality of human rights; that the person's arguments fall within the scope of human rights (regardless of whether or not the argument is technically correct); and that the person engages in 'peaceful action'. However, some essential questions remain, including: To what extent does a defender need to demonstrate that his/her actions are 'non-violent'? To what extent should a defender be expected to demonstrate knowledge of and respect for the universality of human rights? What criteria and process should be adopted to determine this?[43]

Enrique Eguren and Champa Patel[44] (this issue) suggest that the current basis for this definition does not provide enough guidance for those determining if a specific individual, organisation, group or community is a human rights defender. They are concerned that such ambiguity potentially hinders the protection of defenders. Eguren and Patel argue for the development of a critical and ethical framework that focuses on analysing 'what a defender does or does not do in context', making it a *relational* definition rather than one of identity *per se*. This, they assert, provides a clearer framework for decision-making, which increases the effectiveness of protection mechanisms and forestalls misappropriation of the term by states or other aggressors. In their article, they analyse the three 'standards' presented in Fact Sheet 29 to show how critical theory can enable an ethical understanding of who behaves as a human rights defender.

The effectiveness of protection mechanisms

A frequent criticism of protection mechanisms – including by the Women Human Rights Defenders International Coalition – is that they often do not take a holistic, gender-sensitive approach to protection.[45] Defenders and practitioners have also expressed concern about the uneven and inconsistent protection and support provided to defenders, resulting in some defenders from particular groups and those in specific geographic regions being partially or completely excluded. There is scant research evaluating how different protection mechanisms perform for defenders.

Karen Bennett[46] (this issue) examines the effectiveness of the implementation of the EU Guidelines on Human Rights Defenders since the revision of this policy directive in 2008. Drawing upon participatory research conducted in Kyrgyzstan, Tunisia and Thailand, she identifies reasons for gaps in implementation and shortcomings in the integration of the guidelines in the EU's human rights country strategies. Bennett points to good practice in implementation, but also barriers to and constraints upon the capacity and willingness of diplomats to implement the guidance and defenders from accessing the envisaged support. Bennett argues that the EU's policy on defenders needs coherence with other EU human rights foreign policy commitments and that wider foreign and economic policy directives should adopt a rights-based approach that is inclusive of the guidelines. Bennett provides both a 'practice' and 'policy' review of how the implementation of the guidelines on human rights defenders, as an evolving regional mechanism contemporaneous with other EU human rights policy initiatives, can be utilised more consistently in supporting and protecting defenders.

At times human rights defenders at risk have also gained protection from an older, more established international regime – that created for refugees. Martin Jones[47] (this issue) observes there has been little attention paid to the intersection between these two protection regimes. Arguing that direct engagement can be productive, he suggests that the provision of asylum to individuals who flee because they champion human rights causes could provide new ideological currency to the refugee regime, which has seen the gradual erosion of popular support since the end of the Cold War. He also notes that defenders face an additional problem to the difficulties commonly experienced by other refugees – how to remain effective in their human rights work while living in another country. Tracing the development of 'temporary international relocation initiatives' for human rights defenders at risk, Jones suggests that these provide a productive example of the intersection of the two regimes. His contribution underscores the importance of examining the interaction between this evolving protection regime and other more established (protection) regimes.

Repression, activism and tactics for managing risk

A complex relationship exists between the repression of defenders and their defence of human rights; in some cases, repression triggers new forms of mobilisation and activism. The tactics and strategies that defenders use to manage their own security and to respond to risk are diverse, creative and highly adapted to local contexts. As some have observed, there is sometimes a gap between what defenders do and how transnational actors understand and support them, which can lead to ineffective protection and support measures.[48]

Two articles in this collection examine the ways in which human rights defenders have developed and adapted tactics to respond to repression in non-democracies. Elisa Nesossi[49] (this issue) examines human rights practice by China's *weiquan* ('rights-defence') lawyers over a 12-year period (2003–2014), analysing how these lawyers use the courts and the media to protect vulnerable groups, challenge power and highlight problems with access to justice. Noting that the Communist Party has publicly denounced *weiquan* lawyers and that they work in spite of political adversity and direct personal risk, she observes that repression – paradoxically – creates new opportunities for action. In particular, Nesossi observes how *weiquan* lawyers maximise opportunities for change that emerge as a result of repressive action and divisions amongst the political elite; and that they do so with the support of influential allies, by drawing upon the diversification of the media, and through developing social networks.

In a similar vein, Laura Lyytikainen and Freek Van der Vet[50] (this issue) provide useful insight into how two different groups of Russian human rights defenders – youth activists participating in public protest campaigns in Moscow and lawyers bringing the cases of victims of the conflict in Chechnya to the European Court of Human Rights – respond, perceive and manage the high levels of risk involved in their work. Drawing on research conducted from 2005 to 2013, at a time when the Russian State Duma passed a number of laws that significantly restricted the activity of defenders, these authors show how human rights defenders who operate in highly repressive contexts experiment with new tactics to conduct advocacy, manage fear and challenge the boundaries of state power. These tactics include developing flexible work methods, routinising protest, building legal literacy and mental resilience and using vulnerability to demonstrate state violence and repression.

Key reflections and ways forward

Amongst some defenders and practitioners, we see growing consensus about what constitutes 'security' and 'protection', and how this is to be achieved, by whom and for whom. However, while systematisation and standardisation in protection activities can provide some clarity about who should act, how and to what end, there is also a risk that orthodox ways of thinking will result in rigidity and exclusivity in policies and practices. As such, they may fail to keep pace with emerging threats to defenders, the changing nature of civic action, and actors and actions that promote and protect human rights. The five papers in this special issue provide timely and important contributions that raise vital questions about the evolving protection regime for human rights defenders. Yet, critical gaps in knowledge and understanding remain.[51] In particular, these articles point to the need for further research on:

- The construction, function and evolution of the human rights defender protection regime (including changes in its 'strength', 'organisational form', 'scope' and 'allocation mode'[52]). This includes examining: the means and conditions under which state and non-state actors cooperate with each other to strengthen – or undermine – the protection of defenders; how power, interests and knowledge shape the

protection regime; the governance of protection mechanisms and how those that operate at different levels relate to each other; how this protection regime relates to other international (protection) regimes; and how different factors such as technological evolution, regional security concerns, and political alliances influence this protection regime at different levels;
- Issues arising from the institutionalisation of the definition of 'human rights defender'. This includes examining: the benefits and drawbacks of the use of this term; to whom it is applied and to whom it is not; the power-relations, politicisation, inequality and ethical issues that arise from the use of this term;
- Perceptions of and attitudes to risk amongst human rights defenders. This includes: the subjective conceptualisation of 'security' and 'protection'; the relationship between the social construction of risk and identities; the strategic use of risk for advocacy; the security behaviours of defenders in the way they manage their risk; how defenders build resilience and strategies for safety in different types of risky environments; how culture, gender and diversity give rise to protection needs for those who challenge societal and institutional discrimination, especially women and LGBTI rights defenders;
- How the quality, quantity and type of networks – amongst human rights defenders and between them and their supporters – have protection effects. This includes: the relationship between trust, solidarity and security; the way stigmatisation is resisted through counter-narratives and community support; how alliances are built, and how they are weakened; and how local relationships have been reconstituted in the light of the development of the protection regime for human rights defenders.

We strongly encourage the facilitation of collaborative research and the circulation of ideas between academics, practitioners and defenders. This might be through: academic research, seminars and conferences; research embedded in civil society programmes and projects; and more strategic and sustained *foci* in the form of new research hubs that develop theory and practice related to 'risk', 'security' and 'protection'. Such initiatives help us to interrogate how the protection regime for human rights defenders has evolved and strengthens our imagination of what it should be.

Acknowledgements

We wish to thank the external reviewer (Lutz Oette) and associate editor (Lars Waldorf) for their helpful comments on the articles in this special issue.

Disclosure statement

No potential conflict of interest was reported by the author.

Notes

1. Adopted by UN General Assembly Resolution 53/144, 9 December 1998, A/RES/53/144.
2. Michel Forst, *Human Rights Defenders* (Front Line Defenders, 2008), http://www.frontlinedefenders.org/files/en/Background%20to%20the%20UN%20Declaration%20on%20Human%20Rights%20Defenders.pdf.
3. Stephen D. Krasner, 'Structural Causes and Regime Consequences: Regimes as Intervening Variables', *International Organization* 36, no. 2 (1982): 185.
4. UN Special Rapporteur on the Situation of Human Rights Defenders, *Commentary to the Declaration on the Right and Responsibility of Individuals, Groups and Organs of Society to Promote and Protect Universally Recognized Human Rights and Fundamental Freedoms*, July 2011, 5.
5. UN General Assembly Human Rights Council, Resolution 27/31, Civil Society Space, A/HRC/RES/27/31 (3 October 2014); UN General Assembly Human Rights Council, Resolution 24/21, Civil Society Space, A/HRC/RES/24/21 (9 October 2013).
6. Inmaculada Barcia, *Our Right to Safety: Women Human Rights Defenders' Holistic Approach to Protection* (Toronto: Association for Women's Rights in Development, 2014); Asia Pacific Forum on Women, Law and Development, *Claiming Rights, Claiming Justice: A Guidebook on Women Human Rights Defenders* (Chiangmai, 2007); Inmaculada Barcia and Analía Penchaszadeh, *Ten Insights to Strengthen Responses for Women Human Rights Defenders at Risk* (Toronto: Association for Women's Rights in Development, 2012).
7. UN Human Rights Council, *Report of the Special Rapporteur on the Situation of Human Rights Defenders, Margaret Sekaggya, 'Safe and Enabling Environment for Defenders'*, A/HRC/25/55, 23 December 2013.
8. East and Horn of Africa Human Rights Defenders Project, 'Networks for the Protection of Human Rights Defenders: Notes from the Field', *Journal of Human Rights Practice* 5, no. 3 (2013): 522–34; Vanessa Kogan, 'Protecting Human Rights Defenders in the North Caucasus: Reflections on Developments from 2009 to the Present', *Journal of Human Rights Practice* 5, no. 3 (2013): 500–11.
9. Todd Landman, 'Holding the Line: Human Rights Defenders in the Age of Terror', *British Journal of Politics & International Relations* 8, no. 2 (2006): 123–47.
10. For a discussion of these debates see: David Chandler, 'Resilience and Human Security: The Post-Interventionist Paradigm', *Security Dialogue* 43, no. 3 (2012): 213–29; Taylor Owen, 'Human Security – Conflict, Critique and Consensus: Colloquium Remarks and a Proposal for a Threshold-Based Definition', *Security Dialogue* 35, no. 3 (2004): 373–87; Roland Paris, 'Human Security: Paradigm Shift or Hot Air?', *International Security* 26, no. 2 (2001): 87–102.
11. Betty A. Reardon, 'Women and Human Security: A Feminist Framework and Critique of the Prevailing Patriarchal Security System', in *Betty A. Reardon: Key Texts in Gender and Peace*, eds. Betty A. Reardon and Dale T. Snauwaert, Springer Briefs on Pioneers in Science and Practice 27 (Cham: Springer International Publishing, 2015), 109–28; J. Ann Tickner, *Gender in International Relations: Feminist Perspectives on Achieving Global Security* (New York: Columbia University Press, 1992).
12. Barcia, *Our Right to Safety.*
13. Jane Barry and Vahida Nainar, *Women Human Rights Defenders' Security Strategies: Insiste, Resiste, Persiste, Existe* (Ottawa: Urgent Action Fund for Women's Human Rights; Kvinna Till Kvinna; Front Line Defenders, 2008), 88.
14. East and Horn of Africa Human Rights Defenders Project, 'Networks for the Protection of Human Rights Defenders: Notes from the Field', *Journal of Human Rights Practice* 5, no. 3 (2013): 522–34; Kogan, 'Protecting Human Rights Defenders in the North Caucasus'.
15. Barry and Nainar, *Women Human Rights Defenders' Security Strategies*; Jane Barry and Jelena Đorđević, *What's the Point of Revolution If We Can't Dance?* (Boulder, CO: Urgent Action Fund for Women's Human Rights, 2007); IM–Defensoras, 'A Feminist Alternative for the Protection, Self-Care, and Safety of Women Human Rights Defenders in Mesoamerica', *Journal of Human Rights Practice* 5, no. 3 (2013): 446–49; Audre Lorde, *A Burst of Light: Essays* (Ithaca, NY: Firebrand Books, 1988).
16. Daniel Joloy, 'Mexico's National Protection Mechanism for Human Rights Defenders: Challenges and Good Practices', *Journal of Human Rights Practice* 5, no. 3 (2013): 489–99.

17. For a list of such organisations, see: https://ihrfg.org/sites/default/files/Directory_EmergencyResponseGrants_2014.pdf.
18. Federal Department of Foreign Affairs, *Swiss Guidelines on the Protection of Human Rights Defenders* (Bern: Federal Department of Foreign Affairs, 2013), https://www.eda.admin.ch/content/dam/eda/en/documents/topics/aussenpolitik/Menschenrechtsverteidigerinnen_Menschenrechtsverteidiger/2013-Leitlinien-Schutz-Menschenrechtsverteidiger_EN.pdf.
19. Secretary of State for Foreign and Commonwealth Affairs, *Good Business: Implementing the UN Guiding Principles on Business and Human Rights*, September 2013, https://www.gov.uk/government/uploads/system/uploads/attachment_data/file/236901/BHR_Action_Plan_-_final_online_version_1_.pdf.
20. Draft Law Regarding the Promotion and Protection of Human Rights Defenders, adopted by Ivorian Council of Ministers, 4 September 2013, http://www.gouv.ci/conseil_print_1.php?recordID=173. See also International Service for Human Rights, *Côte d'Ivoire: New Law will Strengthen Protection of Human Rights Defenders* (16 June 2014), http://www.ishr.ch/news/cote-divoire-new-law-will-strengthen-protection-human-rights-defenders.
21. European Union Delegation to the United Nations, 'EU Council Conclusions on 10th Anniversary of EU Guidelines on Human Rights Defenders', 23 June 2014, http://eu-un.europa.eu/articles/en/article_15216_en.htm.
22. Organization for Security and Co-operation in Europe, 'OSCE Guidelines on the Protection of Human Rights Defenders', June 2014, http://www.osce.org/odihr/119633.
23. Foreign and Commonwealth Office, *Declaration on Preventing Sexual Violence in Conflict* (London, 11 April 2013), https://www.gov.uk/government/uploads/system/uploads/attachment_data/file/185008/G8_PSVI_Declaration_-_FINAL.pdf.
24. UN General Assembly, *Resolution Adopted by the General Assembly on 18 December 2013: Promotion of the Declaration on the Right and Responsibility of Individuals, Groups and Organs of Society to Promote and Protect Universally Recognized Human Rights and Fundamental Freedoms: Protecting Women Human Rights Defenders*, 30 January 2014.
25. UN Human Rights Council, *Protecting Human Rights Defenders* (UNGA, A/HRC/RES/22/6), 12 April 2013.
26. For example, the Human Rights Council adopted a resolution on *Human Rights, Sexual Orientation and Gender Identity* (A/HRC/27/L.27/Rev.1, 24 September 2014).
27. UN Human Rights Council, *Safe and Enabling Environment for Defenders*.
28. Human Rights Council, *Report of the UN Special Rapporteur on the Situation of Human Rights Defenders*, A/69/259, 5 August 2014.
29. Amnesty International, *Annual Report 2014/15: Republic of India*, https://www.amnesty.org/en/countries/asia-and-the-pacific/india/report-india/ (accessed 16 June 2015); Aloke Tikku, 'Home Ministry Cancels Registration of 9,000 Defaulting NGOs', *Hindustan Times*, 28 April 2015, http://www.hindustantimes.com/india-news/home-ministry-cancels-registration-of-9-000-defaulting-ngos/article1-1341658.aspx (accessed 16 June 2015).
30. United States Mission to the OSCE, 'Statement on Draft Legislation in Central Asia Impacting NGO Operating Space', 22 January 2015, http://osce.usmission.gov/jan_22_15_central_asia.html (accessed 16 June 2015).
31. Thomas Carothers and Saskia Brechenmacher, *Closing Space: Democracy and Human Rights Support Under Fire* (Washington, DC: Carnegie Endowment for International Peace, 2014).
32. The International Center for Not-for-Profit Law, *A Mapping of Existing Initiatives to Address Legal Constraints on Foreign Funding* (Washington, DC: The International Center for Not-for-Profit Law, 1 July 2014).
33. See projects such as the Civil Space Initiative (http://www.wmd.org/projects/civic-space-initiative), the Enabling Environment Index (http://civicus.org/eei/), Lifeline: Assistance Fund for Embattled Civil Society Organisations (https://freedomhouse.org/program/lifeline#.VJoeg7gCB), Making All Voices Count (http://www.makingallvoicescount.org), Digital Defenders Partnership (https://digitaldefenders.org), and the Community of Democracies' Working Group on Enabling and Protecting Civil Society (http://www.community-democracies.org/Working-for-Democracy/Initiatives/Governmental-Bodies/Working-Group-on-Enabling-and-Protecting-Civil-Soc).
34. A leaked report entitled *Concerted Efforts by Select Foreign Funded NGOs to 'Take Down' Indian Development Projects*, from the Indian Ministry of Home Affairs' Intelligence Bureau to Prime Minister's Office, 3 June 2014, was the subject of much media and third-sector

commentary. See: Ram Mashru, 'India's NGO Backlash: Foreign Policy', *Foreign Policy*, 21 July 2014, http://foreignpolicy.com/2014/07/21/indias-ngo-backlash/; Salil Tripathi, 'NGO: Three-Lettered Angels – Livemint', *Live Mint*, 18 June 2014, http://www.livemint.com/Opinion/vqgZM09LRCwmp9erDtKGSI/NGO-Threelettered-angels.html; The Hindu, 'Answering to Law, Not to Caesar', *The Hindu*, 18 June 2014, http://www.thehindu.com/opinion/editorial/answering-to-law-not-to-caesar/article6123746.ece.

35. Archana Pyati, *Karimov's War: Human Rights Defenders and Counterterrorism in Uzbekistan*, ed. Neil Hicks (New York: Human Rights First, 2005). The report notes the government of Uzbekistan's use of the term *Wahhabi* to describe its radical opposition to such Islamic groups perceived as a threat to national security. In April 2014, the Initiative Group of Independent Human Rights Defenders estimated there were 12,000 persons currently imprisoned in Uzbekistan on vague and overbroad charges related to 'religious extremism', with over 200 convicted this year alone. See also Human Rights Watch, 'World Report 2014: Uzbekistan', 2014.
36. Financial Action Task Force, *International Standards on Combating Money Laundering and the Financing of Terrorism and Proliferation: The FATF Recommendations* (Paris: FATF/OECD, February 2012). See also Financial Action Task Force, *Best Practices: Combating the Abuse of Non-Profit Organisations (Recommendation 8)* (Paris: FATF/OECD, June 2013); Financial Action Task Force, *Risk of Terrorist Abuse in Non-Profit Organisations* (Paris: FATF/OECD, June 2014); Human Security Collective, European Center for Not-For-Profit Law, and European Foundation Centre, *The Financial Action Task Force (FATF) Measures to Fight Abuse of NPOs for Terrorist Financing – Draft Position Paper*, September 2014.
37. For example, the UN General Assembly only adopted Resolution 68/181 on Protecting Women Human Rights Defenders on 18 December 2013 after a crucial paragraph was removed – one calling on states to condemn all forms of violence against women and to refrain from relying on tradition, religion or custom to avoid obligations for the elimination of violence against women. This wording had already been agreed upon in a previous resolution. See International Service for Human Rights, *UN Adopts Landmark Resolution on Protecting Women Human Rights Defenders*, 28 November 2013, http://www.ishr.ch/news/un-adopts-landmark-resolution-protecting-women-human-rights-defenders.
38. The language used by these states during debate of resolutions on human rights defenders and on civil society at UNHRC 25 and 27, for instance, repeatedly refers to the 'responsibilities' of human rights defenders and CSOs to 'act within domestic law' (without acknowledging that said domestic laws often contravene international human rights law), accuses human rights defenders and CSOs of allowing themselves to be manipulated by foreign funders seeking to undermine national sovereignty, or of pursuing 'erroneous ideologies', and insists they act 'ethically' and with greater 'transparency and accountability'. Coming from states that use laws to restrict freedoms of association, assembly and expression to criminalise and prevent dissent, this represents an ominous, thinly veiled message.
39. Criticism has been made by NGOs and even UN Special Procedures of states blocking NGOs through deferral by the Committee on NGOs that scrutinises NGO applications for ECOSOC status. See: http://www.ishr.ch/sites/default/files/article/files/letter_to_us_secretary_of_state_re_idsn.pdf (accessed 16 June 2015).
40. See for example: Gwen Burnyeat, 'On a Peak in Darien: Community Peace Initiatives in Urabá, Colombia', *Journal of Human Rights Practice* 5, no. 3 (2013): 435–45; Cynthia Soohoo and Cynthia Hortsch, 'Who Is a Human Rights Defender? An Essay on Sexual and Reproductive Rights Defenders', *University of Miami Law Review* 65, no. 3 (2011): 981–98; Kate Sheill, 'Human Rights, Sexual Orientation, and Gender Identity at the UN General Assembly', *Journal of Human Rights Practice* 1, no. 2 (2009): 315–19; Lauri R. Tanner, 'Kawas v. Honduras – Protecting Environmental Defenders', *Journal of Human Rights Practice* 3, no. 3 (2011): 309–26.
41. Robert M. Cutler, 'De-authoritarization in Uzbekistan?: Analysis and Prospects,' in Irina Morozova (ed.), *Towards Social Stability and Democratic Governance in Central Eurasia: Challenges to Regional Security* (Amsterdam: IOS Press, 2005):120–41.
42. Office of the UN High Commissioner for Human Rights, *Human Rights Defenders: Protecting the Right to Defend Human Rights, Fact Sheet No. 29*, 2004.
43. These questions are raised by Raghad Jaraisy and Tamar Feldman, 'Protesting for Human Rights in the Occupied Palestinian Territory: Assessing the Challenges and Revisiting the

Human Rights Defender Framework', *Journal of Human Rights Practice* 5, no. 3 (2013): 421–34.

44. Enrique Eguren and Champa Patel, 'Towards Developing a Critical and Ethical Approach for Better Recognising and Protecting Human Rights Defenders', *The International Journal of Human Rights* 19, no. 7 (2015): 896–907.
45. Barcia, *Our Right to Safety.*
46. Karen Bennett, 'European Union Guidelines on Human Rights Defenders: A Review of Policy and Practice towards Effective Implementation', *The International Journal of Human Rights* 19, no. 7 (2015): 908–934.
47. Martin Jones, 'Protecting Human Rights Defenders at Risk: Asylum and Temporary International Relocation', *The International Journal of Human Rights* 19, no. 7 (2015): 935–960.
48. Masa Osama Amir, 'A Study of the Experience of Women Human Rights Defenders in Eleven Egyptian Governorates', *Journal of Human Rights Practice* 5, no. 3 (2013): 460–77; Kogan, 'Protecting Human Rights Defenders in the North Caucasus'.
49. Elisa Nesossi, 'Political Opportunities in Non-Democracies: The Case of Chinese *weiquan* Lawyers', *The International Journal of Human Rights* 19, no. 7 (2015): 961–978.
50. Laura Lyytikainen and Freek Van der Vet, 'Violence and Human Rights in Russia: How Human Rights Defenders Develop their Tactics in the Face of Danger, 2005–2013', *The International Journal of Human Rights* 19, no. 7 (2015): 979–998.
51. Alice M. Nah, Karen Bennett, Danna Ingleton and James Savage, 'A Research Agenda for the Protection of Human Rights Defenders', *Journal of Human Rights Practice* 5, no. 3 (1 November 2013): 401–420.; also, notes from the Expert Roundtable on Innovative Thinking for the Protection of Human Rights Defenders – meeting organised by Amnesty International, the University of York's Centre for Applied Human Rights, London Metropolitan University's Human Rights and Social Justice Research Institute, and the International Service for Human Rights, Geneva, 12 March 2014.
52. Stephan Haggard and Beth A. Simmons, 'Theories of International Regimes', *International Organization* 41, no. 3 (1987): 491–517.

Towards developing a critical and ethical approach for better recognising and protecting human rights defenders

Luis Enrique Eguren Fernández[a] and Champa Patel[b]

[a]*Protection International, Brussels, Belgium;* [b]*Amnesty International, London, UK*

The Declaration on the Right and Responsibility of Individuals, Groups and Organs of Society to Promote and Protect Universally Recognized Human Rights and Fundamental Freedoms passed in 1998 by the United Nations General Assembly marked a milestone for the defence of human rights. This article considers some of the limitations around the concept of and term 'human rights defenders', and sets out some considerations for the development of a critical and ethical approach elaborating on criteria in the declaration of how to better understand and define human rights defenders through their practice. This article argues that such an approach, utilising insights from relevant critical theory, should be developed on the basis of the principles and values that recognise that although rights are universal, they are not applied everywhere in the same way or for all individuals equally. This article posits an approach in which the defender is understood, and constructed, as a *relational* agent situated in human rights work. Such a focus, this article argues, can not only help defenders, and those who work with them, to better understand and reflect on their experiences and improve their praxis, but can also lead to tangible improvements in the practices and policies employed for protecting human rights defenders throughout the world.

Historicising the figure of the human rights defender

Since the turn of the twentieth century, and particularly since the inception of the United Nations (UN) in 1945, there has been a rapid expansion of the international governance and human rights system. During this time, countless courageous individuals, organisations and movements have fought for equality, social justice and human rights from early women's rights movements at the turn of the twentieth century, through the decolonisation and civil rights movements of the late 1940s and 50s and the independence movements of the 1960s to the more recent anti-apartheid movement of the 1980s, right up to the Arab Revolutions of 2011–2012. In this respect, it is critical that we understand the emergence and solidification of human rights as a historical phenomenon, which is the product of the interaction of different cultural, political, social and historical situations that have confronted humanity over differing periods of time.[1]

In this context, the figure of the human rights defender (HRD or defender) emerged following protracted political discussion within the UN, a debate that was fuelled by many different actors from outside the institution on the recognition that there was a need to protect those undertaking human rights work often in very difficult environments. When it was ultimately passed by the UN General Assembly in 1998, the Declaration on the Right and Responsibility of Individuals, Groups and Organs of Society to Promote and Protect Universally Recognized Human Rights and Fundamental Freedoms[2] (the UN Declaration on HRDs) was instrumental to institutionalising an understanding of human rights defenders as key agents of human rights change.

Fact Sheet No. 29[3] elaborates on the UN Declaration on HRDs, defining HRDs as:

> a term used to describe people who, individually or with others, act to promote or protect human rights. Human rights defenders are identified above all by what they do and it is through a description of their actions and of some of the contexts in which they work that the term can best be explained.[4]

Interestingly, the document then states that while 'many professional activities do not involve human rights work all of the time' they 'can have occasional links with human rights'. As such, 'they can nevertheless act as defenders on *some occasions* [our emphasis] by working on cases through which they contribute to the promotion or protection of human rights'.[5] It is clear from this definition that the work of human rights defenders cuts across a broad spectrum of interventions by a wide range of actors promoting and protecting civil, political, economic, social and cultural rights. More interesting, however, is the assertion that theoretically every individual could be a human rights defender at any given time. This gives rise to a situation where it is conceivable that someone be actively understood as a human rights defender solely for a specific piece of work or action undertaken rather than the entirety of what they do. Fact Sheet No. 29 further notes that although the 'standard' required of a human rights defender is 'a complex issue', it should meet three requirements: first, the HRD should accept 'the universality of human rights', second, it is not important necessarily 'who is right and who is wrong' (the test is whether the person is defending a human right or not), and finally defenders should aim to engage in 'peaceful action'.[6]

On the one hand, the broad formulation in Fact Sheet No. 29 is advantageous as it recognises the different role of individuals with regard to human rights and allows for wide application in response to diverse political and historical contexts within varying geographical areas. However, the definition is so broad that it is actually a difficult exercise to be clear on who is or who is *not* a defender. It is our contention that the definition and standards outlined in Fact Sheet No. 29 fall short of what is needed to interpret who exactly is a defender and what they do, and this ambiguity may actually hinder defenders' protection. Given the broad scope for definitional interpretation, states have in some instances defined HRDs as those inimical to their own interests or excluded those who are seen as a threat to state practices.

For example, Alvaro Uribe, an ex-president of Colombia, branded some HRDs 'terrorism spokesmen' when they pointed to the human rights violations committed by his security forces.[7] Similarly, in Guatemala, draft public policies arguably define who the state is willing to recognise as defenders in a narrower manner than that allowed by the UN declaration. Such approaches risk exclusion for those who may be legitimately recognised by their actions as defenders under international standards but not within the categories recognised by the state.[8] Likewise, in a similar draft bill proposed for Nepal, there is a reference to a 'code of conduct' to be developed, which might also exclude certain groups of defenders.[9] Although HRDs should be granted formal access to protection mechanisms if they meet the requirements of the UN declaration (i.e. accepting the universality of human rights and not using violence to achieve their objectives), states can exclude HRDs from such mechanisms by setting tight parameters on what activities may be deemed 'right' and 'wrong' – counter to Fact Sheet No. 29.

Such manoeuvres add confusion to an already heated discussion in the media about the defence of human rights, particularly in a context of heavy repression against HRDs. Arguably, having a clearer definition of what constitutes HRD practice would not stop Uribe's politicisation. However, it would provide HRDs with a more solid rebuttal that their activities fall within the scope of the UN Declaration on HRDs and they are eligible for protection mechanisms.

In order to tackle these limitations around the concept of HRDs, this article sets out some considerations to help support the development of a critical and ethical approach, which elaborate on the criteria in the UN declaration and Fact Sheet No. 29 to better understand and define human rights defenders through their practice. This suggested approach could be utilised to better support tailored effective protection strategies rooted in the tangible experiences of HRDs. A more critical and ethical approach could help get past inclusion/exclusion approaches, shifting the focus from who is or is not a defender to analysing what a defender does or does not do in context. By understanding the work of HRDs as a *relational* activity situated in their specific contexts, rather than an identity, we are then able to examine some of the challenges for those working with defenders on recognising who exactly is a defender and what protections they require.

A critical theory approach to human rights practice

But why is a focus on localised human rights practice important to developing more effective protection mechanisms? First, HRDs are key interlocutors in the diffusion of human rights norms from global spaces to local realities. Herrera's concept of 'relational relativism'[10] provides a useful starting point when considering the relationship between human rights policy and practice. According to Herrera, human rights are best understood as:

> A set of dynamic processes of conflicts of interests that strive to have their propositions recognised starting from different positions of power. Human rights should therefore be defined as object systems (values, norms, institutions) and action systems (social practices) that allow arenas of struggle for human dignity to be opened up and consolidated.[11]

Within this relational understanding, the defender is a complex constellation of global norms and local knowledge, constantly constructed and facilitated through local, regional, national and sometimes international networks.

Locating our analysis within such a relational context it is useful to draw on Sikkink's notion of 'agentic constructivism'[12]:

> Social processes where new actors take on and challenge (and sometimes change) existing logics of appropriateness ... These actors don't mindlessly 'enact' or 'perform' scripts, but question them. At rare times, they are capable of not simply 'instantiating structures' but transforming structures. Their actions may be transgressive of existing logics of appropriateness, sometimes intentionally inappropriate. In the end, agency requires the possibility of intention and the possibility of the freedom of subjectivity. This does not mean that all agents are constantly *fully intentional and freely subjective.* The challenge for agentic constructivism in explaining change is to understand which taken for granted structures motivate and inform

> agency, at the same time as we understand which other structures are challenged and sometimes changed.[13] [our emphasis]

Sikkink's analysis has two considerations that are critical to understanding HRDs' work: first, that HRDs' identities are shaped by structural forces interacting dynamically with local, personal experiences; second, that in the process of HRDs' work, they have the ability to redefine those same structural forces through their human rights work. Through this process we see the translation of global norms into local realities – appropriating local languages/cultures and practices into their work in the act of engaging others in human rights work. This is critical to understanding HRD practice in its context as a dynamic, ever evolving dialogue between global norms and local specificities. However, we should be careful not to over-privilege agentic constructivism as an analytical approach. Utilising this mode of enquiry needs to be married to an equal consideration of the ways in which power is constructed, maintained and exercised through structural constructivism. Power dynamics can play out at differing levels (whether it is international or at state level or by third parties such as international non-governmental organisations (INGOs) or donors). What is critical is to locate agentic constructivism within the structural power dynamics in which it operates.

Mark Goodale's concept of 'transnational normativities' provides one way in which to understand some of the structural and ideological tensions that shape HRD practice.[14] He positions 'transnational normativities' as:

> The relationship between the epistemology of human rights practices and the local ontologies in which they are necessarily embedded; the disjuncture between the universalism that anchors the idea of human rights conceptually, and the more modest scales in which social actors across the range envision human rights as part of pre-existing legal and ethical configurations.[15]

For Goodale, human rights are always embedded in 'pre-existing relations meaning and production'.[16] As such, the HRD is constantly mediating and navigating differing transnational norms, which may or may not be in conflict with global human rights norms. While this provides a compelling lens through which to understand the competing narratives and the dynamics and tensions that impact on localised human rights practice, Goodale is less clear on how one would analyse such practices.

Sally Engle Merry offers some insights, from an anthropological perspective, which potentially address this oversight.[17] While Sikkink's agentic constructivism positions international human rights norms as static, against which we measure local actors' practice, Merry, in contrast, argues that international human rights principles and values are redefined and made relevant through local processes of 'translation' and 'framing'. She argues that intermediaries at local levels function as translators and 'refashion global rights agendas for local contexts and reframe local grievances in terms of global human rights principles and activities'.[18] In order to do so, translators 'hold a double consciousness', combining both 'transnational human rights concepts and local ways of thinking about grievances'.[19] She defines framing as a mode of enquiry which considers 'ways of packaging and presenting ideas that generate shared beliefs, motivate collective action, and define appropriate strategies of action'.[20] To extend her approach allows us to bridge Goodale's recognition of the differing ontologies and narratives that can impact on the HRD by providing a frame of reference through which we can understand the HRD as a translator and framer between global norms (human rights or otherwise), competing narratives and local cultural norms and realities.

However, while making a compelling argument for a more dynamic understanding of human rights practice, her scope of enquiry is narrow and focuses on the institutions that facilitate international global norms (mostly states and the UN system) and fails to consider the ethical responsibilities of those who work with HRDs and the role they play in translating and framing human rights norms. I/NGOs, regional entities (such as ASEAN, the African Union and the European Union) and donors can all have an inadvertently negative impact on HRDs. Some of the key challenges include the differences in capacity between often small and voluntary led HRD organisations and large well-funded and well-resourced INGOs, regional organisations and other actors. This difference in capacity is exemplified by negative equality and power dynamics whereby other international actors – because of their own competing missions, agenda and focuses – may create limited spaces for meaningful engagement with HRDs. Yet, HRDs and other local civil society actors may often be approached precisely by these same actors, to provide intelligence and access to the most vulnerable and marginalised groups. As such, we think it is critical to also consider the impact of these actors, who arguably also translate and frame international human rights norms, in the same space as HRDs' localised practices.

With each of the above perspectives, there is a danger of positioning the localisation of human rights practice, whether through an understanding of agentic constructivism, located in transnational normativities mediated through processes of translation and framing, as a coherent framework that sets conceptual boundaries around what are in reality, complex, multi-dimensional and often highly locally specific processes. However, mitigating the limitations of the differing models, it is possible to utilise aspects of Sikkink, Merry and Goodale's thinking to consider HRDs through an agentic constructivism lens (but for this to be understood vis-á-vis an analysis of structural power).

Locating an understanding of HRD practice within such analytical perspectives provides a solid foundation from which to understand HRD practice in context and by extension better understand and meet their protection needs. This can be framed through contextualising and understanding that defenders' experiences are grounded in dense relationships within particular political, social and cultural specificities: HRDs are agents of change and their work both shapes and is shaped by other structures, norms and practices that promote or oppress human rights (whether at the level of individuals, states or the international system). It is at the intersection of these considerations that we begin to analyse the ethical considerations that arise from HRD praxis.

Human rights practice and ethics

While the above analysis enables us to understand HRD practice through a multi-faceted mode of enquiry, there is still a need to interrogate what constitutes ethical practice in such a context. Interestingly, the notion of ethics is only briefly mentioned in the declaration. It specifically states that the defender has to comply with the requirements of professional ethics, if they exist within their profession.[21] A supplementary commentary again only refers in passing to ethics.[22] As noted previously, Fact Sheet No. 29 states that the 'standard' required of a human rights defender has three particular requirements: first, HRDs must accept the 'universality of human rights', second, it is not important to know 'who is right and who is wrong', and finally defenders need to engage in 'peaceful action'.[23]

These three requirements offer an implicit code of ethics for defenders and in practice this is the usual interpretation they receive. However this poses a contradiction between having a loose definition of who can be a human rights defender (based on their actions as and when they occur) and the requirement that a defender should meet all three strands delineated above (or at least not be inconsistent in doing so) at all times. If we were to take the three criteria proposed as the basis for an ethical framework, this could lead to numerous difficulties in trying to apply the criteria to the lived experience of human rights work as 'not all ethical relations are reducible to acts of judgement and that the very capacity to judge presupposes a prior relation between those who judge and those who are judged'.[24] Through considering the potential of the critical approach, outlined in the previous section, to enable a better understanding of who ethically behaves as a defender, we challenge a normative approach that applies an absolute interpretation of the three standards being met concurrently and at all times.

To consider this, it is important to first understand the power dynamics at play in who decides what HRD practice is. There are a number of key questions to be asked: Is it an identity that one chooses or that is designated – even if mutually agreed – by third parties? More pressingly, if the UN states that one does not need to be a defender all the time (as noted earlier), how likely is it in practice that someone would self-identify as a HRD based on isolated activities? We may assume that the other activities undertaken by the defender do not clash with the defence of human rights, but is this assumption a correct one? What about those individuals who would be considered defenders in one aspect of their practice but whose other behaviours may actually be inconsistent with rights they are defending? For example, the case of a lawyer who works for a pharmaceutical multinational that patents medicinal herbs belonging to indigenous cultures in the Amazon, which violates the rights of the indigenous, but who, in his free time, advises a group of women who have been abused.

There is more than one consideration to be taken into account in this instance. The first is the frequency of the defender's action or intervention and the second, whether the action taken undermines other rights. It is our contention that isolated activities are insufficient to make an individual a HRD. There is no established threshold or measurement for determining HRD practice, but intuitively a defender should demonstrate consistency over time using a rights-based approach in their actions to achieve human rights changes. Taking the same example, if the pharmacist patents the herbs with participation from the indigenous community and includes them as central to the process, taking into account impact on gender and vulnerabilities within community, and works toward patenting the herbs in accordance with the international norms and standards, these would be considered actions as a HRD. The human rights lens and approach are both critical here.

The above example touches on the tensions within the first standard in Fact Sheet No. 29: accepting the universality of human rights. The declaration states that 'all human rights and fundamental freedoms are universal, indivisible, interdependent and interrelated and should be promoted and implemented in a fair and equitable manner'. More difficult to navigate, however, is the assertion that '[a] person cannot deny some human rights and yet claim to be a human rights defender because he or she is an advocate for others'.[25] This is reinforced by the former UN Special Rapporteur for Human Rights Defenders, Margaret Sekaggya, who reports that HRDs have the right to protection 'as long as they accept and apply the principles of universality'.[26]

Assuming that most defenders are not in a position, nor have the resources, to work across all human rights in a fair and equitable manner, how exactly does a defender demonstrate universality in practice? A critical first step is to distinguish that the universality of a norm is not the same as the universality of an approach. Locating HRD practices within local specificities could be one way to understand this criterion. Defenders could demonstrate universality through practicing what Tronto calls 'attentiveness', a reflexive tool which requires being open to recognising that the *other* has needs and these should be recognised, acknowledged and responded to.[27] In the case of HRDs, this characteristic would mean that attentiveness towards the human rights violations and an appropriate reaction to them (though not necessarily action) could be expected. As previously noted, HRDs must consistently and holistically take this approach.

HRDs can also develop their skills to be more effective and ethical through a relational model and learn from past experiences. Another tool is to (self) analyse through a lens of otherness. Seeing one's actions through understanding the impact on others is profoundly relational and stems specifically from the defender's perception of the other. Augé points out that a distinction can be made between 'a sense of the other' (understanding what makes sense and is important for 'others', starting from or outside of one's self), and 'a sense for the other', which implies an emotional connection and predisposes a commitment to act (as a distinctive characteristic when compared with a victim, for example).[28]

Another key challenge is where a defender may deny certain rights (towards others). This then raises the ethical question as to whether that person should still be considered an HRD as they no longer meet the requirement of working towards full realisation of all rights. That is not to say that their work has no value, or even that they are not deserving of protection as citizens, but if HRDs are held to a higher standard they must not undermine or deny other rights.[29] Through a focus on human rights practice rather than human rights principles, HRDs, and those who work with them, must recognise the differing external constraints within the operating environment that could limit HRDs' ability to demonstrate universality in practice but instil universality in the ethical approach.

Another requirement in Fact Sheet No. 29 is the need for HRDs to take 'peaceful action'. It should be clarified that while the declaration and Fact Sheet No. 29 talk about 'peaceful action', the Special Rapporteur's office has stated that 'non-violence' is a requirement for a HRD to be afforded the right to appropriate protection.[30] There could potentially be an immediate contradiction in that 'peaceful action' and 'non-violence' are not necessarily synonymous. Broadly understood, the first could refer to an action undertaken without involving violence, while the second could refer to a wider moral and strategic approach to social change.[31] This issue is particularly difficult because human rights work may vary in different contexts in accordance with how the concepts of 'peaceful action' and violence (themselves both poorly defined in the relevant documents) evolve and change.

Relational context is key, as taking a position on just the action itself is of no use if we do not relate the action to the broader dynamics at play and the defenders' agency. For example, we may see throwing stones as a reaction to an overwhelming aggression (such as activists throwing stones against Israeli army tanks in the Palestinian Intifada) in which the direct objective of that action is not to hurt someone and there is no actual peace to be broken. It cannot be compared with throwing a stone with a clear and feasible expectation to harm somebody, as when targeting a nearby person. The intention of throwing stones against tanks as a reaction to previous aggressions is closer to an expression of anger and frustration than a clear expectation to stop such aggression by hurting Israeli soldiers.[32]

In such a scenario, it is actually still feasible for a defender to be considered a defender despite the fact that he or she might engage in actions that could be considered ethically unacceptable in other contexts. In other words, it is not about losing the protection that a defender deserves, but about the ethical acceptance of such behaviour, which should be determined by understanding the broader relational context within which the defender works. The defender's agency in being able to translate, frame and shape the structures within which they operate and the power dynamics at play is what is important here.

The final issue is whether or not it is important to know 'who is right and who is wrong'. Fact Sheet No. 29 is clear that:

> It is not essential for a human rights defender to be correct in his or her arguments in order to be a genuine defender. The critical test is whether or not the person is defending a human right. Human rights defenders must be defined and accepted according to the rights they are defending and according to their own right to do so.[33]

Ironically, the clarification as to whether defenders needed to be 'right' or 'wrong' was deemed necessary as HRDs are often repressed by the governments they criticise. Violations too often occur through national legal frameworks that criminalise HRDs. These frameworks and laws may be contrary to the legislation's original intent. Or the laws (and the agents who enforce them) may target HRDs whose actions may conflict with government policies. Newly created ad hoc laws may also be used to restrain defenders' work by necessitating compliance with complex administrative requirements. There are also strategies that effectively 'criminalise' HRDs, for example the imposition on HRDs of impossible situations of trying to comply with the regulatory demands placed upon them while still being effective in their actions.[34]

It is paramount to counter these increasing attempts to criminalise genuine human rights activity by ensuring states comply with the international standard that a defender does not need to know if their action is 'right' or 'wrong' but that their work should be analysed through the lens of whether their actions are in defence of human rights. This could be not only through supporting legislation but also policies, practices and state engagement with defenders that create an enabling environment for their work. A deeper understanding of the operating environment for HRDs would increase understanding of the structural and cultural barriers that impact practice, and could help stakeholders reflect to what extent negative consequences could have been anticipated or mitigated for, in order to prevent future HRD violations or inform protection agendas. HRD agency, and understanding their role as dynamic interlocutors, could help highlight both the bias the defender is exposed to and the degree to which the HRD can actually shape those external structural forces. For example, while an activity may have a 'bad' outcome when seen as part of a range of interventions, it could still have shifted the ground forward in terms of securing human rights interventions.

Understanding HRD practice as processes of translating and framing, in this respect, could be crucial in locating an analysis of defenders' actions within a spectrum of defending human rights. From a critical perspective, and recognising the difficulties of the working environment, HRD praxis may well be subjected to errors in determining who is 'right' and who is 'wrong' but from an ethical standpoint this could be counterbalanced to see such errors as part of an active process of continual learning and development to improve human rights practice. The bottom line would remain whether the activity was in the service of defending a human right, but analysing the scenario through the proposed critical and ethical approach can surface the particularities and specificities of any situation, which can in turn better define what support or protection strategies are appropriate.

In light of the above analysis of the UN's three standards, we suggest that adopting a purely normative approach may be more limiting than empowering and may fall short of being directly applicable to the complexities of the working context for the HRD. The danger of taking this type of normative ethical approach to the work of defenders presumes that a rational and universal solution could be sought to any ethical issues that arise. In other words, we would have to assume that there can be an ideal and neutral observer whose gaze is capable of encompassing the action taken, its circumstances and all its consequences.

Such an omniscient position does not exist. In the first place, neither the person who is taking the action, nor those observing it, have the ability to know in advance all of the circumstances surrounding the action or its consequences. In the second place, we cannot assume that a HRD is always an autonomous and rational individual, capable of assessing the consequences and impact of every action they take. Finally we cannot even assume that there is a stable external referent, since the logic of the realization of human rights is discursive, highly situational and constantly changing, as illustrated at the outset of this article. Conversely, it could be argued that these limitations actually *reduce* the ultimate responsibility of the HRD, who is faced with a process that is evolving and adapting and which is deeply influenced by context and power relations. It is then paramount to conceive HRDs as agents who evolve over time as their awareness of being a defender grows and they establish relationships with other actors in the context of their work.

Self-reflexive modes of working allow the defender to practice responsibility for the impact of their actions at both an organisational level and in political and social processes, as well as giving them the practical tools – based on experience – to challenge structures of power and privilege. In a relational model, the question shifts then from trying to understand any given situation in terms of 'good' or 'bad'. As Gilligan notes, 'the shift in moral perspective is manifest by a change in the moral question from 'what is just?' to 'how to respond?'[35] Such an approach is to understand that HRDs will keep learning and being shaped by their actions on a daily basis and that mistakes may be made but they are part of a process of evolving towards a more effective and just human rights practice. This reflexivity is crucial to the establishment of a more critical and ethical approach to human rights work: it is the reflective subject, able, at certain moments, to separate him or herself and look at him or herself, who is going to be able to behave ethically when doing human rights work.

But at the same time we must bear in mind that the process of constructing the defender as subject is also emotional, given that he or she is continually confronted with competing ontologies as well as the fear and repression that HRDs themselves suffer because of their work. Such pressures can then make it difficult for the defender to have the space to reflect and for any set of rules or code of conduct to be applied normatively. Protection mechanisms should then ensure that defenders are supported to identify their own secure spaces, such as respite schemes, allowing them to be able to reflect and refine their work.

A way forward – towards developing a critical and ethical approach for HRDs

We believe there needs to be a dynamic, multi-faceted approach to understanding the specificities of HRD practice at the local level. This type of approach, which has critical and ethical considerations embedded at its core, could help HRDs and those who work with them to ensure better application of existing protection mechanisms as well as help support more nuanced discussions on HRD protection needs. This approach, we would argue, needs to locate any understanding of what is needed squarely on the analysis and understanding of human rights practice in context rather than only through human rights principles and commitments as outlined in the UN standards. Our analysis stresses that HRDs are active agents of change working within complex environments, which they may be able to shape and exercise power within to transform human rights agency, but their work can also affect them negatively. Such an exploration needs to increase understanding of the translating and framing processes that take place. HRDs make global human rights norms applicable and relevant in a local context, and in the process, HRDs make difficult choices that may impact on their ability to meet the standards as set out in Fact Sheet No. 29.

We recognise that embedding a critical and ethical approach needs more critique and discussion. While we have outlined some considerations, there are some particularities we have not been able to explore: for example, how gender dynamics can positively or negatively impact HRD practice, or the degree to which HRDs can maintain their 'representativeness' if they are regularly part of transnational networks. There is also a need to further delineate the local realities within which HRDs work, to explore further the critical and ethical considerations in developing HRD protection mechanisms.

In this article we have outlined some initial considerations to better understand and support HRD practice that elaborates on the standards set out in the declaration, Fact Sheet 29 and UN commentary. Carmalt argues persuasively that while human rights law might set universal rules for conduct, what is needed is the 'contextual thickening for their implementation'.[36] It is our hope that the considerations we have outlined in this article provide the beginning of this contextual thickening required in order to inform and improve the practices and policies employed for protecting human rights defenders throughout the world.

Acknowledgements

A former draft of this article was presented at the Research Workshop on Human Rights Defenders (15–17 May 2013), organised by the Centre for Applied Human Rights (York University), the Human Rights and Social Justice Research Institute (HRSJ) at London Metropolitan University, and Amnesty International. The feedback received in the seminar and from peer reviewers and colleagues at Protection International has been invaluable or improving the initial draft.

Disclosure statement

No potential conflict of interest was reported by the author.

Notes

1. A. Belden and W. Narr, 'Human Rights as a Holistic Concept', *Human Rights Quarterly* 14, no. 1 (1992): 4–5.
2. UN General Assembly Resolution 53/144, 1998, http://www.un.org/ga/search/view_doc.asp?symbol=A/RES/53/144&Lang=E.
3. Office of the High Commissioner for Human Rights, 'Human Rights Defenders: Protecting the Right to Defend Human Rights – Factsheet No. 29', 2004, http://www.ohchr.org/Documents/Publications/FactSheet29en.pdf.
4. Ibid., 2.
5. Ibid., 7.
6. Ibid., 8–10.
7. *Semana*, 'La Ira Presidencial', *Semana*, 15 September 2003, http://www.semana.com/nacion/articulo/la-ira-presidencial/60643-3.

8. For example, if a national mechanism for the protection of HRD lists categories of defenders, such as 'human rights defenders, women rights defenders, environmental defenders, etc.' the difficulty is how to define each of the categories as people's work can move fluidly between differing identities and the risk that the process of trying to be comprehensive may in itself end up being exclusionary and restrictive.
9. As above, with no established 'codes of conduct'; for HRDs, any attempt to define one by a state: ibid., 33; and M. Martin and E. Eguren, *Protection of Human Rights Defenders: Best Practices and Lessons Learnt* (Brussels: Protection International Publications, 2009).
10. J. Herrera Flores, *Los Derechos Humanos como Productos Culturales: Crítica del Humanismo Abstracto* (Madrid: Los Libros de la Catarata, 2005), 64.
11. J. Herrera Flores, *El vuelo de Anteo. Derechos Humanos y Crítica de la Razón Liberal* (Bilbao: Desclée de Brouwer, 2000), 52.
12. K. Sikkink, 'Beyond the Justice Cascade: How Agentic Constructivism could help explain change in international politics' (Revised paper from a Keynote Address presented at the Millennium Annual Conference, Princeton, NJ, 22 October 2011), 9; see also K. Sikkink, 'Transnational Politics, International Relations Theory, and Human Rights', *PS: Political Science and Politics* 31, no. 3 (1998): 516–23, http://www.jstor.org/stable/420610.
13. Ibid., 9.
14. Mark Goodale, 'Locating Rights: Envisioning Law between the Global and Local', in *The Practice of Human Rights: Tracking Law between the Global and Local*, ed. Mark Goodale and Sally Engle Merry (Cambridge: Cambridge University Press, 2007), 9.
15. Ibid., 9.
16. Ibid., 36.
17. Sally Engle Merry, 'Transnational Human Rights and Local Activism: Mapping the Middle', *American Anthropologist* 108, no. 1 (2006): 38–51. See also Mark Goodale and Sally Engle Merry, *The Practice of Human Rights: Tracking Law between the Global and the Local* (New York: Cambridge University Press, 2007).
18. Merry, 'Transnational Human Rights and Local Activism', 39.
19. Ibid., 39.
20. Ibid., 41.
21. UN General Assembly Resolution 53/144, 1998.
22. Margaret Sekaggya, *Commentary to the Declaration on the Right and Responsibility of Individuals, Groups and Organs of Society to Promote and Protect Universally Recognized Human Rights and Fundamental Freedoms*, 2011, http://www.ohchr.org/Documents/Issues/Defenders/CommentarytoDeclarationondefendersJuly2011.pdf (accessed 12 July 2013), 84.
23. Office of the High Commissioner for Human Rights, 'Human Rights Defenders: Protecting the Right to Defend Human Rights – Factsheet No. 29', 2004, 8–10.
24. B. Loacker and S. Muhr, 'How Can I Become a Responsible Subject? Towards a Practice-Based Ethics of Responsiveness', *Journal of Business Ethics* 90, no. 2 (2009): 273.
25. Office of the High Commissioner for Human Rights, 'Human Rights Defenders: Protecting the Right to Defend Human Rights – Factsheet No. 29', 2004, 8–10.
26. Sekaggya, *Commentary to the Declaration on the Right and Responsibility of Individuals, Groups and Organs of Society to Promote and Protect Universally Recognized Human Rights and Fundamental Freedoms*, 6.
27. J. Tronto, 'An Ethic of Care', in *Feminist Theory: A Philosophical Anthology*, ed. A. Cudd and R. Andreasen Malden (New Jersey: Blackwell Publishing , 2005), 251–63.
28. M. Augé, *A Sense for the Other* (Stanford, CA: Stanford University Press, 1998), cited in P. Cloke, 'Deliver us from Evil? Prospects for Living Ethically and Acting Politically in Human Geography', *Progress in Human Geography* 26, no. 5 (2002): 590–1.
29. Building on that understanding, it is then possible to also apply Levinas' argument that 'ethics arise first and foremost out of our fundamental responsibility for the other'. For Levinas this is a form of responsibility that is 'unconditional, beyond any "political position" and outside of any social or geographical context'. It is interesting that Levinas stresses the importance of this responsibility, being outside of any context, bearing in mind that HRDs constitute a direct corporal link between the human rights violations that are taking place and the political action that is being taken to stop them. E. Levinas, *Ethics and Infinity: Conversations with Philippe Nemo* (Pittsburgh, PA: Duquesne University Press, 1985), 86; E.J. Popke, 'Poststructuralist Ethics:

Subjectivity, Responsibility and the Space of Community', *Progress in Human Geography* 27, no. 3 (2003): 303–4.

30. Margaret Sekaggya, 'Report of the Special Rapporteur on the Situation of Human Rights Defenders, Margaret Sekaggya, to the Human Rights Council' (Sixteenth Session, Agenda Item 3: Promotion and Protection of all Human rights, Civil, Political, Economic, Social and Cultural rights, including the Right to Development, 2010), 6, http://daccess-dds-ny.un.org/doc/UNDOC/GEN/G10/178/70/PDF/G1017870.pdf?OpenElement.
31. G. Sharp, *Power and Struggle (Politics of Nonviolent Action, Part 1)* (Boston: Porter Sargent Publishers, 1973).
32. Explored in Raghad Jaraisy and Tamar Feldman, 'Protesting for Human Rights in the Occupied Palestinian Territory: Assessing the Challenges and Revisiting the Human Rights Defender Framework', *Journal of Human Rights Practice* 5, no. 3 (2013): 421–35.
33. Office of the High Commissioner for Human Rights, 'Human Rights Defenders: Protecting the Right to Defend Human Rights – Factsheet No. 29', 2004, 9.
34. The Observatory for the Protection of Human Rights Defenders, 'Violations of the Right of NGOs to Funding: From Harassment to Criminalisation', 2013, http://www.omct.org/files/2013/02/22162/obs_annual_report_2013_uk_web.pdf (accessed 3 February 2014); Peace Brigades International, 'Criminalisation of Human Rights Defenders', 2012, http://www.peacebrigades.org.uk/fileadmin/user_files/groups/uk/files/Publications/Crim_Report.pdf.
35. C. Gilligan, 'Moral Orientation and Moral Development', in *The Feminist Philosophy Reader*, ed. A. Bailey and C.J. Cuomo (Boston, MA: McGraw-Hill, 2008), 469.
36. J.C. Carmalt, 'Human Rights, Care Ethics and Situated Universal Norms', *Antipode* 43, no. 2 (2011): 316.

European Union Guidelines on Human Rights Defenders: a review of policy and practice towards effective implementation

Karen Bennett

Human Rights and Social Justice Research Institute, Faculty of Social Sciences and Humanities, London Metropolitan University, London, UK

The European Union Guidelines on Human Rights Defenders (the guidelines) are an EU external relations policy tool providing European diplomats with operational recommendations to support and protect human rights defenders (HRDs) in third country missions, recognising the critical need to protect those working on the frontlines to ensure human rights obligations are enforced in their countries. Implementation of the guidelines by the EU and its member states has resulted in many good practice actions towards the support and protection of HRDs. However the guidelines' recommendations are not systematically implemented by all European member states and implementation in EU mission countries around the world is patchy and inconsistent. This article considers EU commitments to effectively implement the guidelines policy tool in practice, including steps taken to integrate the guidelines' operational recommendations within the relatively new process of planning EU Human Rights Country Strategies in mission countries. Drawing from a study for the European Parliament assessing implementation of the guidelines in Kyrgyzstan, Thailand and Tunisia, the author identifies key areas of stakeholders' concerns, and argues for the need to link the EU's efforts towards coherence in human rights policy with on-the-ground approaches towards the protection of HRDs in third countries.

Introduction

Human rights defenders (HRDs) – who by peaceful means advocate, mobilise and often put their lives at risk to defend the most fundamental freedoms of their fellow citizens – are key agents of change in their own society and make a significant contribution to the international community's efforts to support democracy and human rights. HRDs can face serious threats in their work from both state and non-state actors, including: intimidation, harassment and physical attacks; death threats; illegal imprisonment based on fabricated charges or arbitrary interpretation or application of laws; increasingly sophisticated state surveillance of HRDs' online communications and financial transactions; restrictions on freedom of assembly, expression and movement; torture and mistreatment; incommunicado and prolonged detention; and denial of due process and fair trial.[1] These problems are of particular concern in countries where criminal justice systems are vulnerable to executive interference, arbitrariness and abuse.

Support to HRDs is identified as a major priority of European Union (EU) external policy in the field of human rights. [2] In order to streamline EU actions in this field, the Council of the European Union adopted the European Union Guidelines on Human Rights Defenders in 2004, and revised the guidelines in 2008.[3]

This article addresses how the guidelines, as an EU human rights policy instrument, are utilised in external relations by diplomats of the EU and its member state missions to support and protect HRDs. Analysis of effective implementation of the guidelines is based primarily on viewpoints from experts and stakeholders, including data collected from 48 interviews with European diplomats and HRDs in Kyrgyzstan, Thailand and Tunisia between October 2012 and January 2013.[4] Kyrgyzstan, Thailand and Tunisia are not the worst or most consistent violators of rights against HRDs in their respective regions. All three countries provide legal safeguards enabling HRDs to engage publicly in their practice and (to varying degrees) safely meet with foreign diplomats. However, in these countries, serious offenses have been, and are being, committed against HRDs.[5] These countries have all recently experienced major political transitions (2010–2011), and accordingly, political stability is, to varying degrees, not yet secured, and the work of HRDs in this respect is burdened by high political stakes.[6]

History and context

Providing support and protection to HRDs is a commitment made by many international and regional bodies, governments and national human rights institutions, as described in the 1998 UN Declaration on Human Rights Defenders.[7] HRDs, as civil society actors, are acknowledged as key contributors to a healthy democracy, embedded in the principle of public participation, and recognised in various authoritative international documents and put forth in Article 71 of the UN Charter.[8]

The European Union Guidelines on Human Rights Defenders sets out both policy objectives and practical initiatives to be implemented by the EU and its member states in support of HRDs in third country missions worldwide. The guidelines provide guidance for diplomats to carry out their obligations to promote and respect the rights of HRDs and to protect them from attacks and threats from state and non-state actors. The overall objective is to bring about an environment where HRDs can operate freely.

The Council of the European Union (Council) established a Working Party on Human Rights (COHOM) to take responsibility for shaping the EU's human rights policy in its external relations, including oversight for implementation of the guidelines.[9] EU delegations and member state missions work as the EU's primary interface in third countries in maintaining contact with HRDs, giving HRDs visible recognition, and protecting HRDs through activities such as observing trials. Missions may directly fund projects implemented by HRDs, or assist them in utilising the European Instrument for Democracy and Human Rights (EIDHR), a funding mechanism available to HRDs worldwide.[10] EIDHR also has a small grants programme (up to €10,000) specifically for responding to HRDs at risk. The fund became operational at the end of 2009 and works as a quick response mechanism for HRDs in emergency need.[11]

Since 2004 the EU and its member states have taken a series of measures to translate the guidelines into action. These include elaborating local strategies for their implementation in third countries, increasing the role of EU representation and coordination with member state missions (missions) in the field, and setting up EU delegation offices (EUD) in third countries. In 2006, an evaluation of the guidelines was conducted by the Council under the Austrian presidency, and the Council adopted 64 recommendations.[12] A year later, a set of local strategies developed by the EU under the German presidency were to be implemented. When the EU reviewed the implementation of local strategies in support of the guidelines in 2007, it was found that only 59 out of 124 missions had developed local implementation strategies (the list of countries adopting strategies is not public).

In 2008 the Slovenian presidency called for all missions to develop written strategies, with both long-term and short-term objectives to ensure the protection and sustainability of HRDs, and underlined the need for further commitment to help EU missions to be more proactive and effective (for example, by encouraging diplomats to get out of the capitals and into the regions, and by identifying key areas of focus).

A revision of the guidelines was adopted in 2008, drawing on EU missions' experience of engaging with HRDs, and in response to worsening conditions for HRDs in third countries. The 2008 version incorporates new provisions relating to: the reinforcement of coordination and implementation tools for direct assistance to HRDs; the enhancement of the role of HRDs in planning local strategies and engagement; an increased focus on the means to help facilitate HRDs' work; and the development of the EU's monitoring and protection role, with particular focus on specific risks and groups, such as women HRDs (WHRDs).

The UN Declaration on HRDs is the principle human rights instrument referred to in the EU Guidelines on HRDs,[13] and the guidelines provide a specific operational mandate in 'support for Special Procedures of the UN Human Rights Council, including the Special Rapporteur on Human Rights Defenders'.[14] In December 2008, UN and regional human rights mechanisms' representatives issued a joint statement marking the 60th anniversary of the adoption of the Universal Declaration on Human Rights stating, 'the new decade ahead must be one in which the provisions of the Declaration on Human Rights Defenders are made a reality worldwide'.[15] Consistent with this, we have seen EU missions support the UN declaration being used as an advocacy and education tool by HRDs and human rights advocates. The UN Special Rapporteurs on Human Rights Defenders and HRDs have called for further support to advocate use of the declaration to governments, as a framework document to adopt and implement national laws, policies and protection mechanisms to ensure safe and enabling environments for human rights defenders' practice.[16]

In 2009, during the period of the Lisbon Treaty[17] coming into force and the formation of the European External Action Service (EEAS), there were growing concerns amongst commentators that a lack of consistency in implementation of the guidelines could be a catalyst for worsening the security of HRDs.[18] HRDs and international non-governmental organisations (INGOs) met with EU diplomats at this juncture to advocate for improved consistency in the implementation of the guidelines by suggesting EU missions consider specific benchmarks and indicators by which to assess their actions and effective implementation of the guidelines.[19]

The creation of the EEAS in June 2010 ushered in a renewed 'EU diplomatic corps' responsible for EU foreign policy and managing joint relations with third countries in 140 foreign delegations. The EEAS structure provides EU Delegations (EUDs) in third countries, which includes policy directives to strengthen commitments to improving external actions in support and protection of HRDs. Shifts in functions and staffing of the EEAS, particularly in enabling its delegations in the field to assume more political roles on behalf of the Union, provided potential for advancements in informed decision-making concerning EU member state engagement with human rights problems.[20] However, commentators also found 'it will be necessary for the Union to define more precisely (than in the Lisbon Treaty or in the European Security Strategy) what its foreign policy objectives are and what concrete policy implications they have. This would make the differences and the interplay between self-regarding, collective and other-regarding interests clearer, both for the Union and for third parties.'[21]

The European Parliament resolution of 17 June 2010 On EU Policies in Favour of Human Rights Defenders proposed a number of recommendations to be followed through by the end of 2010.[22] The resolution was critical of the lack of coherent and effective steps by the EU to promote and support human rights defenders in third countries and called on the Office of the High Representative for Foreign Affairs and Security Policy to take immediate action on implementation of specific guidelines' actions.[23] The EEAS responded to the recommendations and investments were made towards systemising implementation of the guidelines within country missions. In 2010, HRD liaison officers were appointed to EUDs or (EU member state) missions, a welcome step in showing the EU's commitment to engage with HRDs. However it was not clear what benchmarks were being set for the HRD liaison officers in this new role, or how this work would be integrated with the designated diplomats' other work priorities.

The EU Parliament continued to call for more coherent, active and effective human rights reforms across the EU, in particular overhauling delivery using a bottom-up, tailored, country-based approach; identifying cross-cutting themes for targeted campaigns; integrating EU external relations policies for achieving greatest impact; building strong partnerships with multilateral cooperation and regional organisations; and speaking with one voice to harness Europe's collective weight. In consideration of 'bottom-up' approaches, a particular need was stressed by the EU Parliament and INGOs that EU diplomatic missions must do better to engage in consultation with civil society, including dialogue with a range of active HRDs representing diverse communities, voices and regions within the mission country.

The EU publicised its pledge to implement fully an integrated and joined up approach towards human rights in its external action policies, as outlined in the Joint Communication to the European Parliament and the Council on 'Human Rights and Democracy at the Heart of EU External Action – Towards a More Effective Approach' in December 2011. Head of the EEAS, Baroness Catherine Ashton, stated 'Human rights and democracy must run as a "silver thread" throughout EU external policies.'[24]

The EU Human Rights Country Strategy (HRCS) objective was published as part of the EU Strategic Framework and Action Plan on Human Rights and Democracy.[25] The Action Plan has a number of actions that have direct or cross-cutting significance to HRDs. Though the Action Plan does not specifically call for implementation of the guidelines on HRDs (or other EU human rights guidelines), it does state that the implementation of the Action Plan is to build on existing policies, notably the EU guidelines.[26] However, the particular direction on diplomatic engagement of EU mission countries with HRDs was vague and patchy in the development of the HRCS process, only requesting the EU consult with HRDs when developing strategy.[27]

When plans for the HRCS process were announced, a consortium of nine international human rights NGOs called for 'minimum standards from the Guidelines to be included in the process: genuine consultations with HRDs on the country strategies; outreach and awareness raising with HRDs; proactive actions for and systematic feedback to HRDs; training to EU and mission staff on the Guidelines; and cooperation between EUD and EU member states, on HRD actions'. Legitimising civil society participation with reticent governments and advocating a human rights-based approach to development were at the core of this campaign.[28]

In December 2012, the European Parliament called for a review of the current Action Plan, urging the EEAS to engage in timely reviews and consultation of actions to be concluded at the end of 2014 with consideration of next steps to be taken in 2015. The parliament raised specific concerns for EU human rights guidelines, urging the EEAS and the Council to consider revisions with a more rigorous review process in order to respond to changing circumstances, and to give particular attention to implementation plans and stepping up training on the guidelines amongst EEAS and EU delegation staff.[29] The European Parliament also established an internal Human Rights Action Unit in 2012, to follow up on implementation of recommendations.[30]

In September 2013 the European Parliament Directorate-General for External Policies of the Union Secretariat of the Sub-Committee on Human Rights held an inter-parliamentary committee meeting with national parliaments to address non-coherence and lack of consistency in human rights policy tools and directives of the EU.[31] In November 2013, the European Parliament called for action:

> [The Parliament] urges the EEAS and the Council to pay particular attention to the issue of proper implementation plans for the Guidelines; recommends further training and awareness raising among EEAS and EU Delegation staff, as well as among member state diplomats; expresses its particular concern regarding the implementation of the Guidelines on international humanitarian law and the Guidelines on torture and other cruel, inhuman and degrading treatment.[32]

Baroness Ashton pledged the EU's continuing commitment to promoting the work of HRDs in June 2013[33] and introduced two new human rights guidelines, both significant in reaffirming EU policy commitments towards HRDs and the groups and individuals they seek to support and protect. The 'EU Guidelines on the Promotion and Protection of Freedom of Religion or Belief'[34] and the 'EU Guidelines to Promote and Protect the Enjoyment of all Human Rights by Lesbian, Gay, Bisexual, Transgender and Intersex (LGBTI) persons',[35] both have explicit reference to protection of HRDs, and to the guidelines on HRDs.

In May 2014, the 'EU Human Rights Guidelines on Freedom of Expression Online and Offline', were introduced, which provide important EU policy direction for the protection of HRDs and their freedom of opinion, expression and privacy, as guaranteed in human rights law.[36] The 'Freedom of Expression' Guidelines are well-developed in providing operational guidance to EU member state missions, including frameworks and operational guidance for protecting rights and freedoms in communication technologies, data protection, best practices of information and communication technologies (ICT) companies, trade measures, and direction for human rights training and capacity building.

The EU has now developed 11 human rights guidelines, articulating EU human rights policy and directives.[37] For diplomatic support and protection to human rights defenders, operational guidance articulated in the EU Guidelines on HRDs is complemented by many of the other EU guidelines' policy directives.

During the 2014 EU Forum Conference entitled 'Protecting Those Who Protect', the EU introduced new and enhanced support mechanisms for protecting HRDs. These include: an enhanced EDIHR budget for 2015–2020; creation of an HRD mechanism to be facilitated by a civil society expert consortium; a new facility of demand driven funding for access to HRDs working in difficult environments; and renewed commitment to the small grant emergency fund for HRDS at risk.[38] The European Council introduced simultaneously at the conference a new toolkit to operationalise a rights-based approach in foreign policy, inclusive of, and stressing the need for, 'continued EU support for human rights defenders, capacity-building of local civil society organisations, and promoting a safe and enabling environment in both law and practice that maximises their contribution to development'.[39] EU recognition of, and engagement with, HRDs as important partners and actors in development, was further elaborated at the conference. However, some HRDs commenting at the conference during a panel session on support for and evaluation of implementation of the guidelines, expressed frustration with the lack of coherent planning for implementation of the guidelines, stating human rights (and defenders) are too often side-lined by other EU policy priorities.[40]

Viewpoints on implementation of the guidelines from Kyrgyzstan, Thailand and Tunisia

Engaging with the guidelines' recommendations

A study assessing implementation of the EU Guidelines on Human Rights Defenders in Kyrgyzstan, Thailand and Tunisia was carried out for the European Parliament between October 2012 and January 2013.[41] Research data were gathered using a participatory approach, primarily from semi-structured interviews with HRDs, European diplomats and representatives of INGOs working in these countries, and with EU representatives in Europe from the EEAS, EDIHR and European Ministry of Foreign Affairs desks responsible for human rights policy. Participants were asked to respond to a series of questions based on recommendations set out in the guidelines.[42]

Findings from the study indicate knowledge of the guidelines' recommendations is limited amongst diplomats and other stakeholders.[43] Out of 41 participants, only 16 reported having knowledge of the contents of the guidelines, 8 reported some familiarity with the guidelines, 13 reported no prior knowledge of the guidelines, and 4 did not comment (or information was not available) (see Table 1).

Diplomats, INGOs and HRDs voiced concern that there was little awareness of the specific content of the guidelines amongst many diplomats worldwide. The diplomats in this study had not received any specific training to gain knowledge of, or strategies for implementation of, the guidelines. Results from the study show technical problems (lack of direction and lack of dissemination) impeding use of the guidelines and inconsistent implementation of guideline recommendations.

HRDs in the study did not find the appointment of focal points for human rights in EUDs resulted in increasing diplomats' engagement with a wider range of HRDs, particularly outside of capital cities. I NGOs in particular welcomed the appointment of HRD liaison officers in EUDs, considering this a significant step in coordinating implementation of the guidelines. However, the time allowed for actually 'liaising with HRDs' in the position has been of concern, as 'liaising' appears to be undefined. Many HRDs did not know how to actually engage with the EU liaison officer.[44]

Table 1. Participants' knowledge of the guidelines in Kyrgyzstan, Thailand and Tunisia

Participants	Knowledge of contents	Some familiarity	No knowledge	No comment
Diplomats	5	6	5	3
HRDs	7	2	8	1
Other	4	0	0	0
Total	16	8	13	4

Notes: Bennett, *Guidelines*, 77. *Knowledge* refers to having read the guidelines – *familiarity* refers to vague understanding of content. The 'others' category represents interviews with INGOs, UN, and Organisation for Security and Cooperation in Europe (OSCE) representatives working in the countries. In addition, consultations were made with a number of human rights experts and INGOs to gather background information for the study.

Some EU country missions taking part in the study had created their own mission-specific 'human rights action plans', providing recommended steps for interaction and support to HRDs. However other diplomats in the study were not aware of these 'action plans', or of any particular strategies to engage with HRDs, and were not aware of the guidelines' recommendations to do so. One EU Foreign Ministry official described the dissemination of their human rights action plan posted on the intranet, providing access to their field operations, but the problem was the action plan was not accessed by diplomats in the field (of those queried in the study).

Suggestions made by some EU and Foreign Ministry officials were to further prioritise support to HRDs as a mandatory requirement of diplomatic work in EU missions. A similar proposal was put forward by a senior EU diplomat at the Conference for Support and Protection of HRDs in 2009, suggesting implementation of the guidelines to be part of the foreign-service job description and part of set criteria for career advancement.[45]

Most diplomats in the study expressed a clear commitment, need and interest to work with HRDs, particularly in countries going through political transition. But some diplomats minimised the need for engagement with HRDs, and one stated that HRDs no longer need protection or support for their empowerment in a country that has already 'democratised'. The majority of diplomats emphasised having an 'open door' policy to the HRD community (which meant HRDs were welcome to take the initiative for engagement with diplomats), noting the utility of diplomats meeting with large numbers of HRD actors being impractical.

Responses from HRDs were generally positive to this open door policy, but many expected more proactive engagement initiated by the EU countries. HRDs made aware of the guidelines' recommendations in the study stated an interest to initiate contact on urgent cases or important human rights issues with EU diplomats, and welcomed the commitment of the EU to provide emergency funds for immediate protection measures.

But many other HRDs felt the initiative should be greater from the EU. HRDs recognised they have a responsibility for their own welfare and to voice their security/protection needs. Even so, the 'open door' policy from EU countries poses questions as to how HRDs can 'engage' to benefit from EU support. Power dynamics in the relationship between diplomats and HRDs exist, and most HRDs interviewed had a lack of understanding on how best to approach diplomatic missions. HRDs also have their own travel and time restrictions that inhibit opportunities to call on embassies or develop relationships.

For some HRDs, direct contact with EU countries is not appropriate. They are cognisant of the possibility of reprisals by state or non-state actors if they are seen engaging with foreign diplomats. Others are hesitant to make contacts with diplomats in a 'world' they are unfamiliar with or uncomfortable in, and there are often language and cultural barriers.[46]

HRDs need to take initiative and communicate their protection needs, and will most often use trusted networks – liaising with family and friends, and possibly INGOs and UN offices (sometimes as a point of contact to access EU support). INGOs in the study recognise they have a role to play in facilitating and working as a bridge between HRDs and diplomats, and HRDs often voiced that INGOs are important facilitators for their support and protection, including their engagement with EU actors.

Good practice approaches and gaps in implementation

Participants in the study indicated a number of good practices by EU missions since the guidelines were revised in 2008.[47] These included: accompanying HRDs to airports to ensure security; monitoring HRD hearings and trials; providing financial and logistical support to HRDs in emergency situations; supporting HRDs needing respite or health-related assistance; challenging laws that criminalise HRDs; developing European diplomats' outreach initiatives to HRDs; supporting HRD protection networks; requesting information from state authorities on HRD cases of serious concern; supporting HRD participation with state and national human rights institutions; and intervening with 'quiet diplomacy' on behalf of HRD cases of concern. In regard to the latter, quiet diplomacy discussions are by their nature never disclosed, and the EU's discretion in this approach can be frustrating for HRDs, their families and support networks, who do not have knowledge of what is being said or done on their behalf. That said it is practice that EU stakeholders would only intervene if the impacted HRD, or the HRD's family members, were in agreement.[48]

Measuring the impact of the EU's strategies and actions is easier in some situations (i.e. visits or meetings with HRDs) and more difficult in others (i.e. diplomatic processes challenging laws and practices that violate human rights/HRDs). Often , responding to a violation against a HRD can be from collective actions taken by a variety of actors, and it may be difficult to discern who or what had a specific impact. However, through increasing EU/EU member state record keeping and documentation of actions and successful strategies, both the initiative of implementing recommendations of the guidelines, and the impact on HRDs, might be easier to discern. For example, research results showed the EU coordinating, and mission diplomats engaging in, trial monitoring in Thailand and Kyrgyzstan, and both INGOs and diplomats gave commentary on this as best practice.[49] Such best practices could be applicable and transferable to other mission countries. If such knowledge-sharing and measures for evaluation of practice were carried out by the EU missions on a systematic basis, this could have a wide impact.[50] The use of indicators and measures for good practice were recognised as a means to help missions effectively implement the guidelines.

There were also suggestions for improvement of EU actions towards HRDs at risk, noted by HRD and INGO participants in the study. The use of public declarations was criticised in some instances as being reactive rather than pre-emptive. There was concern that diplomats often respond only after HRDs are sentenced. There was also criticism that the issuing of 'weak' statements may send a message that the EU is either too pressured to respond or does not care. Participants stressed that EU public declarations should articulate concerns about violations with more detailed reference to the law or specific human rights frameworks.

The complexity of the EU public declaration process needing all member state signatures can result in watered-down messages. HRD and INGO participants noted that in some situations the EU may best refrain from making a statement where member state 'buy-in' is weak, and choose a different means of intervention. When *démarches* and declarations fail, other tactics should be considered to prevent further human rights violations or a worsening situation. Non-EU embassies might be consulted by EUD and EU missions on the appropriateness of interventions on behalf of HRDs. Non-EU countries may share equal concerns to take an urgent stand, and may be better positioned within the host country to make a difference through a *démarche* or public statement. Longer-term political ramifications need careful consideration by the EU when evaluating the impact of EU *démarches*. Releasing a statement that has been diluted through collective member state endorsement can cause political fragmentation across member states, impacting EU cohesion, and possibly causing unintended or negative consequences for HRDs or their practice.

Both diplomats and HRDs reported concern for an absence of engagement with the guidelines' recommendations by diplomats working in other sections of an embassy (non-political sections). This lack of engagement has repercussions on the protection of HRDs when they are involved in human rights issues that intersect with, for example: business, trade and investment policies; security and defence contracting; development planning; and consular services for visas (this may impact issuing visas to HRDs for their professional activities abroad, or for emergency respite needs). Lack of diplomatic engagement with HRDs in these sectors is potentially very dangerous for HRDs. Many international development issues relate to HRDs, and cut across all sectors of diplomatic work. Positive steps to integrate staff across sections might be seen in EU missions that are developing new platforms for engagement with 'environmental HRDs', recognising their role and their vulnerability in development processes.[51]

One diplomat serving as a human rights focal point found engagement with HRDs was mostly taken on by individuals assigned with the task, and not taken up by other diplomats, including those working in embassy departments such as trafficking and border regulation, migration, security and defence, or investment and trade. These embassy sections may be in consultation when preparing input for the EU HRCSs, but it was noted by a significant number of diplomats in all three countries that HRDs normally did not have opportunities to engage with diplomats from non-political sections. The interaction and level of shared information as per the guidelines' recommendations within EUDs and EU missions was not researched in depth in this study, but some diplomats did raise the issue of the lack of attention to HRDs across embassy sectors, expressing that improvement is needed to achieve knowledge of the guidelines internally across all mission staff.

Diplomats who were well-informed about the guidelines mentioned knowledge of their own Ministry of Foreign Affairs national human rights guidance, which they integrate into their work, inclusive of attention to HRDs. These diplomats appeared to have a good understanding of how to effectively manage approaches to support HRDs in their work, and challenges specifically relating to the security of HRDs. Many of these diplomats continue to use best practices from prior diplomatic post experiences, and call for a more coherent approach needed to acknowledge HRDs' contributions to diplomatic missions, and how to support HRDs' work across diplomatic thematic sectors.

A number of diplomats did not engage in facilitating partnerships between government and civil society. HRDs reported that they were supported by the EU in consultations with state officials from time to time, but, with the exception of HRDs in Bishkek, Kyrgyzstan, HRDs felt they needed more support to strengthen their legitimacy and to achieve genuine participation in government. The EU guidelines state:

> The principle of allowing room for independence of mind and free debate on a government's policies and actions is fundamental, and is a tried and tested way of establishing a better level of protection of human rights. Human rights defenders can assist governments in promoting and protecting human rights. As part of consultation processes they can play a key role in helping to draft appropriate legislation, and in helping to draw up national plans and strategies on human rights. This role too should be recognised and supported.[52]

When diplomats were asked of their role to support HRD participation with government, responses were split – some indicated they did not see facilitating HRD engagement as part of their diplomatic work, while others did actively support giving voice and platforms to HRDs in government relations. The mainstreaming of the EU Guidelines on HRDs, and best practices for effective implementation, could be developed in human rights trainings provided for all diplomats, to address any knowledge gaps on EU policy recognising HRDs' contributions to human rights as part of a national political agenda.

A number of HRDs found support to engage civil society in political processes to be driven by particular individuals or small groups of 'rights friendly' missions. When the individual left the mission, HRDs complained that relationship to the mission and its support was lost. Some HRDs did not have knowledge of how to re-engage. Some embassies have taken steps to address this, but more missions reported that when diplomatic posts change, knowledge-sharing of human rights contacts and a process of documentation is needed, to further systemisation across and within missions, and to provide HRDs with ongoing support.

Strengthening support for HRDs in remote areas

European funding streams have been effective in supporting the work of HRDs in each of the three countries studied.[53] However both diplomats and HRDs recognised a number of factors impeding projects being submitted or supported in remote areas. These include: language barriers and knowledge skills needed for the complex project application process; lack of network links to diplomats, INGOs and other HRD partnerships; limited information access and technology available; and the management of large grants impossible or inappropriate for many smaller organisations working in remote areas.

Many HRDs would like to consult diplomats and see them make more effort to visit remote areas and show their interest in the work of HRDs outside capitals. HRDs are concerned that those working in remote areas often do not know of funding available to support their human rights work from small funding streams available through missions or EUDs. Some HRDs thought diplomats pick and choose 'tried and trusted' HRDs to fund, and one HRD noted that 'no new, creative voices will come from this process'.

Tools and actions for mitigating risks for HRDs have been well supported in some geographic areas by the EU. HRDs note methodologies in some situations must be flexible and creative, and HRDs are well situated with ideas and contributions, which could be incorporated in the HRCS process. It is noted that research is lacking in understanding situated protection needs (i.e. for WHRDs in remote areas, HRDs in humanitarian crisis zones, etc.). Building this evidence base for understanding protection needs is vital to their practice and well-being.[54]

Some HRDs in remote areas who already receive funding as recipients of larger projects suggest the local management of projects could be improved to have more impact. There may be projects where impact and value for money can be better achieved in remote areas if efforts are made to identify leadership capacity in those remote areas. Other HRDs in remote areas have suggested more EU investment be made in training and skills building by 'central' partners and international educators to teach those working in remote areas how to meet European standards expected in project management. It is necessary to assess and acknowledge the human rights expertise existing outside of capitals, and their capacity to lead projects, and equally to give attention to those HRDs that would benefit from support and education to increase their capacity to become HRD leaders in their communities.

Another suggestion to enable EU funding to reach remote areas was for EU member state bi-lateral funding streams to initiate smaller projects that could later be matched with EIDHR funds, allowing an easier initial project application process for HRDs to be negotiated with individual missions on the ground. The EUD could monitor the start-up of the project with the member state mission, with the EU providing further funding for sustaining activities beyond the initial start-up period. It was suggested the EU invest more in supporting skills building amongst civil society, for managing projects across a wider range of geographic regions.

Visits to HRDs in remote areas

EU representative visits offer HRDs personal engagement, recognition of their work, and can legitimise their activities in what may be a hostile environment for human rights practice. This engagement can initiate supportive steps that help HRDs feel part of a larger network concerned for their well-being. INGOs noted the importance of security assessments and the consideration of post-visit reprisals, but many HRDs taking part in the study welcomed such visits. Monitoring trials of HRDs in areas outside of capital cities was a particular request from both HRDs and INGOs, as this rarely happens and could impact HRDs receiving fair trials.

Best practice examples from other countries can be useful for diplomats considering their own HRD engagement and outreach. One strategy introduced by a participant in this study was the 'parcelling out' of geographic areas between diplomats to visit HRDs outside of the capital. It was noted that Mexico and the Democratic Republic of Congo have engaged successfully in this strategy. Through knowledge-sharing of each diplomat's experience, this should also increase the level of understanding of human rights situations across the country. This is a practical example of how the limited resources of diplomatic missions can be managed effectively. However, there have been commentators that are concerned with the cohesion and sharing of knowledge amongst missions in forming any 'EU' strategy. There is a danger of geographic information remaining in 'silos' of each specific mission or with individual diplomats, if not documented and shared with colleagues across thematic sections, the larger diplomatic community and with other relevant interlocutors. Such an engagement strategy could be led by the Human Rights Focal Point/HRD liaison officer in the mission country. These best practices indicate some diplomats find value in understanding HRD situations first hand.

Many EU diplomats in this study found direct contact with HRDs important, in addition to relying on INGOs and the UN knowledge of HRD situations in remote areas. However, all participants recognised there remain many HRDs, particularly in remote areas, who work outside of INGO networks or other circles of support and protection. Most of these HRDs do not know of, or understand how the recommendations set forth in the guidelines are intended to impact their lives and their work. Some HRDs interviewed were working and living outside of capital cities, and were not aware they can contact an EU liaison officer to HRDs, and many did not know they can call on EU embassies for support or protection (other than for project funding support). For others, sustaining engagement with the EU proved to be unsuccessful in remote areas.[55] HRDs working with colleagues in remote areas suggested the EU consider a more systemised means to keeping communication lines open to those working on difficult human rights cases, or in contentious environments, far from the capital.

Improving security for WHRDs

The operational directive in the revised EU guidelines states that '[EU] missions should pay attention to particular risks faced by women human rights defenders'.[56] Diplomats, INGOs and HRDs based in country capitals acknowledged their concern for women working in remote areas, noting there could be increased risks for women in particular who work unregistered, or work outside established networks. HRDs noted the evidence base for assessing protection needs of women working in remote areas is lacking. They were concerned violations are unreported and WHRDs themselves are often not documenting abuses they experience. These women may not have access to networks for security when needed. There was no evidence from the study of EU strategies to protect WHRDs in HRCS planning, and most diplomats interviewed were not aware of specific risks to WHRDs.

HRDs in all three countries voiced concerns of the threat of sexual violence against women and intimidation related to cultural stigma and, for some, clashes with Muslim extremist attitudes (reported in the south of Thailand; in both Bishkek and South Kyrgyzstan; and of growing concern throughout Tunisia) with particular concern for WHRDs working in villages, many in relative isolation. WHRDs working in rural communities were considered more vulnerable when challenging power held predominantly by men. LGBTI defenders were also noted as potentially vulnerable and at risk of human rights violations by both state and non-state actors. In Kyrgyzstan, LGBTI and women's rights groups organised a conference on Women's Human Right Defender Day in November 2012, which included a discussion on improving security strategies in their work.[57] At the conference, concern was shared amongst HRD groups that LGBTI rights were increasingly threatened in Kyrgyzstan. Amongst diplomats, only one diplomat in Thailand specifically prioritised LGBTI HRDs as a group that faces risk.

There are a number of publications calling for gender-specific implementation of the guidelines, including a recommendation produced by the World Organisation against Torture in 2013, which is endorsed by 11 INGO groups.[58] Peace Brigades International recently published a report from an international conference in London on WHRDs (October 2012), which engaged EU, UN and HRD representatives to consider more effective implementation of the guidelines in respect to WHRDs.[59]

In November 2013, after a global campaign led by Norway to strengthen international commitments to the protection of WHRDs, the UN adopted a resolution on protecting WHRDs.[60] Consensus amongst states was gained on the last day of deliberations of the resolution, but only through the deletion of a crucial paragraph containing language calling on states to condemn all forms of violence against women and WHRDs and to refrain from invoking any customs, tradition or religious consideration to avoid obligations with respect to the elimination of violence against women.[61] The adoption of this resolution should have resonance and impact on promoting attention to WHRDs within EU missions. HRDs globally are advocating for repositioning of agendas and strategies, urging for increased attention to WHRD protection needs in localised environments. Prominent independent world leaders, women Nobel laureates, and over 70 African CSOs lobbied their country representatives to take WHRD issues seriously.[62]

Utilising the EU protection scheme

Financial assistance for HRDs at high risk is made available through the EIDHR mechanism.[63] Some EU countries provide emergency visas and protection schemes, which have ostensibly saved the lives of HRDs when threatened or at serious risk of harm. There is a current EU initiative creating a more coordinated effort to provide emergency temporary relocation assistance to HRDs in need.[64]

The process for accessing emergency protection for HRDs was not well known or understood by a majority of diplomats and HRD participants in the countries studied. Many diplomats in the study were not aware of an EU funding mechanism for HRDs at risk. A suggested remedy from the study was that EUDs coordinate and convene a briefing session annually with all EU missions in-country, to discuss the tools and processes available to protect HRDs, and how these mechanisms can be accessed by HRDs. Additionally, details of the EU's temporary relocation initiative for HRDs could be disseminated to all diplomats in third country missions.[65] The utility of this scheme and involvement of particular host countries as relocation destinations should be known amongst mission diplomats.

Some HRDs are aware of access and assistance in emergency situations through their partnerships with the UN or INGOs on the ground. But there remain many more HRDs, particularly in remote areas, who are not linked to support mechanisms or real protection networks to assist them when they are in trouble. There are assumptions that HRDs 'know what to do or who to call', but in many instances HRDs do not know how to take appropriate security precautions.

The creation of protection networks, in various bespoke forms, should be a priority in countries where HRDs are at high risk and are working in isolated areas. Regional (multiple country) security networks have been successfully implemented in a number of regions with EIDHR funding, including the Horn of Africa and the South Caucasus. HRDs in the study stated a number of benefits from national, local and particular thematic group networks (e.g. ethnic minority, lawyers, women, LGBTI) contributing to strengthen safe working practices. They also noted that support for bespoke network building is needed, to form better responses to problems through the sharing of experiences, discussing how they manage and mitigate their own risk, and considering means for access to protection mechanisms when needed.

Knowledge sharing

Training available to diplomats on incorporating attention to human rights do not consistently include approaches towards effective implementation of the guidelines, according to evidence from the study. Even where EU member states provide mandatory human rights training, it appears some diplomats have been left out, or personally are not committed, based on the responses given in the study. The EEAS has committed to mainstreaming human rights through mandatory trainings,[66] described by the EU as an important component of EEAS human rights aims to strengthen cross fertilisation of human rights internally.[67]

Commitment to training is one means of instilling the intersections of human rights with coherence of EU priority areas, addressing practically how diplomats can engage human rights matters in the short, medium and long term. Useful training methodologies should provide a structured design to help diplomat awareness of EU and member state commitments to HRDs, and how their actions in missions can be effectively implemented. Trainings should also provide tools for documenting and measuring the impact of actions.[68] A (longer-term) human rights strategic plan of the EU should include appropriately designed training to ensure methods of measuring progress in the implementation of the guidelines. Through improved documentation of actions, the EU can provide further evidence of 'human rights running as a silver thread through a truly integrated range of external policies'.[69]

INGOs have commented that when appropriately designed (and with the commitment of diplomats taking part) mission country trainings developed to engage HRDs and diplomats on implementation of the guidelines can be of value, particularly if the outcome can be measured, such as developing a human rights action plan, or part of the annual HRCS process to develop EU strategy.

The EEAS can utilise the vast experiences of EU human rights focal points and HRD liaison officers to share best practice examples in trainings. Considering new EU commitments to a rights-based approach encompassing all human rights, it is a timely opportunity to systemise a methodology for more regular and mandatory trainings by the EEAS and its partners. There are good examples to draw from. A number of EU member states provide human rights training to diplomats that includes specific methods for support and protection of HRDs. The NGO Frontline facilitates trainings of the guidelines with EU diplomats and HRDs in select mission countries. And universities, INGOs and other forums run in-country training or trainer projects that teach methodologies supporting the protection of HRDs.[70]

Another approach to knowledge sharing is improving the dissemination of the guidelines to HRDs, in a language understandable to targeted groups.[71] The EU has made impressive efforts to translate the guidelines in multiple languages for use across many countries. However, evidence suggests dissemination of the guidelines to HRDs in remote areas of the three countries studied remains poor. HRDs in Thailand mentioned some problems with translation of the guidelines, and the importance of consultation (especially with bi-lingual HRDs working in specific regions) to check the language text and make suitable dissemination plans for reaching remote HRD groups.

Human rights policy coherence

Need for policy coherence

In human rights literature from over a decade ago, Philip Alston and J.H.H. Weiler addressed considerations towards coherence of EU human rights policies in 'An "Ever Closer Union" in Need of a Human Rights Policy: The European Union and Human Rights'. Fifteen years later, many of the same obstacles addressed in their article to achieving human rights coherence in the EU remain a challenge.[72] Gordon Crawford recognised the EU's evaluation methodology lacked analysis of its own promotion of human rights in external relations, and suggested a participatory approach including civil society actors as monitors to improve evaluating EU external relations actions.[73] Schmitter and Brouwer recognised how tracing micro–meso–macro linkages enables evaluators to make more plausible connections between external support and overall political change.[74]

Other commentators suggest cohesion of human rights, development goals and HRD-targeted approaches – all need to be complementary and coordinated, including diplomats' role to support and protect HRDs as partners in democracy building. Academics from the Association of Human Rights Institutes (AHRI) called for the EU to step up its efforts in rights-based approaches in development, including recommendations for the EU to take further actions in their outreach to civil society, particularly in the EU role and actions in UN human rights reforms.[75] The recommendations from the AHRI group note the EU needs inward-looking change to impact their external human rights work.[76]

The need for coherence of EU human rights policy across all human rights (civil, political, social, economic and cultural), and all EU mission thematic sectors (embassy sections or departments) in third counties, was raised at the 2013 EU-NGO Forum on Human Rights, specifically in presentations 'The Fight Against Impunity' and 'Accountability of Economic, Social and Cultural Rights'. The UN Special Rapporteur on the Right to Food stressed the need for the EU to 'practice what it preaches in order to enhance its credibility'.[77]

On International Human Rights Day, 10 December 2013, civil society representatives demanded greater coherence in EU foreign policy, with a specific concern of respecting human rights as a guiding principle in trade relations. Highlighting trade policies and linking EU diplomatic work in this area, groups raised the urgent need of EU support for protection policies of HRDs working on social, economic and cultural rights. Conclusions specified that 'the Guidelines on Human Rights Defenders could become an effective policy tool in the hands of EU Missions to help protect defenders based in remote areas who promote and defend economic, social and cultural rights'.[78]

Consistency in application of human rights principles will solicit the need for rethinking policy objectives at all levels, a tall order for the EU machinery. In rethinking policy shifts and implementation that impacts HRDs, for example, the EU would need to reconsider its general schemes of preferences (GSP) to countries where trade agreements consistently link to non-negotiable human rights clauses. This would entail gauging potential risks to HRDs, while promoting businesses to have meaningful consultations with HRDs to rule out any negative impact on social, economic, cultural and environmental rights.[79] This was to be addressed by the EU Commission and put in force by January 2014.[80] In January 2014, a published report with replies of the commission responded to these challenges in planning for the implementation of the newly revised GSP scheme.[81]

Positions across EU countries on external trade policies may include agreements that are remiss of consistent human rights considerations. It is also imperative to consider the impact of such agreements on human rights defenders and the victims they represent.[82] The dynamics and tensions amongst differing functions of the EU internally will invariably impact such coherence in EU external relations. Arguably the need for improving understanding and actions of rights-based approaches and coherence with human rights policies is then an even greater imperative – it must be vertical (throughout thematic EEAS sections), horizontal (across EU member states), internal (EU Brussels) and external (across all EU external missions).

In June 2014 the Council of the EU adopted Conclusions, stating the EU would intensify its political and material support to human rights defenders:

> … and step up its efforts against all form of reprisals, and will actively support the strengthening of UN monitoring in this regard. The EU is particularly committed to improve its support to vulnerable and marginalised human rights defenders. The EU will intensify outreach to those operating in remote and rural areas. Particular attention is paid to women human rights defenders.[83]

Five INGOs responded to these Conclusions in a collective press release, welcoming this initiative of the EU, but also urging full implementation of the guidelines. They proposed a number of recommendations for concrete actions to be taken, and a more coherent approach of the Council, to include the recommendations in the new EU Action Plan on Human Rights and Democracy for 2015.[84]

The EU is building on its human rights commitments, and may come forth with further steps to mend this coherence gap. It is also noteworthy to consider the multiple layers by which this coherence will need to build over time, and the necessity of measuring the success of implementing these identified policy directives and their coherence in all levels of the EU foreign policy machinery. Implementation includes actions of the EEAS staff working in each sector at HQ level, all of the EU member states contributions, and EU delegations and diplomats' implementation worldwide. In a report examining the feasibility of practical application and policy coherence in development, Michael King et al. write of the increased attention in policy statements and legal documents of the EU (and Organisation of Economic Co-operation and Development) contributing to further conceptualising policy coherence in development. The authors argue that policy coherence can be promoted at five different levels: (1) internal coherence; (2) intra-governmental coherence; (3) inter-governmental coherence; (4) multilateral coherence, and (5) developing country coherence.[85] Not a small feat, but one the EU has now committed to invest in.

Human rights country strategy process

Since the guidelines were revised in 2008 there have been changes in how HRDs practice[86] and how the EU implements its human rights agenda. Notably the EU Human Rights Country Strategy process initiated in 2012 provided a new vehicle for ensuring human rights planning is systematically taken up as a foreign policy priority by EU missions. The EU Strategic Framework and Action Plan on Human Rights and Democracy, including a directive for the HRCS process, sets benchmarks for a three-year period (2012–2014),[87] to be renewed in 2015.

HRCSs are requested from EUDs and member state missions worldwide. The HRCS planning is expected to include consultations with HRDs in providing clear strategies that are monitored and evaluated by the EU. HRCSs are currently internal EU documents. It is difficult to report on attention to HRDs in the planning, and difficult for HRDs and other stakeholders to know of their intended effect. The European Parliament and INGOs have called for a more open process.[88]

In practice, the HRCS process could serve as an opportunity for embedding direction for implementation of the guidelines, considered systematically in the HRCS annual reviews, to improve knowledge of the guidelines and build attention to HRDs consistently in all country strategies. By leaving implementation of the guidelines' recommendations without specific planning benchmarks, and HRD engagement undefined in the HRCS process, use of the guidelines as a policy tool may eventually become obsolete. This could adversely impact EU support and protection to HRDs in areas where it is much needed, but overlooked.

As there is limited time and resources for diplomats to devote to reviewing effective implementation of all policy directives, the EU and its member states might well consider revising or updating the guidelines' operational recommendations on HRDs to include direction and coherence within the HRCS exercise. It was not clear to the author from gathered research data why the EU did not seize the opportunity to systematically improve knowledge and dissemination of the guidelines through the HRCS process when the Action Plan was initiated for 2012–2014. Evaluating outcomes from the first three years of the Action Plan, the EU now has an opportunity to be vigilant in considering integrating and referencing the guidelines' recommendations to support and protect HRDs with new policy directions, and in preparation for the Human Rights Action Plan for 2015 –2017.[89]

The *EU Human Rights and Democracy Strategic Framework* can provide opportunities to strengthen the use of the guidelines as a progressive policy tool. The guidelines provide excellent recommendations, however they must be consistent with current policy developments and the changing HRD landscape, and consistent with the aim of implementing rights-based approaches by the EU institution-wide. But in achieving coherence and mainstreaming the guidelines in HRCS planning processes, the mechanisms and approach must include plans for the guidelines' application to be understood as a policy priority by Foreign Service staff. This would entail a commitment from the EU and partners to devote resources to trainings for Brussels staff and the diplomatic corps. A practical means of training, and a less costly investment, could be building coherence of these policy initiatives through already established processes: the review and updating as necessary of guidelines' recommendations; investment in improving already existing human rights education and training for staff across the EU; and through significant reflection to enhance and strengthen support for EU human rights guidelines in a more robust HRCS process.

Importantly, efforts should be made to reach field staff, to implement cohesion in methods used in missions when best practice methods are identified. This assistance to mission staff should be inclusive of providing tools to help them establish indicators for planning objectives and for documenting actions, and investing in a process for the evaluation of measuring effective implementation and impact of outcomes that show improvement in support and protection of HRDs in mission countries.

Taking a rights-based approach

The EU presented new mechanisms for the protection of HRDs at the European Commission's Conference on Human Rights and Democracy on the 10th Anniversary of the EU Guidelines on Human Rights Defenders in May 2014. The theme was *Protecting Those Who Protect*. The organisers stressed the conference was taking place 'at a key moment when several ongoing EU related initiatives will converge', including the adoption of a 'Tool-box for working towards a rights-based approach (RBA), encompassing all human rights, for the EU Development Cooperation.'[90]

The RBA toolkit references the importance of civil society in development. We also see implicit reference to HRDs, in explaining the third principle of RBA of 'non-discrimination and equal access'. The toolbox, for example, gives reference to a project 'strengthening the trade union movement in Myanmar'[91] and the importance of assessing discrimination beyond gender bias, considering unintended or indirect discrimination, all important to the programming and design stages. The guidance offers no further explanation as to how EU staff might apply the RBA in their work to impact the trade union outcomes of non-discrimination and equal access in the project, or how staff might go about analysis of ensuring the principle of non–discrimination is sustained to impact trade unionists' safe practice for the entire project cycle (and beyond the life of the project). This is where harmonising RBA with the guidelines' recommendations could be important.

If we are to take the Council's recommendations to make use of the HRCS process in the application of RBA, we could, in this same example, consider how the trade unionist movement in Myanmar might benefit from EU engagement with key trade union activists over the years following the project's close. Using RBA principles, and coherence with the EU guidelines' recommendations, EU actions could be benchmarked for planned action, such as meeting engagements with trade unionists, to ensure key objectives of the project are maintained. What the toolbox does not address is how applying RBA principles will support or protect civil society actors. The directive also misses an opportunity to direct EU member states to develop strong linkages with INGO partners, who play key roles as interlocutors with HRDs and often help facilitate their relations to EU missions.

As described in the RBA toolbox working document, RBA changes the analytical and practical lens used to design and undertake actions in all areas to improve (human right) outcomes. If this is to work systematically for the EU in mission countries, explicit guidance for engagement with civil society and human rights defenders, and steps for their protection, is needed.

As mainstreaming rights-based approaches into all EU policies is the aim, again practical steps must be considered. In consideration of the guidelines' implementation, if we make the assumption that RBA is to be mainstreamed in all sectors of EU work (participation with civil society is a tenet of the RBA tool box), and coherence of human rights policy means, in respect of the guidelines and HRCS process, these processes are to be formally linked, we would expect to see HRDs considered (and engaging?) in more diverse diplomatic agendas concerned with human rights, which is in line with EU (and UN) development aims.

One of the more difficult issues for the EU implementation of the guidelines is engaging with HRDs in remote areas and understanding their particular protection needs. This coincides with a priority area of concern for many EU countries in their development and external relations policies – strengthening women's rights in development and addressing violations of sexual violence. WHRDs in remote areas have identified particular protection issues, but identifying best practice approaches to eradicate violations against WHRDs has not been well addressed.[92]

How can application of RBA and coherence with EU strategic planning improve the security problems for WHRDs? In the European Parliament study, Tunisian WHRDs identified increased fear of bodily harm or assault since the Arab Spring revolution of 2011.[93] With gained civic freedoms has also come less certainty of knowing who their adversaries are. Both state and non-state actors may respond aggressively to women advocating for their rights, and WHRDs representing women victims of human rights abuses are on the frontlines and may be exposed to confrontations. There is very limited data available, or reporting on, how the uncertainty (in transitioning political environments) might be impacting WHRDs. Furthering research, with a rights-based approach sensitive to understanding gendered relationships, gender status and how gender is valued, can support better EU strategic planning concerned with the needs of WHRDs.

The European Commission pledges to undertake its first assessment of implementing the rights-based approach in 2016. What is needed from the onset of RBA is giving foreign diplomats genuine benchmarks that require their involvement. This is where coherence and RBA can converge. By embedding the guidelines' recommendations into the EU HRCS process, in consideration of approach in actions to address or engage with W/HRDs (including improving attention to those working in rural areas), implementation of the guidelines might be taken up more consistently by EU partners. With coherence of these human rights policy tools – for planning and benchmarking (via HRCS), for approach (via RBA in all areas of diplomacy work), and in consideration of EU recommendations towards HRDs (via the guidelines), the EU might find means for a systematic, effective implementation of the guidelines around this EU foreign policy priority – the support and protection of human rights defenders.

Conclusions

Changing EU institutional behaviour and establishing frames of reference to define how RBAs can be situated both institutionally at the EU, and how RBAs can be achieved through member state consensus and knowledge of this approach, is a longer process, yet a crucial one in strengthening implementation of all the human rights guidelines.[94] The Council invited the COHOM to continue to regularly review the implementation of the guidelines in June 2014. In its *Council Conclusions on the 10th Anniversary of the EU Guidelines on Human Rights Defenders*,[95] INGOs monitoring the situation of HRDs globally have welcomed the EU's renewed attention to HRDs, but have also made specific recommendations to strengthen coherency of EU policy on HRDs. These include bringing attention to support for all HRDs, including vulnerable and marginalised HRDs, women HRDs and those operating in remote areas; to create safe and enabling environments; and to raise awareness about the guidelines.[96]

In addition to directions for policy coherence with the HRCS process, and introduction of RBA, a revision of the guidelines' recommendations could include new HRD protection concerns,[97] and consideration of diplomats' best practices based on evaluations since the last revision in 2008. In doing so, the EU could strengthen application, relevance and use of the guidelines. This, in turn, could set out to improve diplomats' cohesion in approach to: strengthen communications and task sharing between the EU, missions and the UN on HRD issues; coordinate amongst EU member state missions more efficient monitoring of HRD cases and shared engagement with HRDs; encourage use of indicators and benchmarks to improve accountability of actions taken; contribute to the overall assessment of budgeting for project support to HRDs through improved understanding of HRD needs, particularly in sharing information on and with particular HRD groups; create opportunities for improving RBA actions across missions and thematic departments, to integrate approaches to HRDs in all departments and sectors; and to include more participation across EU mission countries. Advocates and INGOs working for the protection of HRDs have stated their readiness to work with the EU in support of the new EU mechanisms introduced to take action to protect HRDs.

The research study in Kyrgyzstan, Thailand and Tunisia has shown important and successful best practices by the EU, but also wide gaps of engagement between diplomats and HRDs existing in areas where attention to HRDs is needed in an ever-changing, shifting landscape. What the EU must consider from the evidence presented is where missions on the ground are failing in their commitments to support and protect HRDs, and why. The former UN Special Rapporteur on HRDs Margaret Sekkagya's report to the UN General Assembly, *Elements of a Safe and Enabling Environment for HRDs*,[98] provides a framework for considering the protection needs of HRDs by presenting developments that are challenging the security of HRDs and their practice. In the article *A Research Agenda for the Protection of Human Rights Defen*ders,[99] the authors call for further research needed, collaboratively undertaken with HRDs and practitioners, to better understand how to address HRD's security problems. Specific areas needing further research in respect to implementation of the EU guidelines are identified in the research report prepared for the European Parliament.[100]

The EU is at a crossroad with the introduction of these new human rights policy commitments, and at a time when new EEAS leadership is beginning, with the appointment of Ms Federica Mogherini as the new EU Foreign Policy Chief taking office in November 2014. Although challenging, the EU has set its goals for achieving EU policy coherence and agreement of human rights policy as a 'silver lining' in all its diplomatic relations, united amongst EU member states, and across all sectors and political agendas. This process might find help and useful partnerships through supporting a strong and enabled civil society committed to upholding human rights principles and fighting for justice in challenging environments. The practical steps needed – achieving coherence with attention to harmonisation of tools, using practical work methodologies, and EU countries working together to achieve a unified political front where human rights obligations are a priority. In the case of EU commitments to strengthen the legitimacy of defenders, increasing EU engagement with HRDs in country missions, for better informed, well planned and effective human rights strategies that ensure HRD participation, respect for their practice, and measures to ensure their security, are indeed ambitious goals, but worth committed investment.

Acknowledgements

Assessing the Implementation of the European Union Guidelines on Human Rights Defenders: the Cases of Kyrgyzstan, Thailand and Tunisia was a research project carried out by Karen Bennett for the European Parliament Subcommittee on Human Rights. The research report was published on 18 June 2013 (Luxembourg: Publications Office of the European Union).

Disclosure statement

No potential conflict of interest was reported by the author.

Notes

1. On risks and human rights violations HRDs face in their practice, see as examples, situations presented in: analysis of the situation in Indonesia, in A. Nabanan, 'To Protect the Defenders Doing the Most Possible, Continuing to do What Has to be Done', *Netherlands Quarterly of Human Rights* 26, no. 1 (2008): 139–48; analysis of the impact of 'war on terror' to increased violations against HRDs, in T. Landmann, 'Holding the Line: Human Rights Defenders in the Age of Terror', *The British Journal of Politics & International Relations* 8, no. 2 (2006): 123–47; report on the situation of women human rights defenders, 'United Nations Report of the Special Rapporteur on the Situation of Human Rights Defenders, Margaret Sekaggya', Sixteenth Session, Agenda Item 3 (June 2010); and analysis of global trends of violations to HRDs needing further research, in A. Nah, K. Bennett, J. Savage, and D. Ingleton, 'A Research Agenda for the Protection of Human Rights Defenders', *Journal of Human Rights Practice* 5, no. 3 (2013): 401–20.
2. European Union External Action Service, *The EU's Work with Human Rights Defenders*, http://eeas.europa.eu/human_rights/defenders/index_en.htm.
3. European Union, *Ensuring Protection – European Union Guidelines on Human Rights Defenders* (revised 2008), http://www.consilium.europa.eu/uedocs/cmsUpload/16332-re01.en08.pdf.
4. The field research was carried out by Karen Bennett between October 2012 and January 2013. See K. Bennett, *Assessing the Implementation of the European Union Guidelines on Human Rights Defenders: The Cases of Kyrgyzstan, Thailand and Tunisia* (European Union, DG External Policies, Policy Department, June 2013), http://www.europarl.europa.eu/RegData/etudes/etudes/join/2013/410221/EXPODROI_ET(2013)410221_EN.pdf.
5. Bennett, *Guidelines*, 2013.
6. Ibid., see Chapter 3 on Kyrgyzstan, Chapter 4 on Thailand, and Chapter 5 on Tunisia.
7. Declaration on the Right and Responsibility of Individuals, Groups and Organs of Society to Promote and Protect Universally Recognized Human Rights and Fundamental Freedoms, adopted by UN General Assembly resolution 53/144 (9 December 1998). This declaration is commonly referred to as the Declaration on Human Rights Defenders.
8. Charter of the United Nations (26 June 1945); N. Jagers, 'Mainstreaming Human Rights in International Economic Organisations: Improving Judicial Access for NGOs to the World Trade Organization', *Netherlands Quarterly of Human Rights* 24 (2006): 229 –70.
9. COHOM's mandate monitors developments with regard to respect for human rights throughout the world, and missions are expected to carry out monitoring and reporting to COHOM on the position of HRDs, and to make recommendations for appropriate action, such as public declarations or the issuing of *démarches* when HRDs are at risk. COHOM has been responsible for drafting and revising the guidelines as a practical tool to assist EU representations in the field to develop EU policy, and COHOM continues this work within the structure of the EU External Action Service (EEAS). See EEAS graphic representation, October 2013, http://eeas.europa.eu/background/docs/organisation_en.pdf.
10. The instrument supports civil society projects independently, and was reinforced in 2007–2013 with a budget of €1.104 billion , with further budget commitments for 2014 –2020 of €1.332 billion . Europe Aid, European Instrument for Democracy and Human Rights (EDIHR), *How We Finance Aid*, http://ec.europa.eu/europeaid/how/finance/eidhr_en.htm; and Regulation (EU) No. 235/2014 of the European Parliament and of the Council, 11 March 2014,

Establishing a Financing Instrument for Democracy and Human Rights Worldwide, http://www.eidhr.eu/files/dmfile/EIDHR.2014-2020.pdf.

11. Information on EDIHR funding and EU support to HRDs can be found on the European Commission website *Democracy and Human Rights, Human Rights Defenders*, http://www.eidhr.eu/human-rights-defenders.
12. Council of the European Union, *Draft Council Conclusions on the First Review of the Implementation of the EU Guidelines on Human Rights Defenders* 10111/06, Brussels (6 June 2006), http://register.consilium.europa.eu/pdf/en/06/st10/st10111.en06.pdf.
13. EU Guidelines on HRDs (2008), sections 1, 4, 8, 12 and 14.
14. Ibid., section 13.
15. UN and Regional Human Rights Bodies Joint Statement, *Ten Years On, Human Rights Defenders Continue to Pay a High Price*, CommDH/Speech 19 (9 December 2008), https://wcd.coe.int/com.instranet.InstraServlet?Index=no&command=com.instranet.CmdBlobGet&InstranetImage=1135612&SecMode=1&DocId=1344950&Usage=2.
16. In D. Joloy, 'Mexico's National Protection Mechanism for Human Rights Defenders: Challenges and Good Practices', *Journal of Human Rights Practice* 5, no. 3 (2013): 489–99, Joloy provides a detailed account of the practical work involved in developing a national protection mechanism for Mexico from the perspective of a HRD involved in the process, and the challenges remaining for effective implementation of the mechanism. The UN Special Rapporteur on HRDs' (title formerly Special Representative) mandate was first appointed to Ms Hina Jilani (2000–2008) and then Margaret Sekkagya (2008–2014), both very active in actions to support the implementation of the declaration. Michel Forst was appointed to the mandate in June 2014. He has recently stated: 'I am interested to examine the effectiveness of human rights defenders laws and mechanisms recently enacted and established in places such as Mexico and Cote d'Ivoire … The incorporation of the Declaration into national laws and policies is crucial to ensuring a safe and enabling environment for the work of human rights defenders', comments published on the International Service for Human Rights (ISHR) website, 16 July 2014, http://www.ishr.ch/news/new-special-rapporteur-human-rights-defenders-sets-out-his-vision.
17. EU Treaty of Lisbon (2009), http://europa.eu/lisbon_treaty/full_text/.
18. For commentary on EU human rights external relations policy to support HRDs during the period of the formation of EEAS see K. Kinzelbach and J. Kozma, 'Portraying Normative Legitimacy: The EU in Need of Institutional Safeguards for Human Rights', *Perspectives on European Politics & Society* 10, no. 4 (2009); B. Donnelly, 'Europe in the World: All Change or No Change in Foreign Policy After Lisbon?', *The International Spectator* 45, no. 2 (2010): 17 –22; and Front Line, *A Brief Evaluation of the Implementation of the EU Guidelines on Human Rights Defenders* (2010), http://www.europarl.europa.eu/meetdocs/2009_2014/documents/droi/dv/201/201101/20110110_059hrdeval_en.pdf; A. Wetzel, 'The Promotion of Participatory Governance in the EU's External Policies: Compromised by Sectoral Economic Interests?', *Democratization* (July 2011): 978–1000; and Heidi Hautala, *Report on EU Policies in Favour of Human Rights Defenders*, A7-0157 (14 May 2010), http://www.europarl.europa.eu/sides/getDoc.do?pubRef=-//EP//NONSGML+COMPARL+PE-439.063+02+DOC+PDF+V0//EN&language=EN.
19. . K. Bennett, N. Piche, S. Bascon, and L. Mahoney , *Final Report of 2009 Conference report on Security and Protection of Human Rights Defenders* (Peace Brigades International, December 2009), also available at Human Rights and Social Justice Research Institute, London Metropolitan University, https://metranet.londonmet.ac.uk/fms/MRSite/Research/HRSJ/2009-conf/conference-report-2009.pdf.
20. K. Koehler, 'European Foreign Policy after Lisbon: Strengthening the EU as an International Actor', *Caucasian Review of International Affairs* 4, no. 1 (2010): 57–72.
21. D. Mahckne, 'Post-Modern Diplomacy: Can EU Foreign Policy Make a Difference in World Politics?', *EU Diplomacy Papers*, 4/2011 (Bruges: College of Europe, 2011), 22.
22. *European Parliament Resolution on EU Policies in Favour of Human Rights Defenders*, 17 June 2010, http://www.europarl.europa.eu/sides/getDoc.do?type=TA&language=EN&reference=P7-TA-2010-0226.
23. Ibid. The resolution called for creating specific tools for assessing implementation of the guidelines: '… in order to develop more result-oriented action, that the High Representative of the European Union for Foreign Affairs and Security Policy regularly evaluate the

implementation of the EU Guidelines on Human Rights Defenders by each EU delegation in third countries and should prioritise and closely follow up this work, and make recommendations to those missions for enhanced action where the implementation has been noticeably weak; EU institutions to establish an inter-institutional cooperation mechanism on human rights defenders; understands that the creation of such a mechanism could be eased by the setting up of focal points for human rights defenders in all the EU institutions and organs, with such focal points working in close cooperation with those responsible for human rights and democracy in EU missions and delegations; Invites the Council and Commission to explore the possibilities of creating an alert system mechanism to be shared between EU institutions and all other protection mechanisms; Calls on the Commission to follow and monitor regularly the short- and long term implementation of the EU Guidelines on Human Rights Defenders and report back to the Human Rights Subcommittee of the European Parliament.'

24. High Representative of the EU for Foreign Affairs and Security Policy, Joint Communication to the European Parliament and the Council, *Human Rights and Democracy at the Heart of EU External Action – Towards a More Effective Approach* (12 December 2011), http://eeas.europa.eu/top_stories/2012/060112_hr_silverthread_en.htm.
25. EU Strategic Framework and Action Plan on Human Rights and Democracy: *VI. Working with Bilateral Partners, 31 Impact on the Ground through Tailor-Made Approaches*, 11855/12, Luxembourg (25 June 2012), http://www.consilium.europa.eu/uedocs/cms_data/docs/pressdata/EN/foraff/131181.pdf.
26. EU Strategic Framework 5, Preambular paragraphs.
27. The Action Plan calls for EU missions to consult with civil society as part of the HRCS process, and the EEAS encourages EU delegations to address their engagement with HRDs when designing human rights country strategies. The *specifics* of EU engagement with HRDs (for example, which HRDs to engage with – of what profession or geographic regions; the frequency, design and agenda of meetings; the type of support – financial, protection related, facilitating HRD dialogue with state and national institutions, etc. is left to the discretion of individual EU delegations to organise with EU member state mission participation.
28. Amnesty International et al., Letter Re: '"Minimum Standards" for the Implementation of the EU Guidelines on Human Rights Defenders under the Human Rights Country Strategies' to Veronique Arnault, Director, Human Rights and Democracy, EEAS, 25 November 2011, http://www.irct.org/media-and-resources/irct-news/show-news.aspx?PID=13767&NewsID=3395.
29. European Parliament resolution of 13 December 2012 on *The Review of the EU's Human Rights Strategy* (2012/2062(INI), http://www.europarl.europa.eu/meetdocs/2009_2014/documents/droi/dv/p7_ta-prov(2012)0504_/p7_ta-prov(2012)0504_en.pdf.
30. *EU Who is Who: European Parliamentary Human Rights Action Unit*, http://europa.eu/whoiswho/public/index.cfm?fuseaction=idea.hierarchy&nodeID=369146&lang=en.
31. Inter-parliamentary Committee Meeting with National Parliaments, 25 September 2013, *Session Two: Internal/External Coherence on Human Rights*, http://www.europarl.europa.eu/meetdocs/2009_2014/documents/droi/dv/2a_backgroundnote_/2a_backgroundnote_en.pdf.
32. *European Parliament Report on the Annual Report on Human Rights in the World 2012 and the European Union's Policy on the Matter* (2013/2152(INI), Committee on Foreign Affairs (29 November 2013), which includes calls for EU action regarding particular human rights defenders in need of immediate support and protection, and furthering actions on proper implementation plans of EU Human Rights Guidelines, http://www.europarl.europa.eu/sides/getDoc.do?pubRef=-//EP//NONSGML+REPORT+A7-2013-0418+0+DOC+PDF+V0//EN.
33. Remarks by EU High Representative Catherine Ashton on the EU Annual Report on Human Rights, Strasbourg (12 June 2013), http://www.consilium.europa.eu/uedocs/cms_Data/docs/pressdata/EN/foraff/137457.pdf.
34. *EU Guidelines on the Promotion and Protection of Freedom of Religion or Belief*: EU Foreign Affairs Council meeting, Luxembourg (24 June 2013).
35. *EU Guidelines to Promote and Protect the Enjoyment of all Human Rights by Lesbian, Gay, Bisexual, Transgender and Intersex (LGBTI) Persons*: EU Foreign Affairs Council meeting, Luxembourg (24 June 2013).
36. *EU Human Rights Guidelines on Freedom of Expression Online and Offline*: EU Foreign Affairs Council meeting, Luxembourg (12 May 2014).

37. The 11 EU Human Rights Guidelines (as of April 2015) are providing EU policy directives on: human rights defenders (2008); death penalty (2013); torture and other cruel, inhuman or degrading treatment or punishment (2012); promotion and protection of freedom of religion or belief (2013); promoting and protecting the enjoyment of all human rights by lesbian, gay, bisexual, transgender and intersex (LGBTI) persons (2013); human rights dialogues with third countries (2009); children and armed conflict (2008); promotion and protection of the rights of the child (2008); violence against women and girls and combating all forms of discrimination against them (2008); freedom of expression online and offline (2014); and international humanitarian law. See: http://eeas.europa.eu/human_rights/guidelines/index_en.htm.
38. EDIHR Forum Conference, 'Protecting Those Who Protect', Brussels, 12–14 May 2014. EU introduction of Forum 2014: 'Each year the European Commission organises a spring forum dedicated to the reality of Human Rights on the ground and in particular the implementation of the European Instrument for Democracy and Human Rights (EIDHR). Gathering, each year, 400 NGOs from all over the world, this year's edition focused on Human Rights Defenders (HRDs). It timely followed the adoption of the European Instrument for Democracy and Human Rights (EIDHR) for 2014–2020, which gives a strengthened role to HRDs, endowed with additional funding facilities and further protection mechanisms. The objective of this forum was threefold. First, it aimed at defining priorities and avenues for concrete EU operational support to HRDs for the upcoming 7 years and at launching several related initiatives. Second, it aimed, 10 year after the adoption of the EU Guidelines on Human Rights Defenders, at reviewing field operations, operational good practices, concrete lessons learnt and practical adaptation in our support to HRDs. Third, it offered a useful opportunity for HRDs to gather, exchange concrete information, views and contacts, and to network between themselves or with the EU institutions. Therefore, this Forum took place at a key moment when several ongoing related initiatives converged, namely: the launch of a comprehensive EU Human Rights Defenders Mechanism, and the relevant related public procurements; the inclusion of a temporary relocation system for HRDs at risk as a component of this mechanism ("City Shelter"); the selection of new projects on Human Rights and their Defenders in the most difficult situation; the launch of the EIDHR Annual Action Plan (AAP) 2014, and the preparation of the upcoming AAP 2015; the potential adoption of the new EU Guidelines on Freedom of Expression, currently in negotiation; and the adoption of a Tool-box for working towards a Rights-based Approach, encompassing all Human Rights, for the EU Development Cooperation.' The EDIHR Forum presentations are available at: http://www.eidhr.eu/side-panels/what-s-on/events/eidhr-forum-2014/background-documents-and-presentations.
39. Council of the EU, *Council Conclusions on a Rights Based Approach to Development Cooperation, Encompassing all Human Rights*, Foreign Affairs Council Meeting, Brussels, 19 May 2014, http://www.consilium.europa.eu/uedocs/cms_data/docs/pressdata/EN/foraff/142682.pdf.
40. European Union, EIDHR Civil Society Forum, May 12, 2014, Brussels, Belgium: Panel Session on *Improving Support and Evaluation of EU Guidelines on HRDs*, comments from discussion with audience.
41. Bennett, *Guidelines*, 19–21.
42. Ibid., Annex 3-Questionnaire and Study Information Sheet, 93–5.
43. Responses are from interviews conducted with those working in Kyrgyzstan, Thailand and Tunisia. The study was small, thus data provide a limited scope when assessing implementation of the guidelines' recommendations, but the findings do demonstrate that knowledge of the guidelines' recommendations are uneven amongst diplomats and HRDs in these countries. *Knowledge* refers to having read the guidelines – *familiarity* refers to vague understanding of content.
44. The HRD liaison officer details were not found on websites of EU delegations in Thailand or Tunisia at the time of study (accessed 16 December 2012). In Thailand, an INGO reported the EU delegation has appointed a Thai-speaking HRD liaison, but this information was not confirmed by the EU or posted on the EUD website. Kyrgyzstan did provide contact details for the HRD liaison officer on the EUD website (accessed 16 December 2012).
45. Bennett et al., *Conference Report*, 29.
46. These concerns were raised in interviews with HRDs in Kyrgyzstan, Thailand and Tunisia, and with HRDs from Kenya and Sri Lanka.

47. Bennett, *Guidelines*, 66–83. For a full account of best practices and gaps in implementation from the study, please see the full research report, inclusive of country sections and recommendations to the European Parliament.
48. The practice of intervening only with consent from HRDs (or their families) was acknowledged by a number of diplomats interviewed. Also, see EU Guidelines on HRDs, section 10:5, which states: '... EU Missions should therefore seek to adopt a proactive policy towards human rights defenders. They should at the same time be aware that in certain cases EU action could lead to threats or attacks against human rights defenders. They should therefore where appropriate consult with human rights defenders in relation to actions which might be contemplated.' Of the INGOs interviewed, they also emphasised this practice was consistent in their interventions for the protection of HRDs.
49. Bennett, *Guidelines*, 69. The study noted areas for improving trial monitoring of HRD cases included: diplomatic missions registering official notification to the court to attend a hearing or trial; senior diplomats monitoring trials, as this will show level of concern about a case; increasing number of diplomats attending most important trials to show level of concern; consistent monitoring of hearings/trials throughout the court process; increasing diplomats monitoring of trials in outlying areas, outside of capital cities; consistent action when violations are evident against HRDs, and their families.
50. The FRAME Policy Brief on the *Post-2014 EU Action Plan* also provides suggested adaptations for the EU Action Plan 2015 going forward in the use of indicators. Though not specifically addressing the guidelines' implementation, one suggestion is 'the objective of the future Action Plan should be to bolster the credibility of the EU's action in the promotion of its values through the definition of actions which are verifiable in terms of results' (p. 8). The document outlines some direction for the use of indicators, which could be applied to better documentation of the EU guidelines' implementation. See:http://www.fp7-frame.eu//wp-content/materiale/policy_brief/02-FRAME%20Policy%20Brief%20No%202%20–Post%202014%20SFAP%20Policy%20Brief.pdf.
51. Jagers, *Mainstreaming Human Rights*, 229. See also, the UN Office of the High Commissioner for Human Rights published guidance on *Frequently Asked Questions on Human Rights Based Approach to Development Programming*, http://www.ohchr.org/Documents/Publications/FAQen.pdf.
52. EU Guidelines (2008), section 5.
53. HRDs may receive small project support from specific EU member state missions. Larger funding streams are available through schematic calls for proposals and at the Foreign Ministry level. EU funds for HRDs may come from multiple schemes, and as referred to earlier in this article, the EDIHR has recently initiated the *Instrument for Democracy and Human Rights Worldwide Multiannual Indicative Programme (2014–2017)*, which provides a HRD mechanism to further support HRDs at risk, including provision of ad hoc grants in most difficult situations, re-granting, eligibility for non-registered civil society organisations (CSOs) and natural persons (Operating Principles 5: 8), http://eeas.europa.eu/human_rights/docs/eidhr-mip-2014-2017_en.pdf.
54. Nah et al., 'A Research Agenda', 405–6.
55. HRDs working on difficult cases in the south of Thailand were particularly concerned of the lack of attention from the EU, in spite of their request for meetings and support from the EU delegation. HRDs in Thailand also raised concerns regarding only 'drop in' attention given to WHRDs, when the EU specifically promoted their attention to WHRDs in Thailand (when ushering in the revisions to the EU guidelines in 2008). For further information on Thailand, see Bennett, *Guidelines*, 48–56.
56. See: EU Guidelines (2008), section 9.
57. The author was invited by HRDs working for women and LGBTI rights to attend an NGO conference celebrating 'Women Human Rights Defenders Day' in Bishkek Kyrgyzstan on 29 December 2012. NGOs showed video footage of police raids on their work premises. WHRDs discussed how appropriate strategies and international networks can help legitimise their practice, and provide necessary support for ensuring their security.
58. See *Recommendations for Gender-Specific Implementation of the EU Guidelines on Human Rights Defenders*, web-based publication from a civil society consortium: http://www.omct.org/files/2006/11/3790/gender_specific_recomm_for_eu_hrd_241106_eng.pdf.

59. Peace Brigades International UK, *2012 Conference Report – Women Human Rights Defenders: Empowering and Protecting the Change-Makers* (27 August 2013), http://www.peacebrigades.org.uk/country-groups/pbi-uk/pbi-uk-news/news/?tx_ttnews%5Btt_news%5D=3930&cHash=93ec379331f58186d61905505ffac5b7.
60. *UN Resolution on Protecting Women Human Rights Defenders*, adopted by the UN General Assembly, A/C.3/68/L.64 (4 November 2013), http://www.un.org/ga/search/view_doc.asp?symbol=A/C.3/68/L.64.
61. It was argued that this language was already agreed to by the General Assembly in Resolution 67/144 on the Intensification of Efforts to Eliminate All Forms of Violence against Women. The Association for Women's Rights in Development (AWID) monitoring the UN process reported that states who opposed the initial draft resolution asked for the deletion of this paragraph in exchange for the withdrawal of their further amendments. The concession resulted in some member states of the EU withdrawing their co-sponsorship of the resolution. See draft UN Resolution on Protecting Women Human Rights Defenders (with contested language): http://www.un.org/ga/search/view_doc.asp?symbol=A/C.3/68/L.64.
62. A very strong lobby formed in support of the UN resolution protecting WHRDs, including an open letter from *the Elders* group (http://www.theelders.org/news-media/human-rights), http://www.ishr.ch/sites/default/files/article/files/2013_11_open_letter_by_gro_harlem_brundtland_and_hina_jilani_-_unga_reso.pdf; and Nobel women Laureates, http://nobelwomensinitiative.org/2013/11/nobel-laureates-to-un-support-resolution-on-women-human-rights-defenders/; and 71 African CSOs calling on African countries to support the UN resolution, http://www.awid.org/News-Analysis/Announcements2/Letter-calling-on-African-States-to-support-the-UN-General-Assembly-resolution-on-WHRDs.
63. Europe Aid, EDIHR, *How We Finance Aid* .
64. EDIHR, *A Strengthened Comprehensive EU Human Rights Defenders Mechanism*, slides, http://www.eidhr.eu/files/dmfile/HRDsmechanismFORUM2013.pdf.
65. The EU commissioned a report by GHK Consulting on *Mapping of Temporary Shelter Initiatives for Human Rights Defenders in Danger in and Outside the EU* (Luxembourg: Publications Office of European Union, February 2012).
66. Interviews with EEAS participants: see Bennett, *Guidelines*, 28–9.
67. Ibid. See also, F. Benoit-Rohmer et al., 'Report on Human Rights Mainstreaming in the EU's External Relations' (Brussels: European Parliament Publication, September 2009).
68. A. Mihr, *Human Rights Benchmarks for EU's External Policy* (Brussels: European Parliament, December 2011), 16–18.
69. Catherine Ashton's communication *Human Rights: The 'Silver Thread' in Europe's Foreign Policy* (6 January 2012), http://eeas.europa.eu/top_stories/2012/060112_hr_silverthread_en.htm.
70. As an example, the Human Rights and Social Justice (HRSJ) Research Institute at London Metropolitan University runs a number of projects with human rights defenders at risk, designing bespoke training components working with recommendations of the EU Guidelines on Human Rights Defenders. Recent trainings include working with Central Asian HRDs from Kyrgyzstan, Kazakhstan and Uzbekistan, and trainings with lawyers from Darfur, Sudan, including training HRDs on the EU guidelines' recommendations as a protection mechanism.
71. Some diplomats in the study questioned the need for HRDs to be aware of the guidelines, as this was an internal EU policy directed to EU diplomats. Most commentators, and the majority of participants in the study, supported the need for HRDs to be aware of the policy tool directed to support and protect them, particularly as the guidelines call for 'organising at least once a year a meeting of human rights defenders and diplomats to discuss topics such as the local human rights situation, EU policy in this field, and application of the local strategy for implementing the EU Guidelines on human rights defenders'. The HRCS process further supports EU-HRD consultations around implementation of the guidelines (thus inferring the policy document must be disseminated and known amongst HRDs). The EU is in the process of implementing a rights-based approach (RBA) and has provided EU members with an RBA toolbox, intended to provide pragmatic support and guidance to EU staff and partners involved in the implementation of day-to-day EU development cooperation. The EU RBA approach, to be implemented as a coherent approach across all EU foreign policy, promotes 'being closer to citizens and interacting with civil society'.

72. P. Alston and J.H.H. Weiler, 'An "Ever Closer Union" in Need of a Human Rights Policy: The European Union and Human Rights', *European Journal of International Law* 9 (1998): 658–723.
73. G. Crawford, 'Evaluating European Union Promotion of Human Rights, Democracy and Good Governance: Towards a Participatory Approach', *Journal of International Development* 14 (2002): 911–26.
74. Ibid., 920–26, referencing: P.C. Schmitter and I. Brouwer, *Conceptualizing, Researching and Evaluating Democracy Promotion and Protection*, EUI Working Paper SPS No. 9 (Florence: European University Institute, 1999).
75. M. Nowak, T. Hofstätter, and J. Hofbauer, eds, *The Role of the EU in UN Human Rights Reform*, Ludwig Boltzmann Institut für Menschenrechte, Volume 29, EU COST Publication (2013).
76. Ibid.
77. Olivier De Schutter, Speaker at the 15th EU-NGO Forum, 'On Human Rights: *The Fight Against Impunity* and *Accountability of Economic, Social and Cultural Rights*', Brussels, 5–6 December 2013, http://www.eidhr.eu/events/15th-eu-ngo-forum-on-human-rights.
78. Protection International, *Roundtable on National Public Policies for the Protection Of Defenders at the 15th EU-NGO Forum on Human Rights* (6 December 2013), http://protectioninternational.org/2013/12/06/pi-hosts-roundtable-on-national-public-policies-and-protection-mechanisms-for-hrds-at-the-15th-eu-ngo-forum-on-human-rights/.
79. J. Ruggie, UN Special Representative on Human Rights and Transnational Corporations, 'Guiding Principles on Business and Human Rights: Implementing the *United Nations Protect, Respect and Remedy* Framework', Section 17–21 *Human Rights Due Diligence* (2011): 17–24, http://www.ohchr.org/Documents/Publications/GuidingPrinciplesBusinessHR_EN.pdf.
80. Committee, Annual Report on Human Rights in the World 2012 (29 November 2013), 27–30: 11, puts forth a number of calls for change, see: *Human Rights in the EU's Trade Policy.*
81. European Commission, *Replies of the Commission to the Special Report of the European Court of Auditors 'Are Preferential Trade Arrangements Appropriately Managed?'* (EU, 8 March 2014). See section 38: 'The GSP scheme consists of a general arrangement and two special arrangements. The general arrangement is granted to all those developing countries which share a developing need and are in a similar stage of economic development without the need to ratify or implement any international conventions. The EU's GSP+ sub-scheme has been designed to include additional incentives for vulnerable countries willing to take extra steps towards sustainable development and good governance, leaving the choice to those countries whether to seek the additional benefits or not. This approach, endorsed by Council and Parliament, represents a policy choice. The need to ratify and effectively implement international conventions on human and labour rights, the environment and good governance has, therefore, been considered for these 10 countries and not in respect of other beneficiary countries of the general arrangement', http://ec.europa.eu/transparency/regdoc/rep/1/2014/EN/1-2014-194-EN-F1-1.Pdf.
82. Peace Brigades International, *A Dangerous Business: The Human Cost of Advocating against Environmental Degradation and Land Rights Violations*, Conference Report, October 2011, http://www.peacebrigades.org.uk/fileadmin/user_files/groups/uk/files/Publications/A_Dangerous_Business_-_edit_.pdf.
83. EU Council Conclusions on 10th Anniversary of EU Guidelines on Human Rights Defenders, CL14-118EN, 23 June 2014, http://eu-un.europa.eu/articles/en/article_15216_en.htm.
84. EU actions towards enabling environments and protection of HRDs as part of the EU Human Rights Action Plan for 2015 were discussed at the EDIHR Forum, see: http://www.eidhr.eu/events/eidhr-forum-2014.
85. M. King et al., *Measuring Policy Coherence for Development* (Commission report by the Netherlands Ministry of Foreign Affairs and the German Federal Ministry for Economic Cooperation and Development, for the European Centre for Development Policy Management, 2012), 16, http://www.oecd.org/pcd/ECDPM%20Paper_Measuring%20PCD.pdf.
86. One area where human rights defender practice has transformed in recent years is through the use of digital technology, with examples coming from Arab Spring countries' use of social media for mobilising the oppressed to challenge authoritarian political structures. While technology can advance efforts towards improving human rights and democracy, it can also give

rise to new tactics used by aggressing states – control of digital technologies is used to oppress and criminalise HRDs. The guidelines should now be revised to reflect EU policy towards legal frameworks and actions that violate HRD freedoms by, and inhibit civil society free space for, the use of technology. Representatives from EU countries have taken interest on a number of fronts to dedicate efforts around the positive and negative uses of technology, which include threats posed to HRDs through surveillance, censorship and acts of criminalisation through unjust laws used against HRDs.

87. *EU Strategic Framework and Action Plan on Human Rights and Democracy* – 11855/12, Luxembourg, 25 June 2012, https://www.consilium.europa.eu/uedocs/cms_data/docs/pressdata/EN/foraff/131181.pdf.
88. European Parliament Annual Report on *Human Rights in the World 2012 and the European Union's Policy on the Matter* (2013/2152(INI), 29 November 2013, section 25: paras 10–11, on human rights country strategies and human rights focal points: 'regrets, however, the lack of transparency regarding the contents of the country strategies; reiterates its call for public disclosure of, at least, the key priorities of each country strategy, and for Parliament to have access to the strategies so as to allow a proper degree of scrutiny'.
89. Ibid. Human rights country strategies and human rights focal points: 'encourages the EU to produce a public assessment of the lessons learnt during the first cycle of EU human rights country strategies and to identify best practices for the next cycle'.
90. Council of the EU, *Commission Staff Working Document Tool*-Box A *Rights-Based Approach, Encompassing All Human Rights For EU Development Cooperation*, Brussels, 30.4.2014 SWD(2014) 152 final, http://europeanmemoranda.cabinetoffice.gov.uk/files/2014/05/9489-14.pdf.
91. EU Commission, Staff Working Document Tool-Box, 'A Rights Based Approach Encompassing all Human Rights for EU Development Cooperation (Brussels, 30 April 2014, 9484/19), 18.
92. Bennett, *Guidelines*, 74–5.
93. Ibid., 61–2.
94. H. Miller, 'From "Rights-Based" to "Rights-Framed" Approaches: A Social Constructionist View of Human Rights Practice', *The International Journal of Human Rights* 14, no. 6 (2010): 915–31.
95. Council of the EU, Council Conclusions on the 10th Anniversary of the EU Guidelines on Human Rights Defenders, Foreign Affairs, Council meeting, CL14-118EN, Luxembourg, 23 June 2014. Summary Press Statement, http://eu-un.europa.eu/articles/en/article_15216_en.htm.
96. INGO statement (Amnesty International, FIDH, Frontline, Peace Brigades International, Protection International) responding to the EU Council Conclusions on the 10th Anniversary of the EU Guidelines on Human Rights Defenders, http://www.peacebrigades.org.uk/fileadmin/user_files/projects/honduras/files/JOINT_STATEMENT_ON_THE_EU_CONCLUSIONS_ON_THE_10TH_ANNIVERSARY_OF_THE_GUIDELINES_ON_HUMAN_RIGHTS_DEFENDERS.pdf.
97. For example, since the 2008 guidelines were drafted, there have been important changes in how HRDs work and organise. This includes new communication tools and technologies available and used by most HRDs. HRDs' privacy and use of social media may be under surveillance, and access to technology limited and/or controlled by governments (for information on use of technologies for civil society activism see toolkits produced by the tactical technology collective, https://www.tacticaltech.org/). It is the authors' opinion that the newly adopted EU guidelines 'Expression Offline and Online', should be referenced in a revised version of the guidelines on HRDs, as should other human rights guidelines applicable to HRD protection, and updated operational guidance referencing tools for EU engagement with HRDs in the new HRCS process.
98. UN General Assembly, Report of the Special Rapporteur on the Situation of Human Rights Defenders, Mrs Margaret Sekaggya, A/HRC/25/55, 23 December 2013. The report focussed on lessons learnt for 'Creating a Safe and Enabling Environment for the Protection of Human Rights Defenders'.
99. Nah et al., 'A Research Agenda', 401–20.
100. Bennett, *Guidelines*, 81–2.

Protecting human rights defenders at risk: asylum and temporary international relocation

Martin Jones

Centre for Applied Human Rights, University of York, UK

The response of the international community and civil society to human rights defenders at risk has thus far failed to take adequate account of the international refugee regime. The refugee regime can offer a meaningful remedy to human rights defenders at risk. More specifically, human rights defenders at risk seeking asylum abroad can qualify as refugees and receive meaningful protection from the international refugee regime. In a more organised manner, temporary international relocation initiatives (TIRIs) for human rights defenders at risk provide good examples of the emerging regime of protection for human rights defenders intersecting with the international refugee regime. Human rights defenders at risk within and those who manage TIRIs frequently grapple with issues concerning asylum – and the fundamental tension between TIRIs and asylum seeking. However, TIRIs also reveal a set of similarities between the two regimes: their shared recognition of the failure of states to fulfil their human rights obligations; their shared focus on (and contestation) of risk; a similarly shared focus (and contestation) of who is and within and outside each regime; and similar attempts to translate political sympathy into protection. These similarities can assist in charting a more productive, and explicit, engagement between the two regimes in the future that provides for better protection for human rights defenders at risk.

Introduction

> We also thank all those states that have given asylum and assistance to South African refugees of all shades of political beliefs and opinion. The warm affection with which South African freedom fighters are received by democratic countries all over the world, and the hospitality so frequently showered upon us by governments and political organisations, has made it possible for some of our people to escape persecution by the South African government, to travel freely from country to country and from continent to continent, to canvass our point of view and to rally support for our cause. – Nelson Mandela[1]

> [R]elations with the United Nations country teams on the ground and with United Nations bodies and agencies could be strengthened to make their contribution to the protection of defenders more effective, subject to the characteristics of the mandates of each of them. – Michel Forst[2]

The work of human rights defenders is increasingly at risk in many parts of the world. In the face of this growing risk, the international human rights movement has been criticised for failing to provide adequate protection to those defending human rights. The reality for many human rights defenders is that they work in environments that lack effective domestic remedies for human rights abuses. Indeed, it is often their complaints about and advocacy to bring attention to this deficiency that puts them at risk.

In the absence of local remedies, human rights defenders at risk have relied upon a range of tactics to mitigate their risk, including improvement of physical security infrastructure; mutual solidarity with other local and international civil society organisations; engagement with the diplomatic representatives of foreign states; and, international pressure through international human rights mechanisms.[3] Programmes of support from leading international civil society organisations have focused on developing the capacity of human rights defenders at risk to pursue these tactics and to support them in the execution of these tactics.

The response of the international community and civil society to human rights defenders at risk has thus far failed to openly acknowledge an important remedy[4] for human rights violations that pre-exists the contemporary human rights movement: the international commitment to offer asylum to refugees from persecution. The two solitudes of human rights defenders at risk and refugee protection have not always been so unconnected. As the first epigraph indicates, the refugee regime has in previous eras been recognised as protecting those at risk because of their human rights activism; as the second epigraph indicates, efforts are ongoing to better coordinate the protection of human rights defenders at risk, including – potentially – by drawing upon the protection offered by the refugee regime. Temporary international relocation initiatives (TIRIs)[5] for human rights defenders at risk epitomise the way the two protection regimes exist in tension with each other.

This article seeks to explore the protection provided by the international refugee regime and to examine the extent to which the refugee regime can benefit the protection of human rights defenders at risk. After first highlighting relevant features of the emerging protection regime for human rights defenders at risk and the international refugee regime, this article will examine the lack of cross-referencing between the literature and practice on human rights defenders at risk and refugees which occurs despite both regimes sharing a set of key features. An examination of the qualification criteria for access to the international refugee regime demonstrates how human rights defenders at risk can qualify for refugee protection. As a more organised instance of international protection, the nature and operation of TIRIs will be explored as examples of a necessary, imperfect but productive engagement with the international refugee regime by those seeking to protect human rights defenders at risk. The central argument throughout this article is that the international refugee regime can provide a useful tool for states and civil society and an important support for human rights defenders in jeopardy.

The international refugee regime and the emerging regime of protection for human rights defenders at risk

It is useful at the outset to sketch out the basic parameters of both regimes to allow a comparison and a fuller understanding of how they do (and might better) interact.[6] While it is increasingly in competition with other regimes, the international refugee regime provides a set of norms, institutions and processes to regulate and coordinate the international protection of refugees. Although much younger, the developing institutions and processes of protection for human rights defenders at risk also constitute an emerging regime, albeit one that is less formalised and manifests itself at many levels. The key features of both regimes will be highlighted below and common attributes of both regimes will be explored.

Key features of both regimes

The international refugee regime consists of the legal norms and international institutions of refugee protection. The customary and treaty-based norms of refugee protection define the term 'refugee' and define the core protections to which refugees are entitled. These date back to the early contemporary human rights period and were some of the earliest human rights treaties[7] negotiated by the United Nations (UN); the Convention Relating to the Status of Refugees[8] of 1951 and the Protocol Relating to the Status of Refugees[9] of 1967 continue to provide the cornerstones of the refugee regime. These treaties have been supplemented by regional treaties which expand the scope of the term 'refugee' and provide subsidiary protection for other groups at risk of human rights violations. An overwhelming majority of the world's states are party to the treaties that define the international refugee regime.[10]

The principal institution of the regime is the office of the United Nations High Commissioner for Refugees (UNHCR). With an annual budget of around US$4 billion and around 9000 staff in over 250 offices in more than 100 different states, UNHCR is the largest agency by any measure within the UN system. UNHCR also hosts a number of regular fora and processes that continue to articulate best practices in refugee protection and develop the norms of the regime. Regional institutions, such as the European Union's European Asylum Support Office, supplement the UNHCR. These institutions provide a wide range of services to refugees, varying according to refugee population and local context, including assistance with resettlement and family reunification, primary education, basic health care, housing, and some financial support for vulnerable individuals and families. In many countries, the norms and institutions of the international refugee regime have been, respectively, incorporated into and recognised by domestic law. In such states, domestic law has established formal processes whereby individuals seeking recognition as refugees can have their claims to protection determined. There, recognition as a refugee brings with it formal immigration status and an entitlement to various civil, political and economic rights. Other states without such processes often rely upon UNHCR to conduct status determination (and also provide key services to refugees).

Over its 60-year history, the refugee regime (and the international protection it requires for refugees) has both become highly politicised and entered into competition with a number of other regimes that have emerged. During the Cold War, international protection was an extension of the global, Manichean political battle: 'Recognizing persecution and identifying its perpetrators caused no headaches and the grant of asylum was generally used to reaffirm the failures of communism and the benevolence of the West.'[11] The international protection of refugees continues to be politicised, though the refugee identity now often carries with it stigma and states increasingly erect barriers to accessing protection.[12]

In contrast to the long history of the refugee regime, the human rights defender at risk protection regime is much more recent, and perhaps as a result less formalised. It traces its origins back to the Declaration on Human Rights Defenders of 1998 and the creation of a special procedure within the human rights architecture of the UN. The term 'human rights defender' is conventionally dated to the declaration, although the text of the declaration notably does not mention the term.[13] The declaration was the result of a lengthy series of negotiations among states and involving human rights civil society organisations dating back to the mid-1980s[14] and was finally passed by the UN General Assembly on the eve of the 50th anniversary of the Universal Declaration on Human Rights (UDHR).[15] The formal origins of these negotiations are in the same resolution of the UN Human Rights Commission that led subsequently to the creation of the Office of the High Commissioner for Human Rights (OHCHR) and later to the replacement of the UN Human Rights Commission with the UN Human Rights Council.[16]

Since shortly after the Declaration on Human Rights Defenders, the Special Rapporteur on Human Rights Defenders has provided guidance on its interpretation and the implementation of its obligations, in particular in relation to the protection of human rights defenders at risk and the creation of 'enabling environments' for the work of human rights defenders. Inevitably, the Special Rapporteur has had to negotiate his or her position and role both within the UN human rights regime and in relation to other regimes. Unlike the refugee regime, which for much of its history has understood itself as apart from the human rights regime, the protection regime for human rights defenders at risk has been, from its inception, understood as within larger global, regional and national human rights norms, institutions and processes.

Lack of attention to the intersection of the two regimes

Very little attention has been paid to the intersection of the protection of human rights defenders with other regimes of protection, including the international refugee regime.[17] The isolation of the two regimes is mutually constructed: the refugee regime seldom acknowledges the nature and situation of human rights defenders and actors in the protection regime for human rights defenders at risk have been reticent to acknowledge refugee protection as an avenue of protection.

In relation to the former, although human rights defenders are often required to flee their country of origin and activity, they are seldom, if ever, within the refugee regime identified as such – or been identified as such by decision or policymakers. Neither UNHCR nor any state has issued guidelines on the extent to which human rights defenders at risk may qualify for refugee protection.[18] Worldwide, the published refugee jurisprudence consists of only a handful of claims that refer to the category 'human rights defender' and only one decision that determines status on the basis of the identity of human rights defender at risk.[19] While human rights documentation about conditions in countries of origin used in refugee status proceedings increasingly deploy the category 'human rights defender' (in the identification of groups particularly at risk), the term human rights defender is not imported as such into the analysis of refugee decision makers. Indeed, activists within the refugee regime, including refugees themselves, rarely self-identify as human rights defenders.[20]

Similarly, as mentioned earlier, the emerging protection regime for human rights defenders at risk does not openly acknowledge refugee protection as a productive avenue of protection. This lack of acknowledgement is in some ways a continuation of the in-country and transnational advocacy focus of the older literature on the defence of human rights 'activists'.[21] The continuation of this silence into the human rights defender literature is part of a broader inattention to protection: there has been a 'surprising paucity of research on the protection of human rights defenders'.[22] What research that has been done has – unsurprisingly – focused predominantly on elaborating the protection needs of human rights defenders within the institutions and processes of the human rights regime.[23] For example, the recent seminal issue of the *Journal of Human Rights Practice*, which provided the first sustained discussion of 'the protection of human rights defenders', made no mention of refugee protection.[24] The reports of the Special Rapporteur and other organisations working on human rights defenders issues are similarly silent about refugee protection. Thematic reports on human rights defenders neither identify refugees as a potentially vulnerable group of human rights defenders nor raise refugee protection as a viable possibility for protection when domestic remedies fail.[25]

Bringing human rights defenders at risk under the protection of the international refugee regime

A threshold issue for the argument that the two regimes should more explicitly acknowledge each other is the proposition that they share some of the same beneficiaries: that human rights defenders at risk can qualify for and benefit from protection as refugees. The following section outlines how human rights defenders at risk who flee internationally might be understood, generally, to fall within the definition of 'refugee'.[26] It also outlines some of the limitations of refugee protection as a preliminary attempt to understand why human rights defenders at risk do not always seek refugee protection or self-identify as such during the asylum process.

Qualification as a 'refugee'

Do human rights defenders at risk qualify for protection as 'refugees'? And if so, how? In the absence of significant precedent accepting human rights defenders at risk *per se* as refugees, the only way to answer these questions is by conducting a doctrinal analysis of the extent to which human rights defenders at risk fall within the definition of 'refugee' at the core of the international refugee regime.[27]

Article 1(A)(2) of the Refugee Convention defines a refugee as someone who:

> owing to well-founded fear of being persecuted for reasons of race, religion, nationality, membership of a particular social group or political opinion, is outside the country of his nationality and is unable, or owing to such fear, is unwilling to avail himself of the protection of that country[28]

This definition of refugee requires that a refugee satisfy four elements, specifically that he or she (i) is outside of her country of nationality[29]; (ii) has a 'well-founded fear of being persecuted'; (iii) is at risk of persecution 'for reasons of race, religion, nationality, membership of a particular social group or political opinion'; and, (iv) is 'unwilling to avail himself of the protection' of her country of nationality. In addition, other provisions within the Refugee Convention (v) allow certain individuals at risk to be excluded from refugee protection if considered 'undeserving' of protection. Each of these aspects of the definition of refugee (or the exclusion of individuals from it) will be discussed below with a view to assessing whether human rights defenders at risk – in doctrine and practice – fulfil each element. In addition, the analysis will highlight resonances between issues in the refugee definition and issues facing the emerging regime to protect human rights defenders at risk. While one or more of these elements can be contested in individual claims for asylum of human rights defenders at risk and while the interpretation of the definition of refugee varies from jurisdiction to jurisdiction, overall there is a strong prima facie argument that human rights defenders at risk who are outside their country of nationality or habitual residence are entitled to the protection of the international refugee regime.

Outside of her country of nationality

The first element of the definition is satisfied once a human rights defender leaves her country of nationality. Neither the method of departure nor any temporary status in another country would automatically preclude a human rights defender at risk from fulfilling this condition. This element is satisfied even when a defender leaves her country and while abroad faces a problem that prevents her return. Such a '*sur place*' refugee is 'on an equal footing with those who cross a border after the risk of being persecuted is already apparent'.[30]

The ability of human rights defenders to leave their country of nationality has been restricted by states, often as part of the administrative or judicial investigation of defenders. Such restrictions are one manifestation of the 'legalisation' of (use of the law for) the harassment and persecution of defenders. It can often be difficult for a human rights defender at risk to even be able to access a passport both because of political interference and mundane bureaucratic resistance. In extreme cases a state may denationalise a human rights defender and thereby remove any formal entitlement to a passport – and consequent ability to legally travel.

But the restrictions on international travel do not only originate from countries of persecution. Refugee practitioners have noted a growing trend towards the restriction of access through increasingly restrictive visa regimes and interception of potential refugees even before departure.[31] Being forthright about being at risk will generally result in a human rights defender being denied a visa. States can mitigate the problem of access through the facilitation of visas and the creation of special visa categories for human rights defenders. However, in practice, such mitigations have proven difficult to operationalise in the face of securitised borders and immigration bureaucracies.

Well-founded fear of persecution

The second element of the definition requires that there be a 'well-founded fear of persecution'. This requirement can be broken into two independent components[32]: risk and persecution.[33]

In relation to the component of risk, a well-founded fear has been interpreted in the refugee jurisprudence as requiring a 'serious possibility' of persecution. Alternative formulations of the level of risk required include a 'real chance',[34] 'reasonable possibility',[35] and 'real and substantial danger'.[36] What all of these formulations share in common is the recognition that the level of risk facing a refugee does not need to approach certainty or even exceed a balance of probabilities; in statistical terms judges have expressed the level of risk required as around 10%.[37]

In many cases, human rights defenders at risk who have fled their country have already suffered serious human rights violations. In such cases, a presumption will operate that these violations will repeat themselves in the future should the human rights defender return.[38] In other cases without past persecution, guidance can be drawn from the situation of similarly situated individuals, including reports of the mistreatment of other human rights defenders.[39] However, at the end of the day, certainty will be impossible because of the 'forward looking' nature of the analysis.

In relation to the component of persecution, a refugee must face a risk of 'persecution'. Persecution is commonly seen as an act that is 'sufficiently serious by its nature or repetition as to constitute a severe violation of basic human rights'.[40] Human rights defenders at risk face many threats, including arbitrary arrest and indefinite detention; extrajudicial execution; torture; unfair trial; and, discriminatory prosecution. As a general principle, many of these forms of mistreatment will be seen as severe violations of their human rights and would qualify as persecution.

Some of these acts of persecution are specifically prohibited in the Declaration on Human Rights Defenders while others are articulated elsewhere in international human rights law.[41] However, the question arises whether the trials of working in an attritional environment might qualify a human rights defender for refugee protection. Human rights defenders in many states face restrictions on the rights of human rights defenders to freely associate, pursue remedies, protest and express themselves.[42] Defenders also commonly face more mundane interference in other domains of their life as a result of their 'anti-government' activities, including international travel, employment, housing and education.[43] Assuming there is sufficient evidence as to the cause of the mistreatment[44] and the mistreatment is in violation of international standards,[45] there is nothing in principle to stop such acts of mistreatment from constituting persecution either individually or cumulatively.

A key issue that emerges in the analysis of potential refugee claims by human rights defenders – and a common defence by states to claims of mistreatment by human rights defenders – is whether or not the feared acts of mistreatment are simply the result of the prosecution of a law of general application. As the Special Rapporteur has noted, there has been a turn towards the 'legalisation' of the mistreatment of human rights defenders through such acts as prosecution for public disorder, defamation, tax evasion and money laundering. States have a legitimate concern about such activities and are often required by international law to take action against individuals partaking in such activities.[46] If a human rights defender simply faces a lawful prosecution then he or she will not be granted protection as a refugee: 'It should be recalled that a refugee is a victim – or potential victim – of injustice, not a fugitive from justice.'[47]

However, in many cases, such prosecutions are mere pretexts for persecution. At the heart of the analysis of the prosecution must be a review of whether the prosecution is based on a law and conducted in a manner that complies with international human rights law. In relation to the former, prosecution of a domestic law that violates international standards may be persecution. For example, prosecution of human rights defenders for failing to comply with reporting requirements that violate the freedom of association may constitute persecution.[48] In relation to the latter, discriminatory prosecution – in terms of the decision to prosecute, the manner of prosecution, or the punishment following prosecution – may also make an otherwise lawful prosecution persecutory. Even where a human rights defender faces a legitimate prosecution, he or she may nonetheless have a claim to protection on the basis of other feared mistreatment.[49]

For reasons of race, religion, nationality, membership of a particular social group or political opinion

The third element of the definition requires a link between the risk of persecution and one of the five enumerated grounds. In most human rights defender at risk cases, this requirement would be fulfilled by establishing a 'nexus' between the individual's risk and either her perceived 'political opinion' or her 'membership in a particular social group'. While most commonly the nexus provides a causal explanation of the well-founded fear of persecution of a refugee, the nexus may also provide a causal explanation of the failure of the state to protect a refugee.[50]

It is probably not surprising that the historic bias of the international human rights movement towards civil and political rights has influenced the interpretation and the practical application of the 'political' nexus of the refugee definition.[51] The refugee case law and refugee status determination processes have much more easily recognised as 'political' refugees individuals contesting political freedoms and civil rights; individuals pursuing overtly (partisan) political means; and, individuals suffering persecution in the form of violation of their civil and political rights. While many human rights defenders do not overtly identify themselves and their activities as 'political', they are often perceived as such by their agents of persecution. Human rights defenders are, almost by definition, expressing views on matters in which 'the machinery of state, government, and policy may be engaged'[52] and would therefore qualify as having a political nexus.

Human rights defenders may also either work in support of, or themselves be members of, socially marginalised groups. These groups may be defined by race, religion and nationality and will thereby provide a nexus. The final enumerated group, 'membership in a particular social group', would also apply to many human rights defenders as it has been interpreted as 'tak[ing] into account the general underlying themes of the defense of human rights and anti-discrimination that form the basis for the international refugee protection initiative'.[53] Although there remains ongoing debate in the jurisprudence about the proper approach to constructing a 'particular social group', the following groups (amongst others) have been accepted as social groups: sexual orientation, trade unions, women and various groups at risk of human rights violations.[54] Human rights defenders who face risk as a result of their membership in or work on behalf of such groups would have a nexus.

Unable, or owing to such fear, being unwilling to avail oneself of the protection of the country of nationality

The fourth element of the definition requires that the state be unable or unwilling to offer protection to human rights defenders at risk. This element of the definition underscores the surrogacy of the protection offered by the refugee regime: 'the underlying rationale of international protection '[is] as a surrogate, coming into play where no alternative remains to the claimant'.[55] While the jurisprudence has at times suggested that states should be presumed to be able to protect individuals[56] and that individuals should be required to exhaust all opportunities for state protection,[57] the better view is that the adequacy of state protection is a question to be decided on the facts of the case.[58]

In some cases, a human rights defender will be fleeing a non-functioning state or there will be an admission by her state that he or she cannot be protected. More commonly, a human rights defender flees a functioning state that is simply unable or unwilling to offer protection. Ironically, a human rights defender's own criticism of the inadequacy of state mechanisms for protection may be the cause of her risk. The past inability or unwillingness of a state to offer protection, the agent of persecution (and the complicity of a state in the persecution), and the failure of a state to protect similarly situated individuals are factors to be considered. Although yet to be explored in the jurisprudence, presumably the ability of a state to provide protection to a human rights defender is closely linked not only to the operational abilities and willingness of the police, but also to whether or not the state has formal (national or local) mechanisms to protect human rights defenders at risk and the possibilities for protection through national human rights institutions.

Where a human rights defender can find safety elsewhere in her country of origin then protection is available and refugee protection will not be granted. The availability of 'internal protection' is unlikely where the agent of persecution operates throughout the state[59] – or is, indeed, the state.[60] The analysis must also consider the different conditions for human rights defenders throughout a state, including increased risk for defenders faced in particular areas.[61] The federal structure of some states, while complicating the protection of human rights defenders, may also open the possibility of gaining protection in an alternate state or a federally administered district.[62] However, in no case will such an internal relocation be based on the assumption that a human rights defender will be silent or cease her activities. Such an assumption would: 'amount to requiring the "same submissive and compliant behaviour, the same denial of a fundamental human right, which the agent of persecution seeks to achieve by persecutory conduct"'.[63]

Individuals undeserving of protection as refugees

The Refugee Convention not only sets out the previously mentioned grounds for inclusion within its definition of refugee (and the protections of the regime) but also sets out a number of grounds of exclusion, including individuals seen as undeserving of protection as refugees. Articles 1(F)(a), (b) and (c) of the Refugee Convention exclude from refugee protection individuals who there are serious reasons for believing have committed (a) crimes against peace, crimes against humanity, or war crimes; (b) non-political crimes outside of the country of refuge; and (c) acts contrary to the purposes and principles of the UN.[64] These provisions are paralleled, albeit in broader terms, by the exclusion within the Declaration on Human Rights Defenders of those pursuing non-peaceful activities[65] and, the prohibition of acts 'aimed at the destruction of the rights and freedoms referred to in the present Declaration'.[66] Given the broader exclusions of the Declaration on Human Rights Defenders, it is likely that most human rights defenders at risk would fall within the definition of refugee. Given the ongoing struggle to define the term 'human rights defender', it is interesting to note that while the refugee regime excludes *ab initio* active combatants,[67] it has provided protection to former combatants,[68] members of the armed forces of repressive regimes,[69] participants in violent protest[70] and proponents of the violent overthrow of repressive regimes.[71]

Practical benefits of and obstacles to the protection of the international refugee regime

Qualification as a refugee is not an abstract notion. Engagement with the international refugee regime has the potential to bring specific benefits to human rights defenders at risk, including entitlement to various rights, and, international attention and personality. However, as with any regime of protection, the reality often falls short of the promised benefits. There are concrete obstacles to engagement with the international refugee regime, most of which are experienced and well-documented with respect to other refugees. These obstacles include the problem of access, difficulties in status determination, and the compatibility of protection by the refugee regime with continued work as a human rights defender. These aforementioned benefits and obstacles to the engagement of the international refugee regime by human rights defenders at risk are set out in more detail below.

First, refugees are entitled to a series of specific rights to which they would otherwise not be entitled, as enumerated in Articles 3 to 34 of the Refugee Convention. While some of these rights are also enumerated in other international human rights treaties, the Refugee Convention offers various unique guarantees: the prohibition on *refoulement* to persecution,[72] a ban on expulsion,[73] the right to engage in various forms of work,[74] and various forms of administrative assistance.[75] These rights provide a core set of entitlements that are designed to facilitate a refugee's new life in her country of asylum.[76]

Outside of the international refugee regime, a human rights defender at risk has very little legal basis for a claim for protection against any state other than her state of nationality and activities let alone rights sufficient to establish a sustainable residence outside of that state. In contrast, the Refugee Convention provides the right to engage in various forms of economic activity and the ability to move freely within the country of asylum. The broader refugee regime provides assistance with resettlement (to a safe country where life in a refugee's country of first asylum proves unsustainable)[77] and family reunification.[78]

Second, as a refugee, a human rights defender at risk also has a claim to international personality and attention. The principle of comity requires states to recognise each other's decisions about refugee status. In practice, this means that a decision to confer refugee protection on a human rights defender at risk by an individual state is recognised by other states and brings with it a shared interest in the protection of the human rights defender at risk. A concrete expression of this shared interest is the ability of a refugee to travel between states using a 'Convention Travel Document', preventing a human rights defender at risk from being isolated in her state of asylum.

This international interest in the protection of a refugee continues even if he or she returns to her country of nationality. Under Article 1(C)(5) of the Refugee Convention, an individual continues to be recognised as a refugee until she has 're-established' herself in her country of nationality. In terms of the international refugee regime, this means that both the UNHCR and the state of asylum retain an interest in the treatment of the human rights defender at risk even upon her return to her country. While operationalising such an interest can be difficult (and is often contested by the country of nationality), it can provide a form of continuing protection after the human rights defender at risk returns home.

However, invoking the protection of the refugee regime is not without difficulty. First, human rights defenders at risk (and those who support them) must be aware of the regime in order to engage with it. The reality is that many refugees are either completely unaware of or inaccurately informed about the criteria or processes of the refugee regime. Once aware, a human rights defender at risk must be able to access refugee protection. As noted earlier, access to protection has become more difficult. Human rights defenders at risk working in regions where the Refugee Convention has not been widely adopted face particular difficulties in accessing protection.[79] The development of special visas for human rights defenders at risk may partially address the problem of access.

Second, the refugee regime relies upon a necessarily flawed and not always reliable determination of refugee status conducted by states and the UNHCR. Status determination processes in many states (and the UNHCR) have become cumbersome and 'over-sophisticated' – increasingly they are designed to render inadmissible or to impose severe procedural constraints on certain types of claims and claimants. The decision makers in both state and UNHCR refugee status determination processes are frequently poorly informed about the situation in an applicant's country of origin, overworked and cynical. As a result, a significant number of individuals deserving of refugee protection, including human rights defenders at risk, are denied protection.[80] Even at its best, refugee status determination is an emotional and time-consuming process which can leave a human rights defender at risk in 'limbo' for a lengthy period of time. During this period, a human rights defender at risk may be detained and restricted from working.

Third, and most importantly, there are significant obstacles presented by the refugee regime for the continued human rights work of human rights defenders at risk. The refugee regime has long been criticised for its 'exilic bias', offering protection only to those outside their country of nationality or habitual residence.[81] As noted previously, the Refugee Convention causes refugee protection to 'cease' if a refugee re-establishes herself in her state of origin.[82] This provision of the Refugee Convention has been exacerbated by more stringent domestic legislation and policy that further limit the ability of refugees to travel, especially back to their country of origin.[83]

While technology and transnational advocacy networks have provided new opportunities for human rights activities outside of the country of origin, refugees remain physically separated from their community of fellow human rights defenders within their state of origin. There is a political dimension to the separation as well: human rights defenders who have sought asylum abroad may be viewed by their colleagues who have remained in the country as having 'deserted' the (formerly) shared cause.[84] The state may also use a human rights defender at risk's physical presence abroad or her refugee claim to discredit her 'patriotism' or to assert that she has fallen under 'foreign influence'.[85]

In addition to the physical and political obstacles to continued work presented by refugee status, there are also emotional barriers to continued work as a human rights defender. The human rights defender community is not immune to the prejudices that result in social stigma of asylum seekers and refugees in mainstream society. Human rights defenders at risk who have sought refugee protection report having to overcome the opinions of their colleagues that they have 'given up' or that 'there is no dignity' in protection as a refugee.[86]

Temporary international relocation initiatives (TIRIs) and the intersection of the two regimes

Although the two regimes have been described as existing in remarkable isolation from each other, the isolation is not complete.[87] TIRIs provide a concrete and expanding instance of the protection of human rights defenders intersecting with the international refugee regime. The growth in size and number of TIRIs brings together a new tactic within the human rights defender at risk regime and a re-examination of the nature (and length) of protection. An examination of TIRIs exemplifies the need (and productive potential) of further direct interaction between the regimes.

Background on TIRIs and temporary protection

There exist more than 50 TIRIs that endeavour to assist human rights defenders at risk in relocating outside of their state. The largest of these initiatives are run by civil society and exist on a regional level, relocating human rights defenders at risk to other states within the region. However, there are also smaller programmes of international relocation that relocate human rights defenders at risk globally (outside of the region), usually to Europe. These initiatives are managed by a range of civil society actors, ranging from general human rights organisations to organisations specifically focusing on human rights defenders. Almost all of these programmes have been forced to engage the international refugee regime for the protection of human rights defenders at risk when international relocation fails to sufficiently mitigate risk within the time period of hosting.[88]

Although many TIRIs are quite recent in development, the organised provision of international protection by civil society has a long history. In 1933, the Academic Assistance Council (now known as the Council for Assisting Refugee Academics, CARA) was founded to provide support to scholars fleeing persecution by Nazi Germany.[89] Programmes of support have also existed for a long time for specific types of what are now known as human rights defenders at risk, including scholars, journalists and authors.[90]

While the fellowships offered by CARA do not necessarily result in protection as refugees, many of its most famous beneficiaries have used their fellowship as a means to access longer-lasting refugee protection. Since the Declaration on Human Rights Defenders, programmes of protection explicitly for human rights defenders at risk have been developed (or reconceived). A recent mapping of regional and global TIRIs identified more than 50 separate initiatives that were 'diverse in nature and target different groups of HRDs'.[91]

Most TIRIs are institutionalised as a programme within a civil society organisation or network focusing on the protection of human rights defenders at risk (either generally or a specific sub-set of the group). However, there are a few ad hoc TIRIs that have occurred in response to an immediate, one-time crisis and which were therefore not institutionalised. One of the largest and most high-profile of such partnerships occurred following the contested re-election of the Iranian president in 2009. Two European states and Reporters Without Borders cooperated to support (through the respective provision of emergency visas and material support) the flight to Europe of a number of human rights defenders at risk.[92] While TIRIs provide an organised programme of status, shelter and support, there are also other programmes designed to support human rights defenders at risk seeking to flee abroad in a self-directed manner. While not formally TIRIs, such programmes provide financial support for human rights defenders at risk to self-organise temporary international relocation.[93]

Regional networks that provide international relocation for human rights defenders at risk within their region of activity exist in the Middle East and North Africa, East Africa, Southern Africa, Latin America, and Asia.[94] A number of small programmes of support also exist that relocate human rights defenders at risk outside of their region of activity, usually to Europe or North America. The largest global programme of support is the International Cities of Refuge Network (ICORN), a loose network of about 40 cities that provide sanctuary to 'writers at risk'.[95]

Although exact numbers of spaces for human rights defenders at risk within TIRIs are difficult to determine, within the European Union alone there are no more than 300 spaces per year:

The current supply structure for shelter for human rights defenders across the EU Member States, whether these are city shelters, fellowships, NGO relief grants or government financial schemes, are limited and currently represent fewer than 300 temporary shelters a year in the entire EU 27. There are many examples of unmet demand (waiting lists).[96]

Outside of the European Union, there are the aforementioned significant regional networks of protection and some of the global TIRIs also provide international relocation outside of Europe, including Scholars at Risk and some of the ICORN cities of refuge. Although there has been no formal census of spaces, globally TIRIs likely provide international relocation to between a few hundred and around one thousand human rights defenders at risk every year.[97] More ad hoc programmes in support of the self-directed international relocation of human rights defenders at risk probably double this number. While the existing network of TIRIs needs to be rebalanced to better locate human rights defenders at risk geographically closer to where they live and work, the consensus view of those in the sector is that they remain an important, growing and currently under-resourced tool for protection.[98]

In a small number of cases, TIRIs are explicitly seen as pathways to permanent protection, usually through providing access to asylum procedures.[99] However, in most cases, the programmes are conceived as a means to mitigate the risk faced by human rights defenders, through variously the passage of time, the heightened international profile of the human rights defender or their increased capacity to mitigate risk through new tactics of practice.[100] Despite such a conception of their purpose, a recent mapping of these programmes concluded that 'a small number of human rights defenders relocating to existing shelter initiatives have had little choice but to apply for asylum'.[101] The only alternative to seeking asylum is the circulation of human rights defenders at risk amongst initiatives in an attempt to extend their temporary protection until their risk has been mitigated:

While the ultimate goal of existing shelter initiatives are [sic] for HRDs to enjoy safe haven in the EU for a temporary stay and then return to their home countries, the existing picture indicates a risk that many HRDs end up 'relocation shopping' from programme to programme or being forced to apply for asylum or pursue other means of entry.[102]

The rates of asylum seeking amongst TIRIs vary enormously, between 0% and 66%,[103] and there is no direct correlation between the length of the sojourn and likelihood of asylum seeking.[104]

TIRIs and the similarities of the two regimes

An examination of TIRIs highlights the similarities of the emerging regime of protection for human rights defenders at risk and the international refugee regime. The two regimes share four striking similarities that provide avenues for productive cooperation while also highlighting potential tensions. These similarities are (i) there is a shared recognition of the failure of states to fulfil their human rights obligations; (ii) risk is both central to and contested within both regimes; (iii) there is a similar contestation of who is and within and outside each regime; and, (iv) there is a shared attempt to translate political sympathy into protection.

Shared recognition of the failure of states to fulfil their human rights obligations

First, both TIRIs and refugee protection are rooted in recognition that human rights obligations continue to be violated and that the international community has a duty to provide protection to victims of such violations. Unfortunately, TIRIs also underscore the extent to which both the emerging regime of protection for human rights defenders at risk and the refugee regime have failed in fulfilling this duty.

The declaration and the related creation of the category 'human rights defender' were a result of the explicit recognition by the international community of the inadequacy of existing mechanisms for ensuring compliance with human rights obligations. With the creation of the Special Rapporteur on Human Rights Defenders, the international community also recognised its responsibility to human rights defenders at risk. In parallel, the refugee regime was borne out of a pragmatic understanding by the international community of the inadequacy of existing mechanisms for ensuring compliance with human rights obligations.[105] A constant refrain of the refugee regime is that it exists as a 'surrogate' form of protection for individuals who have not been protected by existing (national) mechanisms: 'its general purpose is to afford protection and fair treatment to those for whom neither is available in their own country'.[106] At the core of the definition of refugee is the requirement that a refugee be unable or unwilling to gain the protection of her[107] country of nationality or former habitual residence.[108] As noted earlier, and somewhat controversially, its proponents understand its protection as a form of extraterritorial human rights 'remedy'.

TIRIs justify their often expensive existence based upon an analogous lack of other avenues of protection; TIRIs are a 'last resort' once it is clear there can be no safety in the country of a human rights defender's activities.[109] However, TIRIs also underscore another failure of protection: the failure of other states to offer protection to human rights defenders at risk. TIRIs exist in tension with state immigration bureaucracies designed to keep individuals at risk from obtaining a visa. Indeed, difficulties in obtaining visas were noted as a significant problem facing surveyed TIRIs.[110] Even once a visa is obtained, the fear of not having future access to visas (and, consequently, asylum) often prematurely forces a decision to seek asylum: 'Some HRDs stressed that, due to the short duration of available temporary relocation programmes, they had been forced to apply for asylum.'[111] As Bhaba has pointed out, asylum systems can reveal the disconnect between public proclamations of support and actual protection:

[Asylum advocates] urge governments and courts to be translators of general human rights norms into the minutiae of administrative practice. They test, even expose, the boundaries of domestic insularity and hypocrisy by juxtaposing internationalist public pronouncements with exclusionary and parochial bureaucratic procedures: atrocities that are condemned when carried out at a safe distance suddenly become the subject of a test of the civility and willingness to enforce human rights obligations within the host state.[112]

In a similar way, TIRIs reveal a disconnect between human rights defenders at risk and initiatives to support them. If either in-country initiatives or the asylum provided by the international refugee regime were sufficient, then there would be no need for TIRIs.

Risk is both central to and contested within both regimes

Second, both regimes have at their core a concern about prospective risk – though the exact nature of the risk is disputed within both regimes. In practice, the term 'human rights defender' is deployed almost exclusively in situations where human rights defenders are at risk, contrary to the broader meaning of a defender implied in Article 1 of the declaration. This usage began during the negotiation of the declaration and continued with the work of the Special Rapporteur. The explicitly acknowledged context of the Special Rapporteur is that human rights defenders 'are often subjected to threats, harassment, insecurity, arbitrary detention and extrajudicial executions'.[113] In practice, the activities of the mandate holder have focused almost exclusively on the study of repressive trends and the situation of human rights defenders at risk.[114] Similarly, at the heart of the definition of refugee is concern about the prospective risk of persecution faced by an individual, expressed by the well-worn phrase 'well-founded fear of persecution'.

At first glance, TIRIs explicitly define themselves as providing protection to human rights defenders at risk. However, the exact definition of risk varies from initiative to initiative, and often includes the 'risk' produced by 'working in an attritional environment'. While such a description of risk fits well with the Special Rapporteur's advocacy for broadly construed 'enabling environments', it does not always sit easily with the more technical definition of risk embraced by the refugee regime. Conversely, the disproportionate attention within the human rights defender at risk regime to civil and political rights results in a much narrower conception of risk (and harm) than used by TIRIs.[115] In both cases, TIRIs challenge the existing notions of risk: What level of risk merits international attention? Can suffering risk in itself be sufficient to merit international protection?

Contestation of who is and within and outside each regime

Third, and not unrelated to contestations about risk, both regimes have at their core a contested definition. The term 'human rights defender' is one that the international community has only with some vacillation embraced: the declaration formally goes by a longer title and neither uses the term 'human rights defender' nor mentions the 'defence' of human rights.[116] While the term human rights defender was used repeatedly (and, seemingly uncontroversially) during the lengthy negotiations of the text, it was not until the subsequent creation of the position of Special Representative on the Situation of Human Rights Defenders in 2000 that the international community formally embraced the term.[117] The caveats issued before its proclamation by a group of states[118] and ongoing debate about who should be excluded from the term[119] reflect the continuing fight over who should be the beneficiaries of the regime.

Likewise, the definition of 'refugee' is highly contested, as evidenced by the volume of jurisprudence on its meaning and the complicated (and expensive) state and UNHCR apparatuses to determine refugee status. As Hathaway has noted, a great deal of effort during the first 50 years of the contemporary refugee regime was devoted to interpreting the meaning of 'refugee'.[120] Unlike the declaration, the Refugee Convention contains a definition of 'refugee' – albeit one that has been further expanded by regional refugee instruments. While over the last decade there has been a remarkable transnational convergence in the interpretation of the definition, the application of the definition of refugee to individual cases remains highly contested.

Human rights defenders within TIRIs are unlikely to become victims of these ongoing debates. The selection for such schemes privileges certain categories of human rights defenders, notably writers-at-risk, journalists and scholars.[121] Such individuals are at the uncontested centre of the emerging regime. Equally, their sponsorship by the TIRI (and possibly internationally connected nominating organisations) provides a level of support and credibility that distinguishes them from most asylum seekers. In this case, TIRIs, rather than revealing, actually obscure the definitional contestations of the intersecting regimes.

Translation of political sympathy into protection

Fourth, both regimes represent pragmatic attempts to translate political sympathy for a group of individuals into protection. The obvious *quid pro quo* of leveraging political sympathy for protection is that care must be taken to ensure that the group being protected is politically sympathetic. In the case of refugees, this meant, at the outset of the regime, restricting its core protections to refugees[122] and excluding from its protection individuals who were 'undeserving' of protection.[123] More recently, proponents of the refugee regime have argued against the expansion of the UNHCR's mandate and diluting the hard-gained advantage of the refugee regime by shifting its focus to the broader phenomenon of forced migration.[124] Often these concerns find their way in to the aforementioned debates about the scope of the definition of refugee.

Proponents of protection regimes face a tension between a humanitarian desire to protect more individuals at risk and a pragmatic reality that particular regimes of protection arise from political sympathies that can vacillate as the group being protected grows or changes in composition. The text of the Declaration on Human Rights Defenders already bears signs of this tension, particularly in relation to its frequent caveat that it embraces only those using 'peaceful means'; its negotiating history similarly reveals a desire by some states to limit the advantages that could be leveraged for human rights defenders. While the Special Rapporteur has worked hard to expand the range of civil society actors benefiting from the regime, none of the new beneficiaries bring into question the political sympathy that provides the foundation of the regime.[125]

The development of TIRIs followed a similar strategy to leverage political sympathy into protection, as evidenced by their origins as a response to Nazi violence against public intellectuals, professionals and academics. But this strategy exists in tension with the general lack of political sympathy for refugees. Early efforts allowed would-be refugees to be defined instead by their professional identities: as scholars, journalists and writers. Similarly, the more recent expansion of TIRIs has attempted to leverage these (and other) professional identities and the broader sympathies that the public might have with the defenders of human rights abroad.[126] In the context of the European Union, the support for TIRIs leverages the ideological commitment of the member states (and the European Union itself) to human rights:

There is strong political commitment across the Member States for supporting HRDs. The EU institutions and various Member States in their foreign affairs policies (Finland and the Netherlands, for example) generally recognise the need to support individual HRDs as drivers of democratisation, rule of law and promotion of human rights in third countries.[127]

A similar ideological commitment to human rights defenders at risk and TIRIs has been expressed by other (Western) states.[128] The difficulty with TIRIs emerges when it intersects with asylum: 'The political constraints in some Member States relate almost entirely to the issue of immigration.'[129] The previously noted stigma associated with asylum can undermine the support for human rights defenders within the TIRIs – and even support for the TIRIs themselves. While there are notable exceptions to this proposition, in many TIRIs there is concern that asylum seeking by human rights defenders might undermine the viability of the programme.

Ways forward

Human rights defenders at risk, like so many others at risk, do seek and have been granted protection as refugees. However, within the international refugee regime they are not identified as human rights defenders and neither does the emerging regime of protection for human rights defenders at risk provide sufficient, or even significant, support for accessing refugee protection. The argument of this article is that the community of human rights defenders at risk (and those concerned about their situation) and the emerging regime to protect them must more directly and openly engage with the international refugee regime. Equally, the international refugee regime stands to benefit from greater engagement with the emerging regime for human rights defenders at risk.

As the human rights defender at risk regime develops, any further formalisation should address its nexus with asylum. For example, any future international resolutions or instruments concerning human rights defenders should explicitly recognise the right of human rights defenders at risk to seek and to enjoy asylum. The formalisation of the human rights defender at risk regime may provide an opportunity, to the extent that human rights defenders at risk are seen as a politically expedient group, to progressively develop the right to access asylum, which has become a key issue within the international refugee regime.

There is very little information in the public domain about TIRIs; even the observations made in this article need to be more rigorously documented and examined. However, even from the little evidence available, visa regimes are a crucial determinant of which (and how) human rights defenders at risk can be sheltered within TIRIs. The possibility for longer term ('protection') visas for human rights defenders within TIRIs might remove the need for human rights defenders within such programmes to seek asylum. Having said that, TIRIs should also more formally and proactively address the need for refugee protection for some human rights defenders within their programmes of support. Support is often needed for the transition between participation in a TIRI and the more isolated existence of an asylum seeker or refugee.

Further engagement between human rights defenders at risk and the international refugee regime offers potential benefits not only for human rights defenders at risk themselves. In an era of political polemic about 'bogus' asylum seekers, greater engagement also provides a way to strengthen popular support for the international refugee regime. Since the end of the Cold War, the international refugee regime has lost some of its ideological power.[130] The provision of sanctuary to individuals fleeing because they champion human rights provides a potential new ideological currency to the refugee regime. Recent headlines from the Western media about the popular sympathy for Malala Yousafzai[131] provide an example of a human rights defender whose sanctuary was actively celebrated by the popular media and public. In this sense, human rights defenders at risk, for better and worse, have the potential to become the anti-communists and fellow travellers of the twenty-first century.

The refugee regime should formally recognise the entitlement of human rights defenders at risk to international protection as refugees. The UNHCR regularly issues 'guidelines on international protection' that apply refugee law to particular populations or contentious issues. It would be a useful step for such a guideline to be issued assessing the qualification of human rights defenders at risk for refugee protection and addressing some of the issues around refugee protection identified in this article. Equally, states should pay particular attention to building a jurisprudence of refugee protection for human rights defenders at risk, for example by identifying and publishing refugee decisions that confirm the qualification of human rights defenders at risk per se for refugee protection.

The engagement of the refugee regime with human rights defenders at risk must extend to human rights defenders at risk within asylum procedures, where policies of dispersal, detention and isolation have a significant impact on the well-being of human rights defenders and where there is at best ambivalence – and often open hostility – to human rights defenders continuing their activism as asylum seekers. Within determination systems, the refugee regime must actively seek information about human rights defenders from other branches of government. In the United Kingdom, for example, it has been suggested that 'there could perhaps be scope for a more systemic approach to information sharing between the UK Home Office and the Foreign Office, to take advantage of the latter's knowledge of individual human rights activists, political and religious movements'.[132] Once refugee status is recognised, the refugee regime needs to recognise its 'exilic bias'. Policies need to be reconsidered and revised that prevent the continued engagement by human rights defenders in advocacy and, when safe, their return.

In closing, the refugee regime offers immediate and concrete benefits to human rights defenders at risk, even if engagement with the regime is not always unproblematic. In recent scholarship, the protection offered by the international refugee regime has been described in terms that seem tailor made for the protection of human rights defenders at risk:

Refugee law may be the world's most powerful international human rights mechanism. Not only do millions of people invoke its protections every year in countries spanning the globe, but they do so on the basis of a self-actuating mechanism of international law that, quite literally, allows at-risk persons to vote with their feet.[133]

While access to international protection as a refugee may be more fraught than this quotation suggests, it behooves those developing a new regime for human rights defenders at risk to pay greater attention to the possibilities offered by the refugee regime.

Acknowledgements

A previous version of this article was presented at a workshop on human rights defenders at risk hosted by CAHR, Amnesty International UK, and the Human Rights and Social Justice Institute.

The author wishes to thank the organisers and participants in that workshop for their comments and suggestions that have improved this article, including in particular James Savage, Alice Nah and Lars Waldorf. He also wishes to thank the reviewer of this article [Lutz Oette] whose suggestions concerning its restructuring have produced a more focused article. Of course, any errors remain the responsibility of the author.

Disclosure statement

No potential conflict of interest was reported by the author.

Notes

1. Nelson Mandela, 'Address at the Conference of the Pan-African Freedom Movement of East and Central Africa' (Addis Ababa, 1962). Mandela's speech was his first international public statement and arguably his first as a refugee.
2. 'Report of the Special Rapporteur on Human Rights Defenders: Situation of Human Rights Defenders', UN Document Number A/69/259 (14 August 2014).
3. This range of current tactics can be mapped to the traditional taxonomy of tactics set out before the coining of the term 'human rights defender': Lauri Wiseberg, 'Protecting Human Rights Activists and NGOs: What More Can Be Done?', *Human Rights Quarterly* 13, no. 4 (1991): 525–44.
4. The use of the term 'remedy' to describe what is offered by the international refugee regime underscores the gap between the two regimes. The term has become a legal term of art in international human rights law, typically including access to justice; reparation for harm suffered; and, access to information (see for example, *Basic Principles and Guidelines on the Right to a Remedy and Reparation for Victims of Gross Violations of International Human Rights Law and Serious Violations of International Humanitarian Law*, UN General Assembly Resolution Number 60/147 (16 December 2005)). In contrast, the refugee regime has historically used the term in a more pragmatic way: '[Refugee law] is the only international human rights remedy which can be engaged directly and immediately by at-risk persons themselves. Most important of all, it is a fundamentally practical remedy which can be reconciled to the most basic interests of states.' (James Hathaway, 'Why Refugee Law Still Matters', *Melbourne Journal of International Law* 8 (2007): 89 at 103. See also Justice A.M. North and Nehal Bhuta 'The Future of Protection – The Role of the Judge', *Georgetown Immigration Law Journal* 15 (2001): 479 at 486.
5. These initiatives have been known by a variety of names in the academic and policy literature, including 'protective fellowship schemes', 'sanctuary' initiatives, and programmes of 'international relocation'. The current term is chosen because it highlights the organised, time-limited and international movement of human rights defenders at risk.
6. Regime is understood as the explicit and implicit 'principles, norms, rules, and decision-making procedures around which actor expectations converge', Stephen D. Krasner, 'Structural Causes and Consequences: Regimes as Intervening Variables', in *International Regimes*, ed. Stephen D. Krasner (Ithaca, NY: Cornell University Press, 1983), 1. This approach is consistent with the definition adopted by Karen Bennett et al. in 'Critical Perspectives on the Security and Protection of Human Rights Defenders', *The International Journal of Human Rights* 19, no. 7 (2015): 883–895, (this issue).

7. The idea that these treaties are 'human rights treaties' is of recent origin. As Tom Clark and Francois Crepeau wrote in 1999, '[f]or too long, the [Refugee Convention] has been treated as a piece of international legislation that could only be interpreted according to its own internal logic and objectives in isolation from international human rights law'. 'Mainstreaming Refugee Rights: The 1951 Refugee Convention and International Human Rights Law', *Netherlands Quarterly of Human Rights* 17, no. 4 (1999): 389–410. For a more recent articulation of the Refugee Convention as being part of broader international human rights law see Vincent Chetail, 'Are Refugee Rights Human Rights? An Unorthodox Questioning of the Relations between Refugee Law and Human Rights Law', in *Human Rights and Immigration*, ed. Ruth Rubio-Marín (Oxford: Oxford University Press, 2014); and Colin Harvey, 'Time for Reform? Refugees, Asylum-seekers, and Protection Under International Human Rights Law', *Refugee Survey Quarterly* 34, no. 1 (2015): 43–60.
8. 89 U.N.T.S. 150, entered into force 22 April 1954 [the 'Refugee Convention']
9. 606 U.N.T.S. 267, entered into force 4 October 1967 [the 'Refugee Protocol']. The Refugee Protocol effectively removed the temporal (pre-1951 refugees) and geographic (European only) limitations on the definition of refugee allowed under the Refugee Convention.
10. One hundred and forty seven states are party to either the Refugee Convention or the Refugee Protocol.
11. Gil Loescher, *The UNHCR and World Politics: A Perilous Path* (Oxford: Oxford University Press, 2001), 7.
12. Erika Feller, 'Evolution of the International Refugee Protection Regime', *Washington University Journal of Law and Policy* 5 (2001): 129; Katie Long, 'In Search of Sanctuary: Border Closures, "Safe" Zones and Refugee Protection', *Journal of Refugee Studies* 26, no. 3 (2013): 458–76.
13. UNOHCHR, 'Human Rights Defenders: Protecting the Right to Defend Human Rights' (Fact Sheet 29, n.d.), 2 (n. 2).
14. For an overview of the negotiation of the declaration see 'Breaking the Walls of Silence: Issues at Stake in the Draft Declaration on Human Rights Defenders' (Amnesty International, IOR 40/07/95, August 1995); and Michel Forst, 'Background to the Declaration on Human Rights Defenders: Human Rights Defenders' (Amnesty International, n.d.).
15. The UNDHR (and its 50th anniversary) were explicitly referenced in the UN General Assembly resolution that accompanied the Declaration on Human Rights Defenders and in a preambular paragraphs of the Declaration on Human Rights Defenders itself.
16. The negotiation of the declaration began with the formation of an open-ended working group to negotiate a text by the UN Human Rights Commission in 1984 (Resolution 116/1984 of 16 March 1984).
17. A similar argument could be made about the emerging regime of protection of international criminal law. See for example Markus Eikel, 'Witness Protection Measures at the International Criminal Court: Legal Framework and Emerging Practice', *Criminal Law Forum* 23, no. 1–3 (2012): 97–133.
18. For example, none of the 'country information and guidance reports' published in UK Visas and Immigration in 2014 (used by its officials to make decisions in asylum and human rights applications) identified 'human rights defender' as a discrete actor or category of risk.
19. The only determination of refugee status based explicitly on being a 'human rights defender' found in a search of reported decisions in Australia, Canada, the United Kingdom and the United States, was the decision of the Refugee Appeal Division of the Canadian Immigration and Refugee Board in *MB4-02097* [2014] CanLII 64251 (Maria De Andrade, 9 September 2014).
20. A notable exception is discussed in Katie McQuaid, '"We Raise Up the Voice of the Voiceless": Voice, Rights and Resistance amongst Congolese Human Rights Defenders in Uganda', *Refuge* (forthcoming). A historic reason for this is the very recent embrace of the language of rights by those within the refugee regime, whose actors have traditionally understood their endeavour as humanitarian in nature. Perhaps the relative novelty of the category of 'human rights defender' also reduces the likelihood that activists for refugees will self-identify as and rely in advocacy upon being human rights defenders. See Guglielmo Verdirame and Barbara Harrell-Bond, *Rights in Exile: Janus-Faced Humanitarianism* (Oxford: Berghahn, 2005); and Barbara Harrell-Bond, 'Can Humanitarian Work with Refugees be Humane?', *Human Rights Quarterly* 51 (2002): 51–85.

21. Lauri Wiseberg, 'Protecting Human Rights Activists and NGOs: What More Can Be Done?', *Human Rights Quarterly* 13, no. 4 (1991): 525–44.
22. Alice M. Nah, Karen Bennett, Danna Ingleton, and James Savage, 'A Research Agenda for the Protection of Human Rights Defenders', *Journal of Human Rights Practice* 5, no. 3 (2013): 401–20 at 402.
23. A good example of this is the first report of the current Special Rapporteur which highlighted the need for greater coordination and cooperation (as quoted in the second epigraph) but which focused in its concrete examples exclusively on '[s]trengthening cooperation with other [Human Rights Council] mandate holders'.
24. Nah et al., 'A Research Agenda for the Protection of Human Rights Defenders', 401. More generally see *Journal of Human Rights Practice* 5, no. 3 (2013). Notwithstanding its lack of mention in the publication, the report of the practitioner-academic workshop at which the papers were discussed lists the following question as part of its suggested research agenda: 'What is the effectiveness of protection mechanisms, instruments and methods such as … refugee protection?' Centre for Applied Human Rights, *A Research Agenda on Human Rights Defenders at Risk* (3 February 2012), 4.
25. The exception to this proposition is the recent OSCE (Organization for Security and Co-operation in Europe) Guidelines on the Protection of Human Rights Defenders (Warsaw: OSCE, 2014), which repeatedly mentions the particular risks facing human rights defenders who are refugees or who work on refugee issues.
26. The analysis in this section owes a great debt to the analysis within the recently impressively updated edition of James Hathaway's very influential *Law of Refugee Status* (Toronto: Butterworths, 1991); James Hathaway and Michelle Foster, *The Law of Refugee Status*, 2nd ed. (Cambridge: Cambridge University Press, 2014).
27. It is beyond the scope of this article to conduct a systematic analysis, especially given that notwithstanding the convergence of interpretations of the term refugee there remain interpretative *lacuna* that complicate the analysis. However, the prima facie analysis conducted here can both suggest a provisional conclusion as well as highlight areas for future, more detailed, analysis.
28. While the Statute of the UNHCR defines 'refugee' using slightly different terms, state and UNHCR practice is to treat differences as historical anomalies and to interpret the earlier definition of refugee in the Statute as identical to the definition in the Refugee Convention. Regional refugee instruments have also expanded the core definition of refugee. The beneficiaries of these 'expanded definitions' vary from region to region and the requirements of these new definitions are generally seen as more lenient than those found in the Refugee Convention.
29. The definition of refugee also applies to stateless persons. In the case of stateless persons, the country of reference is her 'country of former habitual residence' and there is no requirement to establish that the state is unable or unwilling to offer protection (the fourth element of the definition outlined).
30. Hathaway and Foster, *The Law of Refugee Status*, 74. See also UNHCR, *Handbook on Procedures and Criteria for Determining Refugee Status under the 1951 Convention and the 1967 Protocol Relating to the Status of Refugees*, UN Doc. HCR/IP/4/Eng/REV.1 (1992), at ¶ 94 et seq; *Minister for Immigration and Citizenship* v. *SZJGV* (2009) 238 CLR 642 (Australian High Court, 30 September 2009); *Win Win* v. *Canada (Minister for Citizenship and Immigration)* [2008] FC 398 (Canadian Federal Court, 28 March 2008).
31. The government of the United Kingdom famously stationed immigration officers at the airport in Prague to prevent Czech nationals of Roma descent from boarding flights to the United Kingdom. See *Regina* v. *Immigration Officer at Prague Airport and Another, Ex parte European Roma Rights Centre and Others*, [2004] UKHL 55 (United Kingdom House of Lords, 9 December 2004). For further information about the broader trend towards restricting access to asylum (including its relationship to the securitisation of borders), see Idil Atak and François Crépeau, 'The Securitization of Asylum and Human Rights in Canada and the European Union', in *Contemporary Issues in Refugee Law*, ed. Satvinder Singh Juss and Colin Harvey (London: Elgar Publishing, 2013): 227–257.
32. The jurisprudence and scholarship has generally rejected attempts to link the two components (for example, to allow a lower level of risk to suffice when the gravity of the feared persecution is greater): 'We were referred to no authority nor any writing on the subject which indicates that the gravity of the risk is to be considered in the balance when determining whether the

asylum seeker has a well-founded fear of persecution', *Puerta* v. *Minister for Immigration and Multicultural Affairs* [2001] FCA 309 (Australian Full Federal Court, 29 March 2001), at ¶ 11.

33. The traditional refugee law analysis bifurcates the 'well-founded fear' element into a subjective and objective component. The current analysis foregoes, for reasons of length and simplicity, explicit attention to 'subjective fear' (which examines the state of mind of the refugee) and incorporates relevant issues that arise in the context of human rights defenders at risk into its discussion of the practical issues in the proof of the two noted elements (risk and persecution) of the objective fear. However, this approach is also consistent with recent scholarship which takes issue with the bifurcation of fear, see for example Bridgette A. Carr, 'We Don't Need To See Them Cry: Eliminating the Subjective Apprehension Element of the Well-Founded Fear Analysis for Child Refugee Applicants', *Pepperdine Law Review* 33, no. 3 (2006): 535–74; and James Hathaway and W.S. Hicks, 'Is there a Subjective Element in the Refugee Convention's Requirement of "Well-founded Fear"?', *Michigan Journal of International Law* 26 (2005): 505.
34. *Chan Yee Kin* v. *Minister for Immigration and Ethnic Affairs* 169 CLR 232 (Australian High Court, 9 December 1989).
35. *Chan* v. *Canada* [1995] 3 SCR 593 (Canadian Supreme Court, 1995).
36. *R* v. *Secretary of State for the Home Department, Ex parte Sivakumaran* [1988] AC 958 (UK House of Lords, 16 December 1987).
37. The formulation of risk in statistical terms has been decried as overly mechanistic. However, the 10% bar does provide a useful reminder that the level of risk required is well below a balance of probabilities. See *INS* v. *Cardoza-Fonseca*, (1987) 480 U.S. 421 at 440 (US Supreme Court, 9 March 1987, opinion of Justice Stevens); and *Abebe* v. *Attorney General* (2005) 432 F.3d 1037 (US Court of Appeal, 9th Circuit, 30 December 2005), at 1042.
38. In the absence of a significant and durable change in material circumstances, there will be a 'presumption' that individuated past persecution will be repeated in the future. Whether this presumption should be treated as factual or legal is much debated, see *Fenandopulle* v. *Minister of Citizenship and Immigration*, [2005] FCA 91 (Canadian Federal Court of Appeal, 8 March 2005).
39. In this respect, the human rights documentation produced by the Special Rapporteur can be very useful to document the situation of human rights defenders, including his or her reports concerning communications, general thematic reports and reports on country visits. The contributions of human rights defenders to the UN Human Rights Council's universal periodic review may also provide evidence of the situation facing human rights defenders.
40. This phrasing was adopted in the legislation setting out the European Union's common European asylum system; it is shared by UNHCR and most common-law jurisdictions. Article 9 of Council Directive 2004/83/EC of 29 April 2004: On minimum standards for the qualification and status of third country nationals or stateless persons as refugees or as persons who otherwise need international protection and the content of the protection granted, *Official Journal of the European Union* L 304/12 (30 September 2004).
41. Even those rights articulated in the Declaration on Human Rights Defenders are generally also articulated in an international instrument or in customary international law. The declaration only articulates a small number of 'new' rights (not articulated elsewhere) which are contestable due to the non-binding nature of the declaration.
42. All of these rights are protected in the Declaration on Human Rights Defenders and guaranteed by international human rights treaty and customary law.
43. None of these rights are protected in the Declaration on Human Rights Defenders though they are guaranteed by international human rights treaty and customary law.
44. A well-founded fear of persecution must be for reasons of one of the five enumerated grounds. For further discussion, see the next section.
45. Refugee law does not distinguish between civil and political rights and social and economic rights: 'breaches of [socio-economic rights] may, in principle, be relied on to found a refugee claim as rights in themselves', in *BG (Fiji)*, [2012] NZIPT 800091 (New Zealand Immigration and Protection Tribunal, 20 January 2012), at ¶ 90.
46. The OECD's Multilateral Convention on Mutual Administrative Assistance in Tax Matters (as amended by its Protocol) requires signatories to cooperate with respect to tax collection. The United Nations Convention against Transnational Organized Crime similarly requires states to

take action against money laundering. Human rights law itself requires states to act against actions 'aimed at the destruction of any of the rights and freedoms'.

47. UNHCR, *Handbook*, ¶ 56.
48. The UN Human Rights Council has called upon states '[t]o ensure that reporting requirements placed on individuals, groups and organs of society do not inhibit functional autonomy' 'Protecting Human Rights Defenders' A/HRC/RES/22/6 (12 April 2013), at ¶ 9(a).
49. The UNHCR, *Handbook*, ¶ 58 states: 'there may be cases in which a person, besides fearing prosecution or punishment for a common law crime, may also have "well founded fear of persecution"'. For a discussion of whether such individuals may be excluded from protection see § 3.1.5.
50. The nature of the causal link is frequently unexamined and inconsistently articulated in the jurisprudence. See Michelle Foster, 'Causation in Context: Interpreting the Nexus Clause in the Refugee Convention', *Michigan Journal of International Law*, 23, no. 2 (2001): 265–340. See § 3.1.4 for a discussion of the failure of state protection.
51. The drafters of the Refugee Convention identified as 'political' refugees a range of persons, all of whom would qualify as human rights defenders explicitly working on and facing threats to civil and political rights: those fleeing from revolution, diplomats thrown out of office and members of an outlawed political party. UN Doc. E/AC.7/SR.172 (12 August 1950), at 18–23; and UN Doc. E/AC.7/SR.173 (12 August 1950), at 5, quoted in Hathaway and Foster, *The Law of Refugee Status*, 405.
52. *Canada (Attorney General)* v. *Ward*, [1993] 2 S.C.R. 689 (Canadian Supreme Court, 1993), at 746. See also *RT (Zimbabwe) & Ors* v. *Secretary of State for the Home Department* [2012] UKSC 38 (United Kingdom Supreme Court, 25 July 2012).
53. *Canada (Attorney General) v. Ward* at 739
54. *Interpretation of the Convention Refugee Definition in the Case Law* (Legal Services Unit of the Immigration and Refugee Board of Canada, Toronto, December 2010), at § 4.7.
55. *Canada (Attorney General)* v. *Ward*, at 692.
56. *Kadenko* v. *Canada (Solicitor General)* (1996), 1996 CanLII 3981 (Canadian Federal Court of Appeal, 15 October 1996).
57. *Carillo* v. *Canada (Minister of Citizenship and Immigration)* [2004] FC 944 (Canadian Federal Court, 30 June 2004). The requirement to have exhausted local avenues of protection bears a superficial resemblance to the requirement for many international human rights bodies that an individual have exhausted domestic remedies. However, the analogy is a false one in so far as a refugee will have no ongoing ability to remedy this defect and the focus of the inquiry in determining refugee status is future (not past) persecution.
58. *A.* v. *Minister for Immigration and Multicultural Affairs* (1999) 53 ALD 545 (Australian Full Federal Court, 23 February 1999). For a fuller rebuttal of the presumption of state protection see Hathaway and Foster, *The Law of Refugee Status*, 519 et seq.
59. *Arboleda* v. *US Attorney General* (2006) 434 F3d 1220 (United States Court of Appeals 11th circuit, 3 January 2006).
60. *Januzi* v. *Secretary of State for the Home Department* [2006] UKHL 5 (United Kingdom House of Lords, 15 February 2006).
61. The Special Rapporteur has identified the particular vulnerability of human rights defenders working in rural areas in many states.
62. For the difficulties of establishing a national protective mechanism in a federal state see Daniel Joloy, 'Mexico's National Protection Mechanism for Human Rights Defenders: Challenges and Good Practices', *Journal of Human Rights Practice* 5, no. 3 (2013): 489–99.
63. *National Coalition for Gay and Lesbian Equality and Another* v. *Minister of Justice and Others*, (1998) 12 BCLR 1517 (South African Constitutional Court, 9 October 1998), at ¶ 130, quoted in UNHCR, *Guidance Note on Refugee Claims Relating to Sexual Orientation and Gender Identity* (21 November 2008), at ¶ 26.
64. Regional human rights treaties have expanded Article 1(F)(c) to include individuals who act contrary to the purposes and principles of regional organisations. See for example Article 1 (5) of the Convention Governing the Specific Aspects of Refugee Problems in Africa.
65. Article 12 of the Declaration on Human Rights Defenders. The UN Office of the High Commissioner for Human Rights has issued guidance that 'the actions taken by human rights defenders must be peaceful in order to comply with the Declaration on human rights defenders',

Fact Sheet 29: Human Rights Defenders: Protecting the Right to Defend Human Rights (UN OHCHR, Geneva, April 2004), 10.

66. Article 19 of the Declaration on Human Rights Defenders.
67. So-called 'refugee soldiers' are generally excluded from refugee protection on the basis of its civilian character and their status as armed combatants under international humanitarian law.
68. There is nothing in the definition of refugee (or subsequent international practice) that excludes former members of a legitimate military force who have renounced their military activities and whose activities (individually and collectively) are within the bounds of international humanitarian law. UNHCR, *Operational Guidelines on Maintaining the Civilian and Humanitarian Character of Asylum* (UNHCR, September 2006), at 32 and 33.
69. *Zoeger La Hoz, Carmen Maria* v. *M.C.I.* and *Contreras Magan, Miguel Luis* v. *M.C.I.* Federal [2005] FC 762 (Canadian Federal Court, 30 May 2005).
70. *Immigration and Naturalization Service* v. *Aguirre-Aguirre* 526 U.S. 415 (United States Supreme Court, 3 May 1999).
71. *Gil* v. *Canada (Minister of Employment and Immigration)*, [1995] 1 FCR 508 (Canadian Federal Court of Appeal, 21 October 1994).
72. Article 3 of the Convention Against Torture and Other Forms of Cruel, Inhuman and Degrading Treatment or Punishment offers a narrower (but unconditional) protection against *refoulement* to torture.
73. Expulsion is forced removal to a country where a refugee would not face persecution. The prohibition on expulsion of Article 32 is limited to refugees lawfully in a state's territory and is subject to several limitations.
74. While the International Covenant on Economic, Social and Cultural Rights famously articulates the 'right to work' (Article 6), this right is significantly qualified by the provisions of Article 2(1) and (3): the recognition that rights can be 'progressively realized' and that states of the Global South may refuse to extend the right to work to non-nationals (including refugees).
75. Refugees often find themselves without access to the ordinary bureaucracies of a state by virtue of their lack of (or holding of unrecognised) civil status, travel and identity documents. The Refugee Convention provides access to necessary documentation and administrative assistance in Articles 25, 27 and 28.
76. As articulated by Hathaway, the architecture of the Refugee Convention seeks to provide a growing set of rights to refugees as they 'attach' themselves (seek to integrate into) new communities of asylum. Hathaway, *The Rights of Refugees under International Law*, 156 et seq.
77. There is no 'right' to resettlement within the refugee regime and only a fraction (less than 1%) of the global population of refugees are resettled. Resettlement typically takes place from the Global South to the Global North and is both a form of 'responsibility sharing' and a mechanism to address the needs of particularly vulnerable refugees.
78. Family reunification is not mentioned in the Refugee Convention but it was articulated as a closing (consensus) recommendation of the conference that drafted the treaty, has been since articulated in a number of resolutions of the UNHCR's Executive Committee, and has been adopted as policy by many states of asylum.
79. Almost all of the four dozen states that are not party to the Refugee Convention are located in a nearly continuous geographic swath from Lebanon through to Indonesia that includes most of the Middle East, all of the states of the Gulf of Arabia, all of the states of South Asia and most of the states of South East Asia.
80. Jaya Ramji-Nogales, Andrew I. Schoenholtz, and Philip G. Schrag, *Refugee Roulette Disparities in Asylum Adjudication and Proposals for Reform* (New York: NYU Press, 2011); Sean Rehaag, 'Judicial Review of Refugee Determinations: The Luck of the Draw?', *Queen's Law Journal* 38, no. 1 (2012): 1–58.
81. B.S. Chimni, 'New Issues in Refugee Research Working Paper No. 2: From Resettlement to Involuntary Repatriation: Towards a Critical History of Durable Solutions to Refugee Problems' (Geneva: UNHCR, May 1999).
82. Article 1(C)(4) of the Refugee Convention.
83. For example, many states issue travel documents under the Refugee Convention that preclude travel to a refugee's country of origin.
84. GHK Consultants, *Mapping of Temporary Shelter Initiatives for Human Rights Defenders in Danger In and Outside the EU Report for Workshop on the Establishment of an EU Temporary Relocation Programme for Human Rights Defenders At Risk* (Brussels, 16 February 2012), 20.

85. Refugee Council, 'Between a Rock and a Hard Place: The Dilemma Facing Refused Asylum Seekers' (Refugee Council, December 2012), 11; GHK Consultants, *Mapping of Temporary Shelter Initiatives for Human Rights Defenders*, 20 and 27.
86. This is based upon conversations with human rights defenders at risk who sought asylum after being part of the TIRI of the Centre for Applied Human Rights.
87. GHK Consultants, *Mapping of Temporary Shelter Initiatives for Human Rights Defenders*, Annexes 4 and 5.
88. This is a result of the inability of the temporary relocation abroad to sufficiently mitigate risk; very few of these programmes have been explicitly designed to provide a route for human rights defenders to access asylum.
89. For more information on the history of the council see http://www.cara1933.org/history.asp (accessed 18 May 2015).
90. In addition to CARA, the Scholar Rescue Fund dates back to 1919 and has provided temporary international protection to more than 400 scholars from more than 40 states. PEN International has a similarly lengthy history (it was founded in 1921) and has been supporting writers needing international protection since 1934 and the founding of its German-speaking Writers Abroad centre in London.
91. GHK Consultants, *Mapping of Temporary Shelter Initiatives for Human Rights Defenders*, 10.
92. Ibid., 20.
93. Annexes 4 and 5 of the GHK Consultants report list more than two dozen such programmes of (largely) financial support.
94. Established regional TIRIs include programmes managed by the Euro-Mediterranean Human Rights Network and the Cairo Institute for Human Rights Studies (CIHR) (in the Middle East and North Africa); East and Horn of Africa Human Rights Defender Programme (EHAHRDP) (in East Africa); Southern Africa Human Rights Defender Trust (in Southern Africa); Sonomos Defensores Programme and a new programme managed by the Consorcio Desarrollo y Justicia (in Latin America); and Forum Asia (in Asia).
95. GHK Consultants, *Mapping of Temporary Shelter Initiatives for Human Rights Defenders*, 57.
96. Ibid., 38.
97. The length of the temporary international relocation offered may vary considerably within this estimate. It has been estimated that there are 'no more than a few dozen long-term [longer than six months] placements' (see Borislav Petranov, *Keeping Defenders Safe: A Call to Donor Action* (New York: International Human Rights Funders Group, 2014), n. 113).
98. . Ibid., 35.
99. A notable example of such a practice is the access to refugee status provided by the 11 member cities of ICORN located in Norway. The aforementioned human rights defenders at risk relocated to Europe from Iran were also brought under the explicit understanding that they would seek (and be granted) asylum. GHK Consultants, *Mapping of Temporary Shelter Initiatives for Human Rights Defenders*, 18.
100. The theories of change for TIRIs have been under-articulated and under-explored; often they are presented simply as humanitarian initiatives responding to immediate threats.
101. GHK Consultants, *Mapping of Temporary Shelter Initiatives for Human Rights Defenders*, 10.
102. Ibid., 19.
103. Ibid., 19 et seq.
104. GHK Consultants, *Mapping of Temporary Shelter Initiatives for Human Rights Defenders* (at 19) suggest a correlation between length of sojourn and likelihood of seeking asylum but this link is confounded by other intervening variables (e.g. those TIRIs that provide a longer sojourn generally are designed for human rights defenders at higher risk).
105. The international refugee regime developed from the 'minorities treaties' that were made a condition of membership in the League of Nations for the successor states of the Austro-Hungarian and Ottoman Empires. See James Hathaway, *The Rights of Refugees under International Law* (Cambridge: Cambridge University Press, 2005), 81 et seq.
106. Lord Hope of Craighead in *Horvath* v. *Secretary of State for the Home Department, ex. parte* [2000] UKHL 37 (6 July 2000) referring to comments by Lord Keith of Kinkel in *Reg.* v. *Secretary of State for the Home Department, Ex parte Sivakumaran* [1988] A.C. 958, 992H-993A.
107. A female pronoun is used throughout when referring to refugees or human rights defenders simply for reasons of stylistic simplicity.

108. Article 1(A)(2) of the Refugee Convention.
109. GHK Consultants, *Mapping of Temporary Shelter Initiatives for Human Rights Defenders*, 1.
110. Ibid., 18.
111. Ibid., 20.
112. Jacqueline Bhabha, 'Internationalist Gatekeepers?: The Tension Between Asylum Advocacy and Human Rights', *Harvard Human Rights Journal* 15 (2002): 155–82 at 158.
113. Resolution of the UN Commission on Human Rights 2000/61 (at the fourth preambular paragraph).
114. In 2008, the mandate of the (new) Special Rapporteur was amended to include, *inter alia*, the 'study ... [of] trends, developments and challenges' facing human rights defenders. The Special Rapporteur has in recent years produced reports on various trends threatening human rights defenders and the current Special Rapporteur has indicated a desire to pay particular attention to the 'most exposed group' of human rights defenders. 'Situation of Human Rights Defenders', UN General Assembly A/69/259 (5 August 2014), at ¶ 48–54.
115. While previous Special Rapporteurs have tried to bring new groups of human rights defenders within the regime, they have generally done so by highlighting the civil and political rights violations of these groups (e.g. the extra-judicial execution of land and environmental activists).
116. The declaration repeatedly refers to individuals who are active in the 'promotion and protection' of human rights. The only use of the term 'defence' is in relation to the right to a legal remedy in Article 9(3)(c) wherein individuals may 'provide professionally qualified legal assistance or other relevant advice and assistance in defending human rights and fundamental freedoms'.
117. Although the resolution is entitled 'Human Rights Defenders' only one of the three specific tasks assigned to the Special Representative makes explicit reference to 'human rights defenders' (see ¶3 of UN Commission on Human Rights Resolution 61 of 2000 on 26 April 2000). The position of the Special Representative was subsequently replaced by a Special Rapporteur (with Resolution 7/8 of 27 March 2008 the UN Human Rights Council).
118. Letter dated 18 November 1998 from the Permanent Representative of Egypt to the United Nations addressed to the President of the General Assembly, UN General Assembly document A/53/679 (18 November 1998) (a letter setting out a restrictive reading of the declaration by Egypt and 25 other states).
119. See the article by Eguren Fernández and Patel in this issue: Luis Enrique Eguren Fernández and Champa Patel, 'Towards Developing a Critical and Ethical Approach for Better Recognising and Protecting Human Rights Defenders', *The International Journal of Human Rights* 19, no. 7 (2015): 896–907.
120. Hathaway, *The Rights of Refugees under International Law*, 1.
121. GHK Consultants, *Mapping of Temporary Shelter Initiatives for Human Rights Defenders*, 1.
122. Initial efforts to draft a treaty that protected the stateless as well as refugees were abandoned in part because of the social stigma of the former in post-World War II Europe.
123. For a discussion of those historically seen as undeserving (and excluded from protection under Article 1(F) of the Refugee Convention see § 3.1.5 below). A current example includes proposals in the United Kingdom to tighten asylum rules to exclude 'extremists'. 'New laws to target radicalization', *BBC News*, 13 May 2015, http://www.bbc.co.uk/news/uk-politics-32714802 (accessed 15 May 2015).
124. James C. Hathaway, 'Forced Migration Studies: Could We Agree Just to "Date"?',*Journal of Refugee Studies* 20, no. 3 (2007): 20.
125. The Special Rapporteur has suggested that various groups of activists should be more explicitly embraced by the regime (and that it should be more sensitive to their particular needs), including women human rights defenders; those working on socio-economic issues; those working on indigenous issues; development actors; and those working in rural communities.
126. The term 'human rights defender' itself can be seen (and has been critiqued) as a 'professional' label and in keeping with the broader trend towards the professionalisation of human rights practice.
127. GHK Consultants, *Mapping of Temporary Shelter Initiatives for Human Rights Defenders*, 24.
128. The US Department of State has also signalled its commitment to human rights defenders at risk at TIRIs through such programmes as 'Defend the Defenders' and its 'Embattled NGO (Assistance) Fund'. Petranov, *Keeping Defenders Safe*, 31.

129. GHK Consultants, *Mapping of Temporary Shelter Initiatives for Human Rights Defenders*, 24.
130. Loescher, *The UNHCR and World Politics*, 6.
131. Malala Yousafzai was a child human rights defender from Pakistan who suffered an assassination attempt as a result of her high-profile public campaigning for access to education for girls. She and her family have been provided with medical care and refuge in the United Kingdom. In 2014, she was awarded the Nobel Peace Prize. Her situation also highlights the difficulties faced by human rights defenders who have sought asylum; attitudes to her in Pakistan are more hostile, where she has been described in the media as 'the good native … the perfect candidate for the white man to relieve his burden and save the native'. Hamida Ghafour, 'Malala Yousafzai: Backlash against Pakistani Teen Activist Spreads in Her Homeland' *The Toronto Star*, 19 June 2013, http://www.thestar.com/news/world/2013/07/19/malala_yousafzai_backlash_against_pakistani_teen_activist_spreads_in_her_homeland.html (accessed 9 May 2015).
132. Adam Hug, 'Introduction: Shelter from the Storm?', in *Shelter from the Storm? The Asylum, Refuge and Extradition Situation Facing Activists From the Former Soviet Union in the CIS and Europe*, ed. Adam Hug (London: Foreign Policy Centre, April 2014), 8.
133. Hathaway and Foster, *The Law of Refugee Status*, 1.

Political opportunities in non-democracies: the case of Chinese *weiquan* lawyers

Elisa Nesossi

Australian Centre on China in the World, Australian National University, Canberra, Australia

The present article examines human rights practice by China's *weiquan* ('rights-defence') lawyers in the years 2003–2014. Notwithstanding the Chinese authorities' hostility and overt repression towards rights defenders, the number of *weiquan* lawyers has increased over the past decade. Most of them are able to bring cases to court, publish in foreign media and cooperate with foreign donors. This article is an attempt to examine why and how this has been possible. It does so by relying on the theoretical framework of the political opportunity structure applied to non-democratic contexts.

Introduction

Since 2003, a scattered group of Chinese lawyers, generally known as *weiquan* ('rights-defence')[1] lawyers has started representing victims of human rights violations and taking up cases with wide social and political significance. Two decades of rapid economic development and social change have been crucial to the development and transformation of human rights practice in the People's Republic of China (PRC). On the one hand, the economic boom experienced by the country has enlarged dramatically the gap between the richest and poorest members of society, creating social tensions and massive discontent among various social constituencies. On the other hand, economic transformation has also facilitated the development of new social forces and created the need for a more stable legal system; these, in turn, have favoured the rise of a stronger civil society and a more pluralistic and diversified discourse on law and human rights issues. It is in this context that at the beginning of the 2000, more rights-aware citizens started to articulate their causes in human rights terms, providing fertile grounds for the emergence and strengthening of *weiquan* legal practice.

In the years 2003–2014, *weiquan* lawyers have helped to raise public attention on sensitive cases and, eventually, to bring them to the consideration of the courts. Their causes vary greatly, but they are all ultimately related to the assertion of the rights of the weakest parties within society, very often against the interests of the Chinese State-Communist Party (generally referred to as State-Party). They have defended and provided legal aid to Tibetans and Uighurs, Falun Gong practitioners, human rights defenders, families of victims of the 2008 Sichuan earthquake and tainted milk powder,[2] migrant and rural workers involved in labour disputes against their employers, victims of environmental pollution, land expropriation and house eviction, defendants in sensitive criminal cases and other public interest cases.

Very often, the significance of the causes they represent extends far beyond the mere gains of an individual case to larger issues of social justice and equality. For these lawyers, the truth is that abused citizens deserve justice and the legal system should provide them with the adequate avenues to have their grievances heard and redressed. The fact that many such cases do not reach the courts or, when they do, are not won,[3] and that those making legal arguments are harassed and maltreated, to them illustrates the continuing political nature of the official understandings of the 'rule of law' and human rights in China, a reality that they want to denounce and fight against.

In just over a decade, the number of *weiquan* lawyers has grown exponentially, from the three prominent names – Xu Zhiyong, Yu Jiang and Teng Biao – involved in the Sun Zhigang accident – the event that marked the start of the rights defence movement[4] – to a list including more than 100 *weiquan* lawyers today. The scope of their actions has expanded as well and has become increasingly complex and diversified, attracting the attention of media, international donors and civil society groups as well as the ire of the Chinese government. On the one side, lawyers confront an authoritarian state, in which legal and political institutions are strictly interdependent and mobilisation[5] from below is highly risky. On the other, they operate amidst the tense state–society confrontations that characterise contemporary China and, in so doing, contribute to the ongoing legal and political discourse focused on change and reform.

The Chinese authorities have interpreted the actions of *weiquan* lawyers as a form of political dissent that could potentially hamper the Communist Party's legitimacy and foment social instability. Hence, in 2012, *weiquan* lawyers figured first in the list of the 'New Black Five Categories of People' that threaten China's social stability and party-dominated top-down reform.[6] Political authorities also have the perception that lawyers are dangerous in view of their participation in the human rights discourse both at the national and international levels. Whilst pursuing human rights claims from below, they become associated with 'foreign' ideas concerning human rights, mainly promoted by the Western organisations they cooperate with.

Yet, the Chinese government has implicitly accepted the fact that *weiquan* lawyers exist, bring their cases to the courts and even publish in foreign media. This has meant that *weiquan* lawyers have continued to operate notwithstanding the repressive political environment, the harassment and the various violent abuses they have been subject to. This article is an attempt to explain why and how this has been possible.

Two intuitive, albeit fairly unsatisfactory, explanations may be given to these vexing questions. The first implies that *weiquan* lawyers have been able to operate because the State-Party has been somehow indulgent towards lawyers and towards *weiquan* activities, even opening up spaces for them to act. The second explanation suggests that lawyers have been responding to an appeal from below. That is, they have been feeling the urge to use legal tools to protect the innumerable victims of abuses and rights violations perpetrated by official agencies and private actors (for example, land developers, enterprise owners, corrupt local officials, police officers). A stronger legal framework, together with an increased visibility of the incongruence inherent in State-Party actions and more vociferous media, has created the spaces for the lawyers to act.

This article is an attempt to provide a more elaborate view on the development and changes in *weiquan* lawyering activities in the years 2003–2014 by reframing and expanding the two broad explanations offered above using the theoretical framework of political opportunity structure. In particular, the article provides an empirical and theoretical contribution to the conceptual challenges posed by Osa and Schock when redefining political opportunities in non-democratic contexts.[7] On the basis of their analysis, I consider the following variables as political opportunities: increasing/decreasing repression, divided elites, influential allies, media access/information flows, and social networks. The case of *weiquan* lawyers explored here proves the high interdependency of the identified variables and illustrates how repression, somehow paradoxically, may create new opportunities for action and, in particular, for change of lawyers' strategic thinking. This model offers a valuable tool to interpret *weiquan* lawyers' activism in China today, as it links knowledge and understanding of the social-legal and political structure with individual and collective choices.

Strictly speaking, this article considers *weiquan* lawyers primarily in their capacity as human rights defenders rather than as legal professionals in a context 'where neither law is strong nor politics is open'.[8] In so doing, it provides a nuanced picture of human rights practices and discourses in contemporary China, in light of the complex and peculiar relationships between law and politics, and between state and society.

The political opportunities structure in non-democracies

In a 2007 article, Osa and Schock offer a re-assessment of the conceptual framework defined as 'political opportunity structure', with the aim of responding to its various critics.[9] In particular, they advocate for its 'resuscitation' and 'correction' to interpret social movements in non-democracies. Hence, they contend, 'in non-democratic systems, political opportunities may be more effective as a theoretical framework because the sources of political opportunity are fewer and narrower in scope'.[10]

Specifically, Osa and Schock put forward a number of conceptual propositions to be tested empirically in non-democratic contexts. First, they claim that in non-democracies, opportunities for mobilisation may stem from institutional failures, from government attempts to increase legitimacy through institutional reforms, or from outside the formal institutions (for example through social networks). Indeed, these circumstances expose the vulnerabilities intrinsic in institutions that are originally designed to concentrate power instead of diffusing or sharing it. Second, Osa and Schock argue that in non-democracies alteration in political opportunities is crucial for initiating mobilisation because of the relatively higher barriers and risks associated with any form of dissent and the limits imposed on political access and independent activism. Third, they state that 'in non-democracies, opportunities for mobilization arise from some combination of the following: divided elites, influential allies, increasing/decreasing repression, media access/information flows, and social networks'.[11] Such variables, they claim, may be highly interdependent.

This article examines *weiquan* lawyers' activism by testing the variables identified by Osa and Schock as part of the theoretical opportunity structure in non-democracies. Indeed, to date, there has been no attempt to test these assumptions and propositions empirically and their appeal has not been widely taken up.

In the Chinese context, social movement theories have been used only sporadically to explain the development of dissent and social organisations. In his 2012 work on social protests in contemporary China, Chen examines how the rise and routinisation of social protests is directly facilitated by the State-Party.[12] He contends that, in the present Chinese circumstances, popular contentions are strictly linked to the limits displayed by the current power structure, and, in particular, to the contradictions and ambiguities within state ideology and institutions, rather than to a decline of the state's capacity. According to Chen, protesters, in order to be effective, need to be able to develop a 'strategic pattern of political opportunism' that balances defiant activities with actions of obedience.[13] In this context, both changes and continuities in the political system may create opportunities.

Hildebrand adopts a similar conceptual approach to explain the development of environmental, HIV/AIDS, and gay and lesbian non-governmental organisations (NGOs) in China. He claims that social organisations have been sprouting because of the 'policy windows' opened by the state when addressing pressing social problems.[14] Both Chen and Hildebrand consider elite divisions and the related opportunities offered by institutional vulnerabilities and ideological discords, approaching the political opportunity structure as devised to analyse democratic contexts.[15] They both agree that such a framework well suits the Chinese context where the authoritarian state plays a pivotal role in determining any form of social activity and any state-society relationships.

Differently from Chen and Hildebrandt, I consider elite division as only one among the various variables creating the political opportunity structure and I take the variable 'increasing/decreasing repression' as the point of departure for analysis. Indeed, while the social and political circumstances that have led to the emergence of the *weiquan* phenomenon have already been discussed among a number of Western scholars,[16] very little attention has been paid to date to the ways in which lawyers respond to repression and the effects that repression has been having on lawyers' activism. In addition, relatively little has been said about the other variables constituting the political opportunity structure in non-democracies.[17]

The conceptual paradox of repression

The effects of repression upon human rights activities do not necessarily lead to predictable outcomes. Tilly explains that repression works by either raising the costs of mobilisation or by directly suppressing actions.[18] However, in non-democracies, studies have demonstrated that repression may generate three effects on dissent: a negative response, whereby an increase in repression decreases dissent[19]; a positive one, whereby repression increases dissent[20]; and 'an inverted-U shaped relationship', whereby dissent is lowest at low and high levels of repression and highest at mid-levels of repression.[21] While a negative response is generally the most intuitive, the latter two deserve a deeper explanation.

Osa and Schock identify three main approaches taken to corroborate such puzzling relations based on three different causal mechanisms at work: the configuration approach, the strategic approach and the rational choice approach.[22] The configuration approach implies that the effect of repression on mobilisation 'depends on the broader configuration of opportunities in which it occurs'. That is, repression may increase or decrease mobilisation depending on the presence or absence of other dimensions of political opportunity.[23] The strategic approach assumes that the strategy adopted,[24] the range of tactics employed, the targets of protest and the organisation of the challenge are of central importance in determining how repression influences mobilisation.

> Since challengers and authorities adapt to each other's action over time, challengers must alter their tactics to prevent demobilization ... Tactical innovation – activists' creativity in devising new non-institutional tactics – facilitates continued mobilization despite increasing repression.[25]

Finally, the rational choice approach is based on the assumption that once a sufficient number of people overtly criticise and defy the government, the costs of dissent drop and mobilisation increases. By joining their voices, dissenters feel united and protected.[26] Lohmnann explains that mobilisation extends when moderate elements of the population realise that the government is less legitimate and the cost of silence is greater than the risk of protesting.[27]

In the case of Chinese *weiquan* lawyers, repression does not dissolve dissent but clearly changes its nature and its modalities of expression. As illustrated in the following sections, *weiquan* activism highlights how the three approaches are not mutually exclusive and can be all equally valid. Indeed, lawyers' activities are made possible by the wider configuration of opportunities offered to them, by the tactical innovation that repression and group enlargement impose, as well as by a rational choice that weight the costs of dissent against that of silence.

Political opportunity 1: repression

Fu claims that in today's China there exists 'a high voltage line' between permissible and prohibited legal practice.[28] Punishment and repression result from crossing this line. The line shifts over time and is drawn differently in dissimilar cases and by various levels of government, according to the perceived political importance of the relevant case.[29] *Weiquan* lawyers seem to have crossed this line frequently.

The preferred coercive tools involve depriving human rights defenders of their fundamental rights through legal and extra-legal means. The key measures taken against *weiquan* lawyers and other activists include[30]: direct actions by the authorities from the Ministry of Public Security, the local public security bureaus and, in particular, the so-called 'domestic security squad' (*guobao*), the Ministry of State Security and its police and local governmental officials; indirect actions, that is measures aimed at restraining or putting pressure upon *weiquan* lawyers through their employers, landowners, family, friends and neighbourhood; legal methods that rely on legal norms and procedures; extra-legal measures, including 'any form or degree of punitive response that is beyond legal review and the legality of which is clearly dubious even by criteria of political crime laws'[31]; severe action in the form of 'physical assault, imprisonment beyond a few days, and/or the loss of material resources for either the resister or persons emotionally significant to the resister, such as relatives, friends and sympathizers'[32]; and other milder reactions. Violence, harassment and intimidation of the individuals or their families very often provide the corollary to such measures and frequently go unreported. While some of these acts may occur only once, others may be recurrent.

While legal measures may expose the state to public scrutiny and have significant political costs, 'measures operating in the shadow'[33] are sufficiently flexible to be used discretionarily by state authorities. Deprivation of physical liberty for example may take the form of imprisonment,[34] 'residential surveillance' (*jianshi juzhu*)[35] and 'soft detention' (*ruanjin*). While imprisonment is regulated by the Chinese criminal legislation, the other two measures lie in a limbo between legal and extra-legal dimensions. When subject to 'soft detention', for example, *weiquan* lawyers (like other activists) are regularly monitored and constrained within their homes or in other places often designated by local state security bureaus.[36] In addition to physical segregation in places of detention or at home, their travel documents can be confiscated and they are routinely prevented from leaving the PRC – even travelling to Hong Kong may often prove problematic.[37]

When harassed or ill-treated on account of their human rights-related activities, *weiquan* lawyers are often dissuaded or prevented from speaking out or writing about their ordeal. Their telephones are frequently tapped and their email traffic monitored; they may be watched and followed by police officers, have surveillance cameras installed near their homes and offices and their neighbours may be recruited to monitor them. Invitations to have tea (*qing he cha*) with the authorities or 'being assigned a guard' (*bei shang gang*) have become a fairly common form of intimidation generating the feeling of being constantly watched over.[38] Organisations founded or operated by human rights defenders are closed,[39] their operations strictly monitored, and their sources of funding rigorously controlled, if not cut off. Their offices and homes are recurrently subject to unauthorised searches and defenders are forced to pay heavy fines for trivial administrative transgressions.[40]

Weiquan lawyers are also targeted in their capacity as legal professionals. Since the mid-1990s, the Chinese authorities have been using the annual licence registration to manipulate the work of lawyers who, if deprived of a licence, are not able to represent their clients in court. Since 2007,[41] various human rights lawyers have seen their licences denied or revoked because of their handling of sensitive cases,[42] and the operations of their law firms frozen or subjected to administrative sanctions. In addition, lawyers have been barred from mass cases and 'discouraged' from taking up cases concerning ethnic and religious groups and other sensitive cases.[43] They are also warned against participating, or encouraging their clients to participate, in petitions to governmental offices and contacting foreign organisations and media.

Years of repression and harassment have not silenced *weiquan* lawyers. Their strategies though have been changing to match available opportunities. Until 2011, the responses of *weiquan* lawyers to repression took a number of different ad hoc forms depending significantly on the nature of the repressive measures as well as on individual attitudes, beliefs and personal circumstances.[44] A number of lawyers – generally not the most radical ones – reacted with silence and self-censorship. Others with stronger contacts – perhaps IT savvy rights defenders – found ways to organise effective virtual networks among themselves and continue their human rights work both secretly and in the open.

Since 2011

I agree with Fu in noting how 2011 represented a strategic turning point in the lawyers' approaches to repression.[45] While repression has continued, and even intensified at specific times deemed particularly sensitive by the Chinese government, a number of high-profile cases demonstrate how *weiquan* activism has changed. During 2011, lawyer Li Zhuang, the defender of the Chinese mafia crime boss Gong Gangmo, became a household name when he was charged, tried and jailed for allegedly helping his client falsify evidence. Strictly linked to the 'Strike Black' campaign against corruption carried forward in Chongqing by the then Party's chief Bo Xilai,[46] the case against Li was widely regarded by China's legal world as a travesty of justice and a significant challenge to the survival of the profession itself. It spurred intense strategic reflections,[47] as it brought out in the open how the law could be easily manipulated to serve the interests of the most powerful in society against any rule of law principle. Chinese lawyers – particularly those involved in criminal defence work – started to reflect more critically on how to become stronger actors in the justice system and, consciously or not, cooperation and collective actions emerged as a possible answer.

Three other cases are worth mentioning here: the Beihai case, the Xiaohe case and the Jiangsanjiang case.

The Beihai case

During a murder trial taking place in Beihai (Guangxi Province) between 2010 and 2011, four defence lawyers seriously challenged the evidence and testimony brought by prosecutors as having been obtained through torture. Two of the four lawyers were arrested for 'witness tampering' (Article 306 of the 1997 Criminal Law) and the two others put under house arrest. The perjury case prompted an outcry among their peers all across China. More than 20 lawyers, including various *weiquan* lawyers, formed the Beihai Lawyers Concern Group and travelled to Beihai to provide legal assistance to their colleagues. While there, they were subject to harassment, beatings and obstruction of their inquiries. That prompted a strongly written letter of protest from the All China Lawyers Association. The case came to an end only in February 2013, when the court decided that the evidence provided by the prosecutors in relation to the murder of Huang was insufficient and the case against the four lawyers was cancelled.

The Xiaohe case

In 2010, Guiyang businessmen Li Qinghong was charged with involvement in organised crime. Li's lawyers claimed that the case was procedurally flawed and the evidence fabricated.[48] Zhou Ze, one of Li's defence lawyers, started revealing the details of the case on Sina Weibo – one of the most popular Chinese microblogs – generating wide attention among Chinese netizens. On 3 September 2011, he published a letter online asking for help, which resulted in more than 30 lawyers from all over China joining Zhou's defence.[49] The lawyers stated that their defence was aimed at protecting not only the defendant's rights but also the future of the Chinese bar as an independent, functioning part of the justice system, as well as wider values of human rights and procedural justice.

Throughout the 47-day trial, the defence posted more than 1000 tweets, some even providing real-time updates during the sessions. In July 2012, Li Qinhong was sentenced to 15 years in prison for leading organised crime. Nonetheless, the cooperation between local lawyers and outsider lawyers established during the trial was considered fruitful.[50] Lawyers from different parts of the country created a cohesive legal team that collaboratively worked on the case defence strategy and they established an informal, albeit highly symbolic, protective network around the local lawyers involved. Several years later, lawyers still consider the case as an example of the crucial role played by collaborative work within the wider project of China's legalisation.[51]

The Jiangsanjiang case

In late March and early April 2014, a group of lawyers and citizens visited a 'legal education base' in Jiansanjiang (Heilongjiang Province) that they suspected to be a re-education through labour camp – such camps continue to exist despite official abolition at the end of 2013[52] – or an illegal black jail.[53] As reported by Human Rights in China, one day after their visit, the local police authorities detained four *weiquan* lawyers (Jiang Tianyong, Tang Jitian, Wang Cheng and Zhang Junjie) as well as an unknown number of citizens. As news of their detention became public, many lawyers and dozens of activists from different parts of the country travelled to Jiansanjiang to press for the release of the lawyers and citizens in custody. Several of the visiting lawyers, including a number of outspoken *weiquan* lawyers, also began a hunger strike to protest the authorities' refusal to let the lawyers see the detainees held at the Qixing Detention Centre.[54] The account by lawyer Tang Jitian to *The Guardian* reports a story of violent abuses by the police.[55] Lawyer Zhang Junjie was released first and the other three lawyers only ten days later.

Overall, these three cases demonstrate how, notwithstanding repression, the actions of *weiquan* lawyers have become increasingly collective even in areas of work that are traditionally more sensitive and problematic like criminal justice.[56] They also show the strategic links that *weiquan* lawyers have been developing with 'mainstream lawyers', the support they have been able to solicit from the Chinese Bar and the crucial role played by virtual social networks.

Political opportunity 2: elite divisions, legitimacy and reforms

One of the reasons explaining *weiquan* lawyers' resilient activism lies in their awareness of the divisions, struggles and contradictions inherent among those in power and their ability to exploit these at times. Paradoxes and ambiguities of the Chinese State-Party started to emerge already at the beginning of the 1980s when the country – after 30 years of authoritarian rule – embarked on a process of accelerated institutional, economic and legal reforms. Drastic changes in various areas of social life and governance exposed flaws and the intrinsic vulnerabilities of a fairly closed political system.[57] In the aftermath of the Tian'anmen massacre, Western scholars started to warn the international community against any simplistic understanding of Chinese political power as monolithic and unified.[58]

As numerous studies on Chinese contentious politics show, the actions of *weiquan* lawyers and other human rights activists within China have been directly affected by the multi-layered structure of the state.[59] Their rights assertions have been facilitated by vertical divisions within the State-Party institutions operating at different levels of authority as well as by horizontal fissures among various agencies at the same level. Lee explains that the State-Party's decentralised legal authoritarianism may generate popular activism 'by furnishing the aggrieved groups with both the vocabulary and an institutional mechanism to express their demands and seek redress'.[60]

Weiquan lawyers have taken advantage of the legal vocabulary that is promoted officially. The language of law has gradually become an instrument of empowerment for both the lawyers and their clients. Indeed, one of the main reasons explaining the emergence of the *weiquan* movement is the fact that lawyers could exploit the gaps existing between the legal rights promised officially by the government and their violation in practice.[61] Since the early 1980s, the Chinese government has been fervently engaged in enacting legislation and promoting legal education. As a result, citizens have become more legally aware, more conscious about their rights and more alerted to the abuses they may be subject to.[62] Government promises and the frequent references to human rights in public statements and official documents have increased citizens' expectations as well as scepticism over official benevolence. Therefore, vulnerable and aggrieved citizens have felt the need for their voices to be heard and their causes to be fought with various means, including legal means.

The use of the law both as a concept and as a concrete instrument for claim-making has brought to light some of the incongruence inherent in the Chinese current power structure, as well as some of the 'contradictions and ambiguities between state institutions and ideology'.[63] Hence, despite the rhetoric of the rule of law – promoted as a fundamental principle of governance under Xi Jinping[64] – legal institutions, including the legal profession at large, are regarded by Chinese leaders as but one of the many functional departments of the State-Party.[65] As such, they face intractable ethical quandaries and have to choose between abiding by the national law, upholding values like human rights and the rule of law and, at the same time, preserving harmony and stability. Judges, for example, are caught in the difficult struggle of working for justice whilst advancing their careers.[66]

For years, there has been a debate among lawyers as to whether they should work within the system or challenge it from the outside; whether and how they should exploit its inherent tensions and uncertainties; and whether they are entitled to use the law to achieve larger political objectives.[67] Throughout the decade, responses have been inconsistent.[68] Radical lawyers have claimed their full opposition to the system and rejected any form of collaboration with the authorities. Moderate ones have adopted a more diplomatic approach and engaged with the authorities in putting forward specific suggestions for reform.[69] According to Fu, the repressive episodes against *weiquan* lawyers in 2010–2011 have modified the stakes and changed traditional thinking. Instead of bypassing the courts and not engaging with legal institutions, 'there is now a more critical engagement between judges and lawyers both online and offline. The common understanding is that the court is now a significant battlefield and a significant entry point into the system and a platform on which to speak to power.'[70] In the Beihai and Xiaohe cases, for example, the lawyers were quite vocal in defence of their endangered peers because they could leverage the legislation and rhetoric by central government authorities on the prohibition on torture. In particular, they knew that local courts were adjusting their adjudicating practices in view of the official attention paid to the problem of confession extracted through torture and the impact that wrongful convictions could have had on judges' ranking and promotions.[71]

Political opportunity 3: influential allies

As in other developing countries and non-democracies,[72] Chinese *weiquan* lawyers have been able to develop and sustain their activism through the support of influential allies, in particular, foreign allies. Controlled by the state, potential domestic allies – like the ACLA and local bar associations – have been precluded from responding to the plight of *weiquan* lawyers. International allies, on the other hand, offer resources, information and political leverage that human rights lawyers would not be able to mobilise on their own – except in very rare circumstances (such as the Li Zhuang and Beihai cases for example).

International organisations, funding agencies and NGOs – primarily based in Europe and the United States and sometimes with offices in China – have been providing expertise and economic assistance to the work of *weiquan* lawyers. Foreign NGOs have organised training on international human rights standards (for example, on the prohibition of torture, freedom of religion,[73] freedom of expression), internet security and gender equality. Some have invited human rights lawyers to travel abroad to attend trainings on human rights, offering them the opportunity to meet international peers. Within China, they have also facilitated lawyers' gatherings in the form of salons and contributed to the design of lawyers' lectures to law students in law schools around the country. Foreign religious organisations – in particular Christian organisations based in the United States – have offered financial support, legal training and Christian rights education to the numerous Chinese Christian *weiquan* lawyers.[74] Foreign diplomatic officers and representatives from international organisations have been frequently meeting rights defenders to understand their working environment and personal situations; they have paid visit to those in distress, often bringing defenders' plights to the open in the context of human rights dialogues, official state meetings and through the voice of foreign media.

Alliance with foreigners has not always been easy; hence, it has taken time to develop and consolidate. Mutual needs had to be understood and re-interpreted to adapt to the local working circumstances of *weiquan* lawyers. Indeed, initially lawyers were not used to working in partnership beside individual networks of friendships and, very often, they established alliances with foreigners with both parties knowing very little about each other's expectations. The language and practices of lawyers were not familiar to foreign donors, sometimes creating misunderstandings and a sense of frustration at both ends. Foreign allies have been approaching *weiquan* lawyers with ideas about possible projects. These were shaped by their knowledge of the Chinese circumstances but also by the narratives built by foreign media and human rights groups about the conditions in which such lawyers were operating. In this context, their aim was that of supporting the nascent Chinese civil society and contributing to the discourse on liberal rights that was seemingly happening within China. At times though, international partners have been complaining about lawyers' lack of strategic thinking.

Though mostly kept secret, alliances with foreign donors sometimes might have also increased the level of sensitivity of the activities of *weiquan* lawyers. The Chinese authorities have associated lawyers' activities with a sensitive and hostile political agenda promoted by foreign organisations under the guise of human rights protection.

Cases of repression of prominent *weiquan* lawyers well-known to the international community prove that international allies do not hold political leverage strong enough to deter the deployment of coercive measures. Indeed, they are believed 'to create noise but, only a politicised and fairly rudimentary noise that does not really have significant political weight'.[75] Other potentially more powerful allies, like businesses or professional organisations, have not offered their support to the activities of *weiquan* lawyers, remaining silent when repression occurred.[76]

Political opportunity 4: media access/information flow

Journalism started to develop in China at the beginning of the 1980s[77] when cuts in government subsidies led newspapers, magazines and television to enter the free market for revenue. Notwithstanding the state's continued control over information and expression,[78] the media landscape has become progressively more diversified. Today, with more than 2000 newspapers and 9000 magazines published annually,[79] the print media includes publications with different degrees of independence and outreach, varying from state-owned newspapers under the strict control of the Chinese Communist Party (CCP) (for example, the *People's Daily* and *Guangming Daily*) and various ministries in the government (for example, the *Legal Daily* and *China Public Security Daily*) to more independent ones (for example, *Southern Weekend*). Marketisation and diversification have facilitated the development of a public sphere infused with new ideas and values and have played a crucial role in defining the contours of the politics of justice in China.

Greater transparency has come about with more opportunities for victims and their advocates to openly reveal information about cases of injustices. Indeed, to generate revenue, 'commercial media need story that sell'[80] and, 'legal matters help to sell papers'.[81] It is in this context that investigative journalism emerged in the early 2000s. Investigative journalism in China entails 'negative reporting' about power abuses, official misconduct and injustices with the aim of 'asking for accountability, fighting for justice, and promoting certain visions of justice and equality in society'.[82] Investigative journalists, often working together with lawyers, have reported about legal cases of wider social impact and political relevance, exposing the wrongs of those in power. Svensson, Saether, and Zhang explain that disenchanted citizens have sought out lawyers and journalists when other institutions have let them down.[83]

Notwithstanding their collaboration with investigative journalists, *weiquan* lawyers and their most sensitive cases never figure in Chinese domestic newspapers. Thus, the lawyers have two main channels to make their causes known: foreign journalists and the social media. Those who work in alliance with international partners may be put in touch with foreign journalists who may report about their stories and create awareness and mobilisation around their causes.[84] The majority though mainly rely on social media, including blogs and microblogs. Indeed, mobile communications enable them to share information rapidly and bring violations to the attention of the extensive online community.[85] Staying one step ahead of the internet censors, bloggers are required to constantly set up new blogs as old ones are closed down the moment they stray across the ill-defined boundaries of what is permitted. In particular, in times of high political tension and when the perceived sense of risk is quite high, lawyers use microblog communication not only to express their opinions but, crucially, to report to their peers and their followers every event in their daily life that might be a potential source of risk. For example, in the early months of 2011, when anonymous calls for a 'Jasmine Revolution' were spreading online, or during the month leading to the 25th Anniversary of the 1989 Tian'anmen protest, *weiquan* lawyers were targeted for repression and made to disappear by the authorities. At these times, microblogs like Twitter and Weibo were used by the lawyers to inform their peers and followers about police visits and 'invitations for tea', about the circumstances of their meetings with the police and, sometimes, the details about their detention.

Political opportunity 5: social networks

In non-democracies, networks offer real opportunities for mobilisation even in the most repressive circumstances as they stimulate cohesion and create a sense of solidarity and security.[86] In the Chinese context, recent cases of repression have demonstrated how networking has become crucial to the survival of human rights lawyering.

The scope of networking between *weiquan* lawyers and mainstream lawyers has been changing over time. At least until 2010–2011, the fact that many *weiquan* lawyers expressed very critical views of the government and engaged in sensitive political activities induced mainstream lawyers to distinguish themselves from the *weiquan* lawyers, especially from the radical ones, who were perceived as non-strategic and unable or unwilling to identify effective tactics for cooperation with existing institutions at the expenses of their clients and their own safety.[87] After various perceived attacks on the profession – in the Li Zhuang case, for example – an increased number of lawyers have started to identify a common professional identity built around shared interests and values. In pursuing the same objectives of rule of law and accountable government, lawyers are reaching out to each other and increasingly cooperating in high-impact cases. They are attempting to link with their peers, with institutional actors and NGOs.[88]

Weiquan lawyers have often offered support to Chinese NGOs. According to Fu, such relationships have become stronger and more diversified over time.[89] In particular, Fu identifies two ways of networking with NGOs. The first is led by NGOs themselves. That is, those well-organised and structured NGOs – Yirenping, for example[90] – match legal expertise with specific legal needs by reaching out to individual lawyers and providing a platform for legal intervention in public events. Where NGOs lack the necessary capacity, lawyers tend to be more proactive in connecting with NGOs and identify their particular legal needs. 'Lawyers need NGOs to reach the sources of problems so as to bring cases which are otherwise invisible to legal attention, and NGOs need lawyers to bring new strategies and opportunities on board.'[91]

The internet has also served as a powerful tool to overcome the isolation of rights defenders from the outside world. While poor language skills still pose a challenge to effective communication of their experience to an international audience, Chinese human rights defenders may count on a strong network of civil society organisations that help support their cause and spread word about their plight. Indeed, in the last decade, in addition to the various organisations that have been traditionally working on Chinese human rights issues, other ad hoc organisations – like China Human Rights Defenders[92] or the China Human Rights Lawyers Concern Group[93] – have also been established with the aim of offering support to human rights defenders and their families.

In addition to virtual networking, Chinese human rights defenders still value 'real' discussions and gatherings in restaurants and teahouses. Indeed, China's many restaurants with private rooms and the tradition of eating out enable activists to meet and share their experiences, provided the timing is not 'sensitive'. Such informal gatherings often take the form of salons in which information is shared and human rights actions discussed. Lawyers have also devised a system whereby prominent lawyers travel around the country to meet their peers in person and discuss matters relating to the cases they are working on. Leading figures are also offering lectures concerning public interest cases to law students, in order to create wider knowledge and followers on issues of public interests.

Conclusions

This article takes up the conceptual challenges posed by Osa and Schock in 2007 in relation to non-democracies and demonstrates how in the contemporary Chinese context all the five political opportunity variables – repression, divided elites, influential allies, media access/ information flows and social networks – are highly interdependent and make lawyers' mobilisation possible notwithstanding the risk of repression. As discussed by Osa and Shock, changes in relation to one variable reflect on the others and produce a mechanism of evolving action with new opportunities arising.

Notwithstanding the authoritarian nature of the Chinese government and its ongoing repression of dissent, mobilisation is actually possible even without a clear and coherent strategy for action. While it is hard to use quantitative measures to say whether repression has had a significant impact on the number of lawyers involved in *weiquan* activities, it is fairly safe to say that repression has changed the dynamics of mobilisation among *weiquan* lawyers, potentially even facilitating the emergence of other opportunities and, as a result, new forms of mobilisation.

The case study of *weiquan* lawyers demonstrates that the three approaches devised to clarify the paradoxical link between repression and increase of mobilisation – the configuration, the strategic and the rational approach – are all equally valid and useful in explaining why and how repression changes the forms of dissent. In the case of *weiquan* lawyers, repression triggers lawyers to create strong alliances with their peers, with the foreign community of donors and with domestic and foreign NGOs; it makes them also heavily reliant on journalists. With time, it has made lawyers reflect critically on their strategies and on the difficult relationship between law and politics that exists when supporting the causes of the weakest parties in society. Furthermore, to prove Lohmann's argument, repression, when extreme and unjustified, has raised the attention of domestic professional associations and provided the opportunity to create new alliances with domestic 'mainstream' peers who consider the costs of repression less onerous than the ones attached to silence.

Disclosure statement

No potential conflict of interest was reported by the author.

Notes

1. Benney provides a detailed account of the changes that have occurred in the use of the term *weiquan* in China. Jonathan Benney, *Defending Rights in Contemporary China* (London and New York: Routledge, 2013), 12–34.
2. The scandal involved Sanlu, a Hebei-based dairy company, whose melanine-contaminated baby milk formula had sickened thousands of babies around the country. Litao Zhao and Tin Seng Lim, 'The Tainted Milk Formula Scandal: Another Hard Lesson for China', EAI Background Brief No. 406, 29 September 2008, http://www.eai.nus.edu.sg/BB406.pdf.
3. Lawyers may occasionally win in administrative courts or in general courts, but to win special conditions should be created. See: John Givens, 'Sleeping with Dragons? Politically Embedded Lawyers Suing the Chinese State', *Wisconsin International Law Journal* 31 (2013): 734–87; Mary E. Gallagher, '"Use the Law as Your Weapon!" Institutional Change and Legal Mobilization in China', in *Engaging the Law in China: State, Society, and Possibilities for Justice*, ed. Neil Jeffrey Diamant, Stanley B. Lubman, and Kevin J. O'Brien (Stanford, CA: Stanford University Press, 2005), 54–83; Alex Wang, 'The Search for Sustainable Legitimacy: Environmental Law and Bureaucracy in China', *Harvard Environmental Law Review* 37 (2013): 365–465.
4. Verna Yu, 'A Blow For Freedom: The Campaign In Memory Of Sun Zhigang, 10 Years On', *South China Morning Post*, 14 May 2013, http://www.scmp.com/news/china/article/1236973/blow-freedom-campaign-memory-sun-zhigang-10-years.
5. In this article, I use the word 'mobilisation' in its broadest sense, as defined by Osa and Corduneanu-Huci, whereby mobilisation in non-democracies includes all manifestations of high risk/high cost political action. Maryjane Osa and Cristina Corduneanu-Huci, 'Running Uphill: Political Opportunity in Non-Democracies', *Comparative Sociology* 2 (2003): 612.
6. Peng Yuan, 'Zhongguo zhenzhen de tiaozhan zai nali' [Where Are The Real Threats To China], *Sina.com*, 31 July 2007, http://news.sina.com.cn/pl/2012-07-31/035924873558.shtml. For a translation of the article see: Geremie Barmé, 'The Five Vermin Threatening China', *The China Story Journal*, 4 November 2012, http://www.thechinastory.org/2012/11/the-five-vermin-五蠹-threatening-china/.
7. Maryjane Osa and Kurt Schock, 'A Long, Hard Slog: Political Opportunities, Social Networks and the Mobilization of Dissent in Non-Democracies', *Research in Social Movements, Conflicts and Change* 27 (2007): 123–53.
8. Frank W. Munger, Scott L. Cummings, and Louise G. Trubek, 'Mobilizing Law for Justice in Asia: A Comparative Approach', *Wisconsin International Law Journal* 31 (2013): 396.
9. Jeff Goodwin and James M. Jasper, 'Caught in a Winding, Snarling Vine: The Structural Bias of Political Process Theory', *Sociological Forum* 1 (1999): 27–54; Doug McAdam, Sidney Tarrow, and Charles Tilly, *Dynamics of Contention* (Cambridge: Cambridge University Press, 2001).
10. Osa and Schock, 'A Long, Hard Slog', 142.
11. Ibid., 143.
12. Xi Chen, *Social Protest and Contentious Authoritarianism in China* (New York: Cambridge University Press, 2012).
13. Ibid., 192.
14. Timothy Hildebrandt, *Social Organizations and the Authoritarian State in China* (New York: Cambridge University Press, 2013).
15. Ibid.; Chen, *Social Protests and Contentious Authoritarianism.*
16. Eva Pils, 'Asking the Tiger for His Skin: Rights Activism in China', *Fordham International Law Journal* 30 (2007): 1209–87; Hualing Fu and Richard Cullen, '*Weiquan* (Rights Protection) Lawyering in an Authoritarian State: Building a Culture of Public-Interest Lawyering', *The China Journal* 59 (2008): 111–26; Eva Pils, 'Rights Activism in China: The Case of Lawyer Gao Zhisheng', in *Building Constitutionalism in China*, ed. Stéphanie Balme and

Michael W. Dowdle (New York: Palgrave MacMillan, 2009), 243–60; Hualing Fu and Richard Cullen, 'Climbing the *Weiquan* Ladder: A Radicalizing Process for Rights-Protection Lawyers', *The China Quarterly* 205 (2011): 40–59; Eva Pils, *China's Human Rights Lawyers: Advocacy and Resistance* (Abingdon: Routledge, 2014).

17. Fu and Cullen, 'Climbing the *Weiquan* Ladder'; Hualing Fu, 'Can Lawyers Build a Legal Complex for the Rule of Law in China?', *Human Rights in China*, 25 July 2014, http://www.hrichina.org/en/china-rights-forum/can-lawyers-build-legal-complex-rule-law-china.
18. Charles Tilly, *From Mobilization to Revolution* (Englewood Cliffs, NJ: Prentice Hall, 1978), 100–2.
19. Mark Lichbach, 'Deterrence or Escalation? The Puzzle of Aggregate Studies of Repression and Dissent', *Journal of Conflict Resolution* 31 (1987): 266–97; Mark Lichbach, *The Rebel's Dilemma* (Ann Arbor: University of Michigan Press, 1995); Mancur Olson, *The Logic of Collective Action* (Cambridge MA: Harvard University Press, 1965); Neil Smelser, *Theory of Collective Behavior* (London: Routledge and Kegan Paul, 1962).
20. Charles Brockett, 'A Protest-Cycle Resolution of the Repression/Popular Protest Paradox', *Social Sciences History* 17 (1993): 457–84; James de Nardo, *Power in Numbers* (Princeton, NJ: Princeton University Press, 1985); Marwan Khawaja, 'Repression and Popular Collective Action: Evidence from the West Bank', *Sociological Forum* 8 (1993): 47–71; Marwan Khawaja, 'Resource Mobilization, Hardship, and Popular Collective Action in the West Bank', *Social Forces* 73 (1994): 191–220; Johan Olivier, 'State Repression and Collective Action in South Africa, 1970 to 1984', *South African Journal of Sociology* 22 (1991): 109–17; David Snyder and Charles Tilly, 'Hardship and Collective Violence in France, 1830–1960', *American Sociological Review* 37 (1972): 520–32.
21. Terry Boswell and William J. Dixon, 'Marx's Theory of Rebellion: A Cross-National Analysis of Class Exploitation, Economic Development, and Violent Revolt', *American Sociological Review* 58 (1993): 681–702; Edward N. Muller, 'Income Inequality, Regime Repressiveness, and Political Violence', *American Sociological Review* 50 (1985): 47–61; Kurt Schock, 'A Conjunctural Model of Political Conflict: The Impact of Political Opportunities on the Relationship between Economic Inequality and Violent Political Conflict', *Journal of Conflict Resolution* 40 (1996): 98–133.
22. Osa and Schock, 'A Long, Hard Slog', 135–7.
23. Ibid., 135.
24. As claimed by Meyer and Staggenborg, 'strategy includes decisions about tactics, claims, targets, and alliances, and these decisions are interrelated'. David S. Meyer and Suzanne Staggenborg, 'Thinking about Strategy', in *Social Movements, Protest, and Contention, Volume 37: Strategies for Social Change*, ed. Gregory M. Maney, Rachel V. Kutz-Flamenbaum, Deana A. Rohlinger and Jeff Goodwin (Minneapolis; London: University of Minnesota Press, 2012), 6.
25. Ibid., 136.
26. Timur Kuran, 'Sparks and Prairie Fires: A Theory of Unanticipated Political Revolution', *Public Choice* 61 (1989): 41–74; Timur Kuran, 'Now Out of Never: The Element of Surprise in the East European Revolution of 1989', *World Politics* 44 (1991): 7–48.
27. Susanne Lohmann, 'The Dynamics of Informational Cascades: The Monday Demonstrations in Leipzig, East Germany, 1989–1991', *World Politics* 47 (1994): 42–101.
28. Fu and Cullen, 'Climbing the Weiquan Ladder', 51.
29. Ibid., 52.
30. I follow here the methods of classification of repressive measures identified by Turk. See Austin Turk, *Political Criminality. The Defiance and Defence of Authority* (Beverly Hills, CA: Sage Publications, 1982).
31. Ibid.
32. Ibid.
33. Eva Pils, '"Disappearing" China's Human Rights Lawyers', in *Comparative Perspectives on Criminal Justice in China*, ed. Mike McConville and Eva Pils (Cheltenham, UK: Edward Elgar, 2013), 418.
34. Charges such as 'subversion' and 'inciting subversion of state power' (Article 105 of the 1997 Criminal Law), along with 'splittism' and 'inciting splittism' (Article 103), and 'leaking of state secrets' (Articles 111 and 398) are generally characterised as crimes of 'endangering state security' and punished with relatively long periods of imprisonment. Other vague provisions such as

'creating disturbances' (Article 293) or 'gathering a crowd to create public disturbance' (Article 291) are also frequently used to silence rights defenders.

35. The 1979 Criminal Procedures Law (CPL) and its later revisions (1996, 2012) allow two distinct forms of residential surveillance, which differ depending on the location where the measure is carried out – either in or around the criminal suspect's place of residence or, in exceptional circumstances, in a residence designated by the police (*zhiding jusuo*). When there is 'no fixed residence' or 'in cases involving offences of endangering state security, terrorism or extremely serious corruption' (Article 73, 2012 Criminal Procedure Law), the law does not require for notification of the families about the detainees' whereabouts or the charges they face. Over time, such exceptions have been used to widen the scope of 'residential surveillance', which has merged with other extra-legal measures including enforced disappearance or *incommunicado* detention.
36. Human Rights Watch, 'China: End Unlawful Practice of House Arrest', 24 October 2012, http://www.hrw.org/news/2012/10/24/china-end-unlawful-practice-house-arrest.
37. Under the 2006 Passport Law (Article 13(7)) and the 2012 Entry-Exit Law of the PRC (in force from 1 July 2013) (Article 12(5)(6)), officials may prevent Chinese citizens from travelling abroad when they believe that this might harm 'state security' or harm or cause 'major loss' to national interests. The meaning and scope of 'harm to state security' or 'harm or loss to national interests' are left purposely undefined to allow a broad degree of official discretion and arbitrary enforcement. China Aid Association, 'Three Lawyers Barred from Leaving China to Attend US Human Rights Forum', 2 January 2011, http://www.chinaaid.org/2011/02/three-lawyers-barred-from-leaving-china.html.
38. Yaxue Cao, 'Drinking Tea with the State Security Police – Who Is Being Questioned?', *Seeing Red in China*, Comment posted 11 March 2012, http://seeingredinchina.com/2012/03/01/drinking-tea-with-the-state-security-police-who-is-being-questioned/.
39. Tania Branigan, 'China Officials Shut Legal Aid Centre', *The Guardian*, 18 July 2009, http://www.theguardian.com/world/2009/jul/18/china-shuts-legal-aid-centre.
40. Human Rights Watch, *Walking on Thin Ice*.
41. In 2007, the Law on Lawyers was amended and in 2008 the Ministry of Justice issued the Methods for the Management of Law Firms and the Methods for the Management of Lawyers' Practice imposing an 'annual inspection and assessment process' (*niandu jiancha kaohe*).
42. One of the most extreme cases is represented by the disbarment from the profession of the two Beijing lawyers Tang Jitian and Liu Wei in 2010. Human Rights in China, 'Beijing Judicial Bureau Revokes Licenses of Two Rights Defence Lawyers', http://www.hrichina.org/en/content/398.
43. Following the release of the Guiding Opinions on Lawyers Handling Collective Cases in 2006.
44. Fu and Cullen and Pils offer a systematic classification of *weiquan* lawyers according to 'a pyramid of *weiquan* lawyering' including moderate, critical and radicals. Moderate represents the majority of the lawyers, those who try to protect the rights and interests of the Chinese citizens without significantly challenging the legal and institutional constraints defined by the state. Critical lawyers are those who criticise China's current legal and political conditions, but who express their criticism with a certain degree of caution. They work at an individual-case level, but they also propose longer-term legal and political reforms. Lastly, radical lawyers challenge both the legal and political status quo by taking up extremely sensitive cases which involve the so-labelled 'enemies' of the state. Legal defence is accompanied with radical criticism of the political and legal systems. Fu and Cullen, 'Climbing the Weiquan Ladder'; Fu and Cullen, '*Weiquan* (Rights Protection) Lawyering in an Authoritarian State'; Pils, 'Asking the Tiger for His Skin'.
45. Fu, 'Can Lawyers Build a Legal Complex'.
46. Susan Trevaskes, 'The Ideology of Law and Order', in *The China Story Yearbook 2012. Red Rising, Red Eclipse*, ed. Geremie Barmé (Canberra, Australia: Australian National University, 2012), 66–87.
47. Rongjie Lan, 'Killing the Lawyer as the Last Resort: The Li Zhuang Case and Its Effects on Criminal Defence in China', in *Comparative Perspectives on Criminal Justice in China*, ed. Mike McConville and Eva Pils (Cheltenham, UK: Edward Elgar, 2013), 304–21. See also the articles on: http://special.caixin.com/event_0422_1/index.html.
48. On Zhou's approach to law and justice at the time the cases presented here unfolded see: Trevaskes, 'The Ideology of Law and Order'.

49. Yueran Zhang, 'China's All-Star Legal Team Pleads for Defendants' Rights on Social Media', *TeaLeafNation*, 25 July 2012, http://www.tealeafnation.com/2012/07/bilingual-brew-chinas-all-star-legal-team-pleads-for-defendants-rights-on-social-media/.
50. Ibid.
51. 'Yuanyu fangfan yu lüshi zuowei' (Preventing Wrongful Imprisonment and the Role of Lawyers), *Xinpo pinglun*, 22 December 2013, http://news.sina.com.cn/pl/2013-12-22/08222 9050181.shtml.
52. Re-education through labour (RTL) was a form of administrative detention administered by the public security organs, allowing detention without trial for up to three or four years for prostitutes, petty thieves, those judged to have disrupted social order, people involved in unlawful religious activity and even petitioners. The system was formally abolished at the beginning of 2013.
53. Black jails are unlawful detention facilities where individuals, very often petitioners, could be held incommunicado. See: Human Rights Watch, 'China: Secret "Black Jails" Hide Severe Rights Abuses', 12 November 2009, http://www.hrw.org/news/2009/11/02/china-secret-black-jails-hide-severe-rights-abuses.
54. Human Rights in China, 'Lawyers Detained in Jiansanjiang, Heilongjiang', 26 March 2014, http://www.hrichina.org/en/citizens-square/photos-lawyers-detained-jiansanjiang-heilongjiang.
55. Associated Press, 'Four Chinese Rights Lawyers Allege Torture by Police', *The Guardian*, 16 April 2014, http://www.theguardian.com/world/2014/apr/15/chinese-rights-lawyers-police-torture.
56. On the difficulties experienced by Chinese lawyers in criminal defence work, see: Elisa Nesossi, *China's Pre-Trial Justice. Criminal Justice, Human Rights and Reforms in Contemporary China* (London: Wildy, Simmonds and Hill, 2012), 136–72; Elisa Nesossi, 'Compromising for "Justice"? Criminal Proceedings and the Ethical Quandaries of Chinese Lawyers', in *Comparative Perspectives on Criminal Justice in China*, ed. Mike McConville and Eva Pils (Cheltenham, UK: Edward Elgar, 2013), 256–78; Hualing Fu, 'When Lawyers Are Prosecuted ... The Struggle of a Profession in Transition', *The Journal of Comparative Law* 2 (2007): 95–133.
57. On the risks associated with reformist projects, see: Osa and Schock, 'A Long, Hard Slog', 128–9.
58. Craig Calhoun, *Neither Gods Nor Emperors. Students and the Struggle for Democracy in China* (Berkeley and Los Angeles: University of California Press, 1994); Dingxin Zhao, *The Power of Tiananmen: State-Society Relations and the 1989 Beijing Student Movement* (Chicago: The University of Chicago Press, 2001).
59. Kevin J. O'Brien and Li Lianjiang, *Rightful Resistance in Rural China* (New York: Cambridge University Press, 2006); Elizabeth J. Perry, *Challenging the Mandate of Heaven. Social Protest and State Power in China* (New York: M.E. Sharpe, 2002); Chen, *Social Protests and Contentious Authoritarianism.*
60. Ching Kwan Lee, *Against the Law: Labor Protests in China's Rustbelt and Sunbelt* (Berkeley and Los Angeles: University of California Press, 2007), 17.
61. Pils, 'Asking the Tiger for His Skin'; Hualing Fu and Richard Cullen, '*Weiquan* (Rights Protection) Lawyering in an Authoritarian State'.
62. Lianjiang Li, 'Rights Consciousness and Rules Consciousness in Contemporary China', *The China Journal* 64 (2010): 47–68; Mary Gallagher, 'Mobilizing the Law in China: "Informed Disenchantment" and the Development of Legal Consciousness', *Law and Society Review* 40 (2006): 783–816; Merle Goldman, *From Comrade to Citizen. The Struggle for Political Rights in China* (Cambridge, MA; London: Harvard University Press).
63. Chen, *Social Protests and Contentious Authoritarianism*, 16.
64. Yinan Zhao, 'Xi Pledges to Implement Rule of Law', *China Daily*, 12 May 2012, http://www.chinadaily.com.cn/china/2012-12/05/content_15985873.htm.
65. Benjamin Liebman, 'China's Courts: Restricted Reform', *The China Quarterly* 191 (2007): 620–38.
66. Nesossi, *China Pre-Trial Justice.*
67. Fu, 'Can Lawyers Build a Legal Complex for the Rule of Law in China?'
68. Fu and Cullen, '*Weiquan* (Rights Protection) Lawyering in an Authoritarian State'; Pils, 'Rights Activism in China'; Nesossi, 'Compromising for "Justice"?'
69. Consider, for example, the suggestions sent to the National People's Congress (NPC) by lawyers Xu Zhiyong, Teng Biao and Yu Jiang that led to the abolition of the system of 'custody and

repatriation' (*shourong shencha*) in the aftermath of Sun Zhigang's death, or, the 2013 suggestions sent to the NPC by 11 *weiquan* lawyers calling for the revision of the 1990 Regulations on Detention Centres. See: Keith Hand, 'Using Law for a Righteous Purpose: The Sun Zhigang Incident and Evolving Forms of Citizens Action in the Peoples' Republic of China', *Columbia Journal of Transnational Law* 45 (2006): 114–95; Xinhuawang, '11 ming lüshi jianyi xiugai "kanshousuo tiaoli" jinzhi qiangpo laodong' (Eleven Lawyers Suggest Revising the 'Detention Centres Regulations' and Prohibiting Forced Labour), *Xinhua News*, 18 March 2013, http://big5.xinhuanet.com/gate/big5/news.xinhuanet.com/legal/2013-03/18/c_124471564.htm.

70. Fu, 'Can Lawyers Build a Legal Complex for the Rule of Law in China?'
71. See, for example: Carl Minzer, 'Judicial Disciplinary Systems for Incorrectly Decided Cases: The Imperial Chinese Heritage Lives On', *New Mexico Law Review* 39 (2009): 63–88; Ira Belkin, 'China's Tortuous Path toward Ending Torture in Criminal Investigations', *Columbia Journal of Asian Law* 24 (2011): 273–302.
72. See Boaventura de Sousa Santos and Cesar Rodrigues Garavito, *Law and Globalization from Below, Toward a Cosmopolitan Legality* (Cambridge: Cambridge University Press, 2005); Margaret E. Keck and Kathryn Sikkink, *Activists beyond Borders. Advocacy Networks in International Politics* (Ithaca, NY: Cornell University Press, 1998); Osa and Schock, 'A Long, Hard Slog', 131.
73. See, for example, the work done by CHINAaid on freedom of religion: http://www.chinaaid.org/2014/03/law-and-religious-training-seminars.html.
74. Gerda Wielander, *Christian Values in Communist China* (Oxon and New York: Routledge, 2013), 140.
75. From private conversations with Chinese *weiquan* lawyers.
76. Nicola Macbean and Elisa Nesossi, 'Living Up to Human Rights Responsibilities: Lawyers and Law Firms in the Chinese Authoritarian Context', in *Human Rights Protection in Global Politics: Responsibilities of States and Non-State Actors*, ed. David Karp and Kurt Mills (London: Palgrave Macmillan, forthcoming 2015), 180–200.
77. As of 1979, there were only 69 newspapers in the country, all fully controlled by the State-Party and reporting primarily political propaganda. See: Benjamin Liebman, 'Watchdog or Demagogue? The Media in the Chinese Legal System', *Columbia Law Review* 105 (2005): 17; Marina Svensson, Elin Saether, and Zhi'an Zhang, eds, *Chinese Investigative Journalists' Dreams. Autonomy, Agency, and Voice* (Lanham, MD: Lexington Books, 2013), 7.
78. Karin Deutsch Karlekar and Jennifer Dunham, 'Freedom of the Press 2014. Press Freedom in 2013: Media Freedom Hits Decade Low', *Freedom House*, http://www.freedomhouse.org/sites/default/files/FOTP2014_Overview_Essay.pdf.
79. China.org.cn, 'Mass Media', http://www.china.org.cn/english/features/Brief/193358.htm.
80. Qiang Gang and David Bandursky, 'China's Emerging Public Sphere: The Impact of Media Commercialization, Professionalism, and the Internet in an Era of Transition', in *Changing Media Changing China*, ed. Susan Shirk (Oxford: Oxford University Press, 2011), 40.
81. Benjamin L. Liebman, 'Changing Media, Changing Courts', in *Changing Media Changing China*, ed. Susan Shirk (Oxford: Oxford University Press, 2011), 153.
82. Svensson, Saether, and Zhang, *Chinese Investigative Journalists' Dreams*, 1.
83. Ibid., 7.
84. See for example: Biao Teng, 'China's Growing Human Rights Movement Can Claim Many Accomplishments', *The Washington Post*, 18 April 2014, http://www.washingtonpost.com/opinions/chinas-growing-human-rights-movement-can-claim-many-accomplishments/2014/04/18/7c5fb650-c707-11e3-bf7a-be01a9b69cf1_story.html.
85. The Chinese authorities appreciate the power of the internet and are strictly controlling it. Thus, Section Five of the 1997 Computer Information Network and Internet Security, Protection, and Management Regulations approved by the State Council provides, among others, that the internet should not be used to 'incite splittism' or 'destroy the order of society' – vague clauses that are easily abused in cases involving individuals who are deemed politically sensitive. Since 2010, new legal and institutional structures have been created to further strengthen the state's control over the internet.
86. Osa and Schock, 'A Long, Hard Slog', 137.
87. Nesossi, 'Compromising For "Justice"?'
88. Fu, 'Can Lawyers Build a Legal Complex for the Rule of Law in China?'
89. Ibid.

90. Beijing Yirenping Center, http://www.yirenping.org/.
91. Ibid.
92. China Human Rights Defenders, http://chrdnet.com.
93. China Human Rights Lawyers Concern Group, http://www.chrlawyers.hk.

Violence and human rights in Russia: how human rights defenders develop their tactics in the face of danger, 2005–2013

Freek van der Vet[a] and Laura Lyytikäinen[b]

[a]*Aleksanteri Institute, University of Helsinki, Finland;* [b]*Department of Social Research, University of Helsinki, Finland*

Between 2005 and 2013, the Russian State Duma passed legislation restricting the activity of human rights defenders (HRDs). Although these measures complicate their work, this study contends that Russian HRDs creatively manage constraints. Through an interview study, this article contributes to the literature on human rights defence in dangerous circumstances by identifying the coping practices of two groups of HRDs: opposition youth activists in Moscow and human rights lawyers in the Northern Caucasus. Here, we argue that those activists at high risk often reinvent their tactics to counter curtailing legislation, experiment with the boundaries of police violence and manage the fear of fellow activists.

Introduction

Defending human rights in Russia can be perilous. One only needs to recall the killings of human rights defenders (HRDs, *pravozashchitniki*), investigative journalists and lawyers like Anna Politkovskaya, Stanislav Markelov, Anastasia Baburova or Memorial activist Natalia Estemirova. Opposition activists also face physical danger. In February 2015 Boris Nemtsov, an opposition leader and former first deputy prime minister during Yeltsin's second presidency, was shot dead near the Kremlin in Moscow. Moreover, some organisers and participants of demonstrations have faced prosecution and imprisonment.

Not all HRDs in Russia face these physical threats, yet most HRDs have to confront legal constraints to their work. Since 2005, the Russian authorities have implemented legislation isolating the political opposition and curtailing the funding of HRDs. The State Duma passed the 'foreign agent law', or law No. 121-FZ, in 2012 in an attempt to restrict the activity of non-governmental organisations (NGOs) that receive foreign funding and engage in 'political activities'. These laws affect the whole spectrum of civil, cultural and human rights associations, yet, Tatiana Lokshina, a Human Rights Watch (HRW) representative in Moscow, is concerned that 'those behind the [2012 NGO legislation] most likely meant it to be used selectively, against particularly bold critics of the government'.[1] In March 2013 local prosecutors launched inspections into the offices of organisations and began preparing administrative and civil lawsuits against those who refused registration.[2]

In this article we argue that an analysis of state restraints and violence contributes to our understanding of how HRDs choose to reinvent their human rights practices in response to dangerous circumstances and legal restraints. While they certainly limit the activity of HRDs, constraints to human rights work can also be an opportunity for the innovation of new tactics. Research repeatedly shows that HRDs (along with intergovernmental human rights institutions) are key actors who define how rights are practiced at the local level.[3] HRDs choose to develop their tactics during their interaction with the government authorities and the police. International reports often ascertain that new political constraints directly impact the conduct of HRDs in Russia.[4] Nevertheless, this study argues that the effects of such measures are slower and that repression facilitates how HRDs strategically calculate the development of new activities.

In this article, we analyse the tactics of two groups of activists in two separate areas of contention: young protest leaders in Moscow who defend the right to freedom of assembly and an international network of human rights lawyers that provides free legal aid to victims of grave atrocities in the Northern Caucasus. The recent legislation, as explained in the next section, affects all NGOs and social movement organisations, including those HRD groups and protest activists that openly criticise the government.[5] However, the two groups in this study face different degrees of risk, with the physical risk of HRDs in the Northern Caucasus being many times higher than the dangers faced by youth activists.[6] Another difference is the arena in which these HRDs operate: while protest activists make claims in the public space and media, lawyers prefer more ‘quiet’ strategies such as litigation and often shun the public space because of a fear of coming across as ‘partisan’. A final difference between these cases is that, while the protest movement activists challenge the authorities in the public sphere and wish to remain anti-institutional, the lawyers working in Chechnya work ‘behind the scenes’ and rely on legal institutions to achieve justice. In addition, while activist groups rarely represent individual cases of human rights violations, lawyers work to promote human rights protection through legal aid to individuals.

Despite their apparent differences, we chose these case studies because they illustrate the wide spectrum of challenges faced by HRDs and opposition activists in contemporary Russia. This article aims to dissolve the division between analyses of legal and public protest in Russia by examining the repertoires of youth protesters and HRDs and how they choose to interact with government actors and the police and how they strategically calculate their responses to new legislation. This article aims to categorise the challenges to HRDs in Russia from 2005 to 2013 and map out the HRDs’ responses to it. By comparing these two apparently separate groups of HRDs, this article highlights how HRDs working under the same restrictive legal conditions have come to employ comparable tactics to challenge and change the legal and political system in their country. Human rights work is a practice that involves a great amount of strategic planning. In particular, it defines the HRDs’ common responses to three challenges of high-risk activism: (a) how to organise advocacy and protest in risky situations, (b) how to manage risk and fear, and (c) how to use domestic and international legal mechanisms in a repressive state?

Accordingly, the article consists of five sections. The first section theorises the constraints of human rights activism under Russia’s contemporary political regime. The subsequent three sections present how these two groups of HRDs respond to the three challenges mentioned above. The conclusion discusses the implications of these findings for the protection of HRDs across the world.

Legislation, danger and activism

The regulation of activism in Russia, 2005–2013

Russia's political system is a hybrid – located between an authoritarian and a democratic system. Vladimir Gel'man specifies that this political system of 'electoral authoritarianism' combines aspects of a democratic system (elections with meaningful competition) with features of authoritarianism (manipulating ballots and curtailing the activity of political opposition).[7] Richard Sakwa brands Russia a 'dual state': a normative state defined by constitutional order and law, combined with an administrative regime defined by informal relations, such as exchanging favours (*blat*) for administrative benefits or material goods.[8]

This hybrid political system has had its effect on the development of a civil society sector. Some have argued that the Putin administration had a plan to design civil society from the 'top down'[9] or redefine state–society relations.[10] Yet, recent endeavours by the authorities to limit foreign funding and curtail civic activity are certainly not a novel trend in Russia. It is part and parcel of a political system's technique of safeguarding the status quo.[11] Daucé argues that these measures intend to make a clearer divide between political party activities and civil society activities as well as cut the financial links between foreign funding agencies and NGOs.[12]

The most recent legal reforms of civil society fall into two periods. The first period, from 2005 to 2006, starts with the introduction of an anti-extremism law in 2005. This legislation raised concern with the international community because its vague language invites broad interpretation.[13] In 2006, the State Duma passed another round of legislation regulating the national registration of NGOs and cultural associations with the Ministry of Justice.[14] It limited the foreign funding of political parties and NGOs and increased the powers of authorities to inspect and intervene in the activities of NGOs. These laws created the Federal Registration Service, which has the mandate to investigate the accounts of any organisation and can ultimately close down associations.[15] Carothers famously labelled these measures part of the global 'backlash against democracy promotion'.[16] Some argue that limiting the foreign funding to activist groups was to avert a possible 'colour revolution' of the sort that had spread across Eastern Europe during the 2000s.[17]

The law also had a much wider impact on civil society with criminal charges against organisations or their leaders, police inspections and the arbitrary use of extremism legislation.[18] For instance, the Nizhny Novgorod Province Court ordered the dissolution of the Russian-Chechen Friendship Society under the extremism law in 2007. Moreover, the lawyers of the Centre for International Protection, an organisation that provides legal aid to prisoners, were prevented from representing victims before the European Court.[19] According to state representatives, some of these lawyers were allegedly involved in fraud and fabrication of their powers of attorney.[20]

The second period of legal reform followed the mass protests after the 2011–2012 parliamentary and presidential elections. For the first time since the political reforms and protest in the 1990s, a large number of citizens had protested against election results (this time, the re-election of Vladimir Putin).[21] To counter the growing public demonstrations, the Kremlin adopted a harsher stance towards the renewed collaboration of opposition movements after Putin's inauguration as president in 2012.[22] The new laws increased the fines for participation in unauthorised public demonstrations, modified existing laws on treason and recriminalised libel. In July 2012, the Duma adopted law No. 121-FZ – or, foreign agent law – which stipulates that NGOs that engage in 'political activities' and receive financial funding from abroad are required to register as a 'foreign agent' (*inostrannyi agent*) with the Ministry of Justice. NGOs which register as foreign agents are subject to further reporting restrictions. The law defines political activity as participating 'in organizing and implementing political actions aimed at influencing the decision-making by state bodies intended for the change of state policy pursued by them, as well as in the shaping of public opinion for the above mentioned purposes'.[23] While many NGOs resist registration as foreign agents, the laws have subjected NGOs to public vilification.[24] For instance, in November 2012, 'Foreign Agent' and a heart with 'USA' were sprayed on the walls of Memorial's office.[25]

Human rights monitors and academics are divided over the impact of these legal measures during these two periods. HRW predicted that the laws would curtail the development of a healthy civil society and threaten freedom of assembly.[26] Sean Roberts states that 'the Putin administration is trying to intimidate with laws intended to shock opponents with their potential for use'.[27] In contrast, Javeline and Lindemann-Komarova argued that the existing interpretations on the relation between the legislation and the 'crackdown' of Russian civil society in the period 2005–2006 fail to assess the impact of these laws, as they focus on the accounts of a handful of high-profile defenders working in Moscow.[28] Moreover, Richter reveals that few NGOs receiving funding from abroad were banned after 2006.[29] Quoting Javeline and Lindemann-Komarova, Richter underlines that the legislation was still more supportive of civil society than that under the Yeltsin regime.[30]

Richter argues that the reforms did not intend to suppress NGOs, but 'sought to redefine the relation between state and society [...] to coordinate Russian social organizations in the interests of the whole'.[31] Especially in the regions, NGOs often nurture a fruitful cooperation with local authorities to provide welfare benefits and services to citizens, such as distributing medication.[32] Before 2012, opportunities and risks for civic activism in Russia depended heavily on whether the NGOs would oppose the state or cooperate with it to provide social services.[33] Reflecting on the period after 2012, Daucé argues that the foreign agent law has had an ambiguous effect. On the one hand, the law intends to cut financial links with foreign funders and brands human rights organisations as 'foreign agents'. On the other hand, the state is providing its own funding for these groups.[34] This duality and the vagueness of the laws creates confusion amongst organisations as, first, they have to choose to submit or oppose the law, and second, it limits cooperation between NGOs as they are forced to respond to the new legislation on their own.[35]

HRW reports that some of these observers 'sorely underestimate the effect that these combined measures have had on civil society'.[36] HRW reports that the political environment for HRDs has deteriorated even further since 2012.[37] After Putin returned to the presidency in May 2012, the Russian government tightened its grip over political and human rights activism. According to a HRW report: '[t]he authorities have introduced a series of restrictive laws, [they have] harassed, intimidated, and in several cases imprisoned political activists, interfered in the work of nongovernmental organizations (NGOs), and sought to cast government critics as clandestine enemies, thereby threatening the viability of Russia's civil society'.[38] The Bolotnaya 6 case illustrates the restrictive legal environment that anti-government protesters operate in. Several demonstrators were arrested and prosecuted for mass rioting and violence against police after a demonstration at the Bolotnaya Square on 6 May 2012, which was organised to protest Putin's inauguration as president. Hundreds of protesters were arrested, 26 people were placed under investigation, and 12 were put on trial. Ten accused were sentenced to 2.5–4.5 years in prison in February 2014.[39]

In the Bolotnaya 6 case, observers reported numerous violations of Russian law and the rights of the defendants.[40] In November 2013, when detention of the accused was extended to February 2014, the defendants' lawyers claimed that the extension violated the principles established by the European Convention on Human Rights.[41] The European Court of

Human Rights (ECtHR) requested information from the Russian state about the conditions of the detained.[42]

The following section discusses the impact of the legislation on the work of HRDs and activists in Russia. In particular, it reassesses the connection between repressive measures and the high costs of participation in civic activism.

Reassessing risk in activism

HRDs frequently work under violent, life-threatening circumstances. They challenge the state by revealing hidden or denied violations. As a result, HRDs often become targets of persecution themselves.[43] They are often arbitrarily arrested, detained, threatened, killed and targeted by judicial investigations.[44] Charles Tilly defines repression as an action '... which raises the contender's cost of collective action'.[45] These repressive 'actions' can include: legislation to increase the reporting duties of human rights organisations to the state, rules that enable authorities to inspect organisations, or the criminalisation of participation in public demonstrations. Due to these repressive measures, human rights and protest activism are often classified as high-risk activism.[46] The potential cost of involvement in high-risk activism for the activist – and one's household or family – is potentially higher than the benefits of openly opposing power-holders.[47]

The social movement literature on high-risk activism suggests that participation in activism entails an assessment of the costs and likely risk of participation – the 'anticipated dangers of engaging in a particular type of activity'.[48] Yet, high-risk activism involves more than a rational choice on behalf of the individual activist; participation often involves a deep emotional engagement and, in dangerous environments, a management of fear despite the high costs.[49] Participation in high-risk social movements results from the personal biography of the activist and his pre-existing networks.[50]

HRDs creatively choose to respond to the constraints on their work and actively manage fear, build legal literacy and mental resilience to counter the high costs of activism. The behaviour of activists is therefore only indirectly influenced by repressive measures. Instead HRDs, at times, use their own vulnerability towards state violence as a technique to draw public attention to their causes or try to find alternative ways of developing their organisation's strategies.

These strategies remain hidden as they are invented by practitioners and protest leaders 'off stage'.[51] Erving Goffman introduced the terms 'off stage' and 'on stage' to describe how humans present themselves depending on the public audience they face. The off stage is where people prepare for their performance or where they can abandon the roles they play in everyday life.[52] This distinction between on and off stage remains useful as it shows that activism is not as spontaneous as it first appears: it needs careful planning, networking and management to keep participants safe. For HRDs, the 'off stage work' creates a safe environment where fear and risk are managed and where activists are educated on legislation and interactions with the police. Similarly, Goodwin and Pfaff found that movement leaders often engage in behind-the-scenes 'emotion work' to manage the fears that participants have to cope with before they attend a public demonstration.[53] Other examples of behind-the-scenes work include the preparation of satire and humour in protest against the state.[54] Therefore, while the claims of human rights organisations may appear coherent and adamant from the outside, in fact HRDs have to overcome internal dilemmas: which rights to protect over others, which victims to represent, and whether to cooperate with or confront state authorities.[55] Their work involves a great amount of strategic deliberation on how to solve these dilemmas. These dilemmas and the strategic choices leading to their resolution often remain invisible as they are managed off stage.

This article aims to analyse some of these behind-the-scenes choices and dilemmas through examining the strategies of Russian youth activists and human rights lawyers and how they respond to three challenges: (1) how to do advocacy under risky circumstances; (2) how to manage fear and assess risk; and (3) how to use the domestic legal mechanisms in a repressive state? Before answering these questions, we will first introduce both case studies.

Case studies: Moscow's youth leaders and HRDs in Chechnya

Youth activists and opposition demonstrations in Moscow

In late 2009, Eduard Limonov, a popular author and leader of the National Bolshevik Party and the Other Russia Coalition, initiated the Strategy-31 protests in Moscow's Triumfalnaia Square. On the 31st day of every month, protesters rallied to remind the authorities to respect their right to freedom of assembly, guaranteed under Article 31 of the Constitution of the Russian Federation. Throughout 2010, various oppositional groups and public figures joined the Strategy-31 movement, for instance Boris Nemtsov of the Solidarity movement and Liudmila Alekseeva, leader of the Moscow Helsinki Group. Subsequently, the rallies spread to other cities, such as St Petersburg and Yekaterinburg. The city authorities never authorised Strategy-31 demonstrations and frequently arrested dozens of participants.

This case analyses the practices in Strategy-31 from the point of view of the activists of the liberal oppositional youth group *Oborona* ('Defence') which organised and participated in the Strategy-31 rallies.[56] The Strategy-31 organisers responsible for the earlier protest cycles transferred their protest tactics to the more recent post-electoral protests.[57]

HRDs in Chechnya[58]

Russian human rights practitioners seeking redress for victims in the Northern Caucasus face exceptional challenges and threats to their work.[59] Several HRDs and investigative journalists – Anna Politkovskaya, Stanislav Markelov and Natalia Estemirova – were killed allegedly owing to their involvement in investigating grave atrocities in the Northern Caucasus or representing victims before domestic courts. Gilligan argues that the two conflicts in Chechnya (1994–1996 and 1999–2009) are among the most violent conflicts in contemporary world history.[60] Human rights monitors found both the federal military forces and the Chechen armed forces responsible for committing grave abuses, primarily enforced disappearances, abductions, extrajudicial killings, indiscriminate bombings and torture.[61] For this article, we focus on lawyers who give legal aid in post-conflict Chechnya and lawyers who assist their clients to lodge applications with the ECtHR.

A handful of human rights practitioners provide legal aid to victims and pursue state accountability through filing cases before the ECtHR. The majority of these lawyers work for renowned NGOs, for instance the Memorial Society in Moscow, which has monitored human rights violations in the Northern Caucasus since the first Chechen conflict.[62] The British European Human Rights Advocacy Centre in cooperation with Memorial (EHRAC-Memorial) and the Dutch-Russian Stichting Russian Justice Initiative (SRJI) continue to assist victims in the Northern Caucasus with their claims before the ECtHR.[63] Both NGOs have offices in Moscow and representatives in the Northern Caucasus. In addition, the Committee against Torture in Nizhny Novgorod also gives domestic legal aid to victims of recent abuses in Chechnya, but mainly represents victims of torture and ill-treatment during police detention.

The following sections examine how HRDs manage constraints and how they interact with the police and state authorities. It categorises the HRDs' responses to three challenges in human rights work.

Tactics for advocacy in dangerous situations

In this section, we examine the first challenge: how both groups of activists do advocacy under risky circumstances. The Moscow protesters adapted to and routinised the arrests during public demonstrations, while a group of HRDs adopted a mobile working group to give legal aid in post-conflict Chechnya.

Routinising demonstrations and arrests by Moscow's youth activists

While the Moscow city government rarely authorises demonstrations of the opposition, protest leaders continue to participate and organise these protests. Demonstrations remain important as they are the movement's only 'facade' through which it is seen by others.[64] By persistently organising protests to protect the freedom of assembly, the activists have established a routine and accumulated experience in organising unsanctioned protest events. Youth activists perceive unsanctioned demonstrations to be a necessity:

> [Participating in unsanctioned meetings] is not always a pleasant experience, because there are actions where arrests are almost guaranteed. But we must understand that it is absolutely necessary, anyway, once in a while to participate.[65]

Other activists perceive that 'hooligan activities' and provocation are a means to promote their goals and to draw media attention.[66] One of Oborona's leaders and a member of the organising committee of Strategy-31 claims that getting arrested can be a goal in itself:

> Sometimes, among your tactical goals is that you get arrested. It's normal; already Gandhi used this tactic a lot. But then you have to be arrested in a way that you expected.[67]

However, he argues that if the goal is to be arrested, it has to happen within control of the activists. When a demonstration's goal is to march from one location to another, then unwanted arrests are a failure. However, he states that getting arrested is sometimes more beneficial for publicity than a small peaceful march, which would not draw attention from the media.[68]

Some of the interviewed activists speak about arrests with either enthusiasm or anxiety. Though, after a while, the excitement of getting arrested wears off and they start to see the experience as a nuisance: 'it's usually boring. We are detained for several hours, and then released'.[69] Experienced activists anticipate their arrests and carry some additional clothing or even sleeping bags with them to make the night in jail more comfortable. Following a demonstration, activists who are not detained gather outside the police stations to wait for the release of the detained or bring them food and water. The procedure of getting arrested becomes a routine to many. In fact, some participants become so familiar with the police that they even discuss and joke with them in the detention centre. One of the activists noted this in his Facebook profile: 'interestingly, the same policemen who beat and drag people in the street, completely support us in private conversations'.[70] Routinising the arrests and getting familiar with the police lowers the threshold of participation in an unsanctioned demonstration and, thus, is a tactic aimed at helping people to join and stay in high-risk activism.

Providing frontline legal aid in Chechnya: the Joint Mobile Group

Like the protesting activists in Moscow, HRDs in Chechnya have created routines to minimise the risks and dangers of their work. After the abduction and killing of human rights activist Natalia Estemirova in 2009, the political environment changed dramatically for practitioners working in Chechnya. Estemirova was working on behalf of relatives of the disappeared for Memorial in Grozny. After her death, the President of the Chechen Republic, Ramzan Kadyrov, initiated a defamation case against Memorial's Director, Oleg Orlov, concerning Orlov's public claims about the Chechen authorities' involvement in Estemirova's abduction. The legal procedures against Orlov lasted for two and a half years until his acquittal in June 2011.[71] Owing to Estemirova's death and the heated court procedures against Orlov, Memorial closed down its Grozny office and scaled down its activities in the region.[72]

After Estemirova's death, it was deemed too dangerous for local HRDs to continue monitoring grave abuses in the region. Consequently, defenders were forced to adopt a flexible method in order to continue working in the region. A small group of HRDs provides legal aid in Chechnya with the Joint Mobile Group (JMG; *Svodnaia Mobil'naya Gruppa*). The JMG is a group of lawyers who travel to Chechnya for short periods to assist victims of recent violations with their claims to local courts. According to one member, 'the reason for setting up [the JMG] is clear: the purpose was to try and carry out civic investigations'.[73] The JMG mainly consists of HRDs who work for the Committee against Torture (*Komitet Protiv Pytok*, CAT), an NGO working in five regions.[74] CAT represents victims of torture and degrading treatment before domestic courts and the ECtHR. One practitioner reflects on his observations of the fear in post-conflict Chechnya:

> Last year I went for three weeks on a shift of the Joint Mobile Group. I, of course, was astonished. Probably, such a hopeless situation never existed there before. [...] Behind the facades [of the renovated city of Grozny] a fear exists that I even did not encounter during the worst days of the war when you needed to crawl on all fours to move around.[75]

The JMG employs various tactics: it consists of three to four HRDs who do not stay for more than a few months at a time to decrease the chances of violence against them.[76] Moreover, practitioners always travel together. In addition, video monitoring is an attempt to guarantee their safety in their apartment in Grozny and during transportation.[77] *The New York Times* reports that in 'their little car, they can activate a video camera and microphone in case of trouble and push a small red button on their dashboard to transmit sound directly to their main office 900 miles away'.[78]

Most of these practitioners face several challenges to providing assistance inside the Chechen Republic in comparison to giving legal aid in other regions. One lawyer elaborates on this difference:

> It's emotionally very hard to be under constant pressure. To be working there for three months is very difficult. When I am working [in Nizhny Novgorod] I only work on the European Court. There, I give legal aid. [...] How does it work in Chechnya? There, the investigation department is a concrete fortress, surrounded by a high fence. You will not be able to enter if the investigator does not come for you at a checkpoint where passes are issued. You need to

> call the investigator to get through. If he knows that you are there to complain about him, he will not pick up the phone. You say 'through my power of attorney I want to get acquainted with the materials'. He replies, 'we do everything according to law, we do not let you get access to the material, you can go to complain before the court'. This process takes a great deal of time.[79]

Throughout 2012, the pressure on both the CAT and JMG increased. In June 2012, members of the JMG were invited to a meeting with Chechen President Ramzan Kadyrov, where he expressed his anger about the activities of the JMG in the Chechen Republic.[80] Internationally, the group received praise for its work in the Northern Caucasus. In May 2011 Frontline Defenders, the international foundation for the protection of human rights defenders, gave JMG the Front Line Defenders Award.[81] In 2013 the JMG received the Martin Ennals Award for Human Rights Defenders.

Other practitioners who conducted research on human rights violations committed during the conflict in Chechnya were prosecuted due to their involvement in 'extremist' activities and publications. For instance, in December 2012, the Nizhny Novgorod's prosecutor filed a petition to ban the monograph 'International Tribunal for Chechnya' claiming that its authors were involved in 'extremist' activities.[82] The book promotes the establishment of an ad hoc international criminal tribunal for Chechnya.[83] One HRD involved in this project notes that: 'in case of harassment or pressure, there is no need to be afraid [...], instead we need to make sure that the club hitting us will hit them too'.[84] In July 2013, however, the Dzerzhinsk City Court in Nizhny Novgorod rejected the petition by the prosecutor's office which argued that the book had 'extremist' content. Instead the court accepted an expert report offered by the activists that argued that the book was a judicial and academic publication.[85]

Thus, the lawyers have enacted a strategy that uses the institutional legal framework for their own benefit: De Certeau refers to this as 'the weak' manipulating the framework created by 'the strong'.[86] The HRD states that the criminal charges brought public attention to the book:

> [...] The struggle against all these attacks takes time. It is emotionally exhausting. If they do initiate a criminal case, it is also good for us, because it is the best advertisement. [A colleague] already jokes about this to me: 'are you paying them for advertising you?' [...] Because, if there is a criminal case a lot of reporters come here [...].[87]

This is not to downplay the daily dangers for HRDs working in Chechnya. The JMG creatively adopts its way of working as a method for managing the risks and fear involved in providing legal aid in Chechnya. As with the youth organisation Oborona, the lawyers engage beyond their professional legal activities in 'emotional work' and routinise their visits to the Chechen Republic. Mobility is of vital importance to minimise constant pressure. The rotation of members, on the other hand, deflects target attacks to individuals within the group, which has a vertical, hierarchical structure. Despite these precautions, the JMG's office was burned down in December 2014. According to the activists it was set on fire by attackers, but the Chechen police reported it as an accident.[88]

Managing fear and risk

This section discusses the local tactics of HRDs in managing the fear in activism by building legal literacy and managing the dangers of applying to the ECtHR.

Building legal literacy and mental resilience before protests

HRDs further manage these hazardous circumstances through using law as a source of protection. The young activists participating in unsanctioned demonstrations in Moscow recognise the threat of violence and harm, for example getting fired from their jobs or suspended from university. They are familiar with the harassment of independent journalists and recognise that oppositional activists can face attacks as well:

> Being a journalist is very dangerous. In general, engaging in public activities is also fairly dangerous. At least, you should always keep in mind is that this [violent attacks] can happen.[89]

Besides facing violence from the police, participants in demonstrations face violence from unidentified hooligans, who they suspect of being paid by pro-Kremlin groups:

> […] a week ago, three or five mobsters attacked a picket. They looked like skinheads or hooligans. They were armed with chains and the strange thing was that there were no police around. […] They always bring the riot police even to our smallest actions.

However, he continues:

> Of course it [violence] won't prevent us from holding our actions but it may prevent many people from participating. Because not everybody is ready to be attacked physically by some skinheads armed with chains for just coming to a picket or a meeting.[90]

Despite the threat of violence against them, activists claim that they are not afraid and will not cease their activities. Goodwin and Pfaff argue that social movement leaders actively mitigate the fears of participants to generate courage and risk-taking behaviour.[91] Moreover, Russian youth activists have created tactics to manage their fear through their repetitive, and frequently violent, encounters with the authorities. Another activist reflects on this:

> One of the biggest benefits [of activism] is that I stopped being afraid of the police. I was really scared before. […] My knees used to shake [when meeting with the police]. Now I know how to communicate with them. I know what I need to say to them, [and] where to remain silent, and that gives me confidence. I'm not afraid of them.[92]

These encounters with the authorities have also created a feeling of confidence and 'legal literacy' for some of the activists:

> It's such a great experience. At least, I am not completely defenseless in the legal sense, if a police officer tries to inspect me.[93]

In special seminars, leaders and guest speakers train activists to be aware of their rights and how to defend them. These seminars are also open to the public and the activists hope to convey this 'legal literacy' to all Russians so that they would not be afraid and 'would understand their rights and learn how to defend them'.[94] Activists often claim that fear and vulnerability vis-à-vis the authorities and the state 'system' are the roots of the apolitical mentality of Russians.

Furthermore, humour and irony are efficient ways to manage fear and to challenge apathy.[95] Russian youth groups often use humour, ridicule and irony in smaller-scale actions or flash mobs, in their self-made placards in demonstrations and on their websites.[96] According to one of the youth movement leaders, using humour is like judo, Putin's favourite sport, in regard to using the opponent's power against him.[97] Sharp defines this practice as 'political jiujutsu'.[98] Activists build their mental resilience by becoming literate about their legal rights and how to use humour in protest as a way of deflecting violence. They train in how to counter the police and can therefore routinise the experience of being arrested, which helps them to overcome part of the fear of violence. Humour, in addition, gives the police a human (and often ridiculous) face.

Managing the fear of litigating before the ECtHR

The activists involved in public protests build legal literacy and resilience to manage fear in protest events. Lawyers in Chechnya also aim to create strategies to manage their clients' fears and to prepare them to face threats from the authorities.[99] One significant opportunity spurred organisations to seek justice across Russia's borders: Russia's ratification of the European Convention of Human Rights in 1998. This watershed event allows for HRDs to litigate before the ECtHR on behalf of victims from the second conflict in the Chechen Republic. Two organisations are their main representatives: EHRAC-Memorial and SRJI. They aim to seek state accountability and individual remedies related to indiscriminate bombings, enforced disappearances, torture and extrajudicial executions.[100] Between 2005 and 2014, the court found violations of the convention in over 250 of their applications. By applying to the ECtHR, the practitioners evade the non-cooperation of the Russian state in domestic investigations, and force the authorities to comply with the convention and provide remedies to victims. While the Russian state follows through on paying financial compensation, both organisations continue to advocate for further implementation of the ECtHR's judgments, such as the re-opening of investigations.[101] Consequently, the ECtHR's mounting judgments become leverage to pressure the state to comply with the convention or to initiate truth-seeking processes on the violent conflict.[102]

Applications to the court can be dangerous for lawyers and their clients.[103] SRJI describes the various perils that lawyers encounter:

> Any travel requires crossing numerous military checkpoints where soldiers routinely solicit bribes. Private persons do not have telephones, email or other modern means of communication. Material evidence of human rights violations often does not exist or is almost impossible to obtain. Witnesses often feel vulnerable and intimidated, and are reluctant to step forward.[104]

For instance, relatives of victims of enforced disappearances were unlawfully detained after they had lodged a claim before the ECtHR.[105] A lawyer explains that when they select a new case, the client's awareness of the danger has an impact on their choice:

> It happens that some applicants just drop their cases. Then, everything we did on the domestic level […] was in vain. To avoid this, we try from the start to agree with the applicant that he will not abandon his appeal […] Now, only a part of our applicants abandon their cases. But mostly the applicants waive their cases due to threats from the authorities.[106]

In this sense, the lawyers have to manage the expectations of their clients and inform them about the procedures of the court.[107] As with the youth group Oborona, the lawyers engage in building their clients' legal literacy of their human rights.

Consequently, an application before the court entails a strategic selection by the lawyers of those applicants who are willing to pursue their claim until the end, even when they are in danger of receiving threats or are made offers to abandon their claims against the Russian authorities.[108] Therefore, making applications to the court includes a risk that is managed by the practitioner.[109] The lawyers explain from the very beginning that an application can be dangerous.

Using legal mechanisms against the state

This section examines the tactics that involve obedience or disobedience to law and the use of alternative registration of NGOs. Some HRDs use legal mechanisms as a means of protection, while others consciously challenge the boundaries by using their own vulnerability.[110]

Demonstrating police violence during protests

HRDs aim to challenge the state by seeking protection in domestic legal mechanisms. The objective of the Strategy-31 demonstrations was to draw attention to the Russian constitution that guarantees the right to peaceful assembly, but which the state does not respect. Despite the small size of the gatherings, protesters managed to attract the attention of journalists, bloggers and foreign media.

The liberal oppositional groups employ Gandhian non-violent resistance tactics that diffused from the American Civil Rights movement to activists in Eastern Europe's 'colour revolutions'.[111] One inspiration for them is Gene Sharp's *From Dictatorship to Democracy*, a popular non-violent resistance handbook first published in Burma in 1993.[112] To perform their own non-violence and to demonstrate police violence against peaceful protesters, the activists consciously put themselves into a situation in which violence is anticipated. The protesters play different roles during a protest event; some push through to the heart of the demonstration, shout and fight the police. Familiar faces to the police are regularly arrested. Behind this front line of participants are other protesters and bystanders that observe and shout slogans but try to stay out of contact with the police. According to one of the author's observations, the protesters in Strategy-31 demonstrations test the boundaries and tolerance of the authorities by pushing through areas closed to the public or by challenging police orders. Frequently, this disobedience leads to arrests. Some protesters fiercely resist arrest while others lay immobile on the ground forcing several policemen to carry them to the police vans. The protester who resists arrest usually faces police violence.[113]

Following the protest event the activists claim that these arrests and police violence was illegal and disproportionate. After a demonstration, protest participants and activist-journalists publish a selection of pictures on blogs and on social media sites about the violent treatment by the police, especially against young people, women and the elderly. For example, the arrest of the elderly Liudmila Alekseeva received worldwide condemnation after pictures of the arrest spread through the internet.[114] In subsequent demonstrations, the police did not interfere when Alekseeva walked into areas closed to other protesters. Some activists note that the police do not arrest women because they are afraid of a 'scandal':

> Police arrest mostly young men, they tend to not touch young women. It would be a big scandal if something happens to them [women]. Therefore, usually the girls stay, and young men are taken away somewhere.[115]

Even if most of the protesters are men, women and other groups represented as 'weak' play an important symbolic role in demonstrating police violence. Kuzio argues that young women played an important role in Serbian protests in 2000, breaking down the distrust between law enforcement and the revolutionaries.[116] Women protesters were usually marching in front of a demonstration because the police were less likely to attack women. And if women were beaten, pictures with blood-stained young women in newspapers and on the internet worked in favour of the opposition.[117] The gendered practices of Russian protesters draw on a patriarchal understanding of gender differences that remains influential in contemporary Russia and shapes the roles men and women play in political activism.[118]

In addition, the lodging of lawsuits by arrested demonstrators is a related practice. While the chance of winning a case is small, filing several claims after a demonstration is a way to burden the authorities and use their own legal framework against them. Frequently these cases are not opened for investigation, but the activists consider that they 'should do everything [they] can to make their [the authorities] lives more miserable'.[119]

Exploring legal alternatives: NGO registration and protection by the ECtHR

HRDs in Chechnya and elsewhere in Russia use legal mechanisms to find alternatives to the burdensome registration procedures enacted by the state between 2006 and 2012. The annual reporting is an increasing bureaucratic burden to NGOs.[120] Especially since the adoption of the 'foreign agent law' in 2012, NGOs and individual HRDs have been the target of administrative and civil lawsuits for their failure to register as a foreign agent. In some cases, NGOs were able to win these lawsuits.[121] Some organisations chose to shut down, for instance, the Anti-Discrimination Center Memorial in Saint-Petersburg and JURIX Lawyers for Constitutional Rights and Freedoms.[122]

Before the adoption of the 'foreign agent' law, it appeared to be easier for NGOs to work around their problems with registration within the boundaries of the law. The Ministry of Justice has the power to strike out a foreign NGO from its registry; it cannot strike out a Russian NGO without a court hearing. One HRD indicated that the establishment of their NGO in 2001 was initially risky, but with the aid of HRW's experts, they could register as a foreign NGO working in Russia:

> We are a fund. The organization is Dutch. In other words, in the beginning when the organization was founded, the idea was to investigate crimes in the Northern Caucasus and the lodging of cases with the [European] Court. It was difficult back then to establish such an organization in Russia, because of the ongoing conflict and military operations in the Caucasus. [...] Through the support of Human Rights Watch the decision was made to set up a fund in The Netherlands in Utrecht. To have all the registrations there, so that they would not shut us down.[123]

Another HRD adds that 'there has never been a permanent office in Utrecht. So it is just a matter of the configurations that will allow you to work most efficiently and get around the restrictions.'[124]

The NGOs are careful to conform to the restrictive NGO laws and stay within the law. Despite these precautions, in 2012, due to a mistake in its registration report, SRJI was struck off the registry by the Ministry of Justice[125]:

> The NGO law that came into force in 2006 has much more restrictive or draconian provisions for regulating the activities of foreign NGOs. One of those provisions has to do with the actual registration of the office. What happened to us was that we made a mistake in our reporting requirements. We acknowledged this mistake: it was not intentional, but a human error. But

> still, they struck us out of the registry, just like that. They have the power to do that under Russian law […] It was quite a shock when we received the letter that stated that 'you don't exist anymore'.[126]

As a precaution, the organisation created a partner organisation as a back-up if the organisation were to face problems with its annual registration: '[they] can only strike out a Russian NGO through court. So you have a little bit more protection'.[127] One lawyer explains that:

> Well, the shell of it already did exist, which was fortunate. Basically it was the foresight of some former staff members. The organization already had registration problems in 2006–2007 when the NGO law came into force and all the foreign NGOs were obliged to reregister. We failed to reregister twice as a branch office. So, after the second rejection they set up this [organization] as a backup, but then we were registered on the third attempt.[128]

Resource centres for civil society organisations in Russia have proposed alternative tactics. A representative of the St Petersburg Human Rights Resource Center (HRRC) explored several possible tactics to get around the foreign agent law, for instance by registering an NGO as a commercial entity.[129] The HRRC also continues to report on the effects of the law in St Petersburg and give legal aid to NGOs affected by it.[130]

Besides using the domestic legal system, the ECtHR mechanisms provide a vital international protection mechanism for HRDs. On 6 February 2013, 11 NGOs (including Memorial and the Moscow Helsinki Group) lodged an application with the ECtHR alleging that the 'foreign agent' law violates their freedom to expression and assembly guaranteed under Articles 10 and 11 of the European Convention on Human Rights.[131] Although it is too early to tell the potential impact of this case, it highlighted to an international audience the law's potential debilitating effect on Russian civil society. In the immediate wake of their complaint, prosecutors started inspections into the activities of Russian organisations and began to prepare administrative and civil lawsuits against a selection of those who refused to register in March 2013. From May 2014 onwards, the Ministry of Justice was given the authority to register NGOs as foreign agents on its own initiative.

Conclusion

This article explored how HRDs behave in a hybrid political regime and how they choose to interact with police, courts and government officials. In particular, the article categorised the various responses of two groups of Russian HRDs to three challenges of high-risk activism in the period 2005–2013: (a) how to organise advocacy and protest in risky situations, (b) how to manage risk and fear, and (c) how to use domestic and international legal mechanisms in a repressive state. By comparing two separate areas of contention – public protest and litigation before courts – this article goes beyond studies on institutional politics in hybrid authoritarian regimes and highlights how HRDs working under the same restrictive legal conditions have come to employ comparable strategies. We have argued that despite international concern on new restrictive legislation, Russian HRDs use the remaining legal opportunities and develop tactics to manage fear, assess risk and voice grievances on behalf of marginalised communities.

These findings do not underestimate the dangers to their work. While this article covers the period 2005–2013, the pressure on NGOs and HRDs has increased over 2014 and the beginning of 2015 when domestic prosecutors decided to launch a series of lawsuits against

NGOs refusing to register as 'foreign agents'. Since then the legal and political environment in which the HRDs work has changed. These changes diminished NGO cooperation and further complicated cooperation with government institutions.[132] How the opposition activists and HRDs have adapted to these changes falls beyond the scope of this article but demands further research. We emphasise that those HRDs who are at risk have no choice but to respond to the political curbs by routinising the experience of danger and fear during protest through legal education, by confronting new laws, by testing boundaries of police violence, or by seeking legal alternatives to registration.

This discussion suggests two broader implications to the study of human rights defenders across the world. First, this article reshapes the way we commonly perceive HRDs as being 'heroic' and coherent in their actions. Instead, human rights work is a practice that involves behind-the-scenes strategic calculation: HRDs have to overcome dilemmas and fear in their daily work through craftiness and creativity.[133] Second, in a legal system where laws are ambiguous, they can be interpreted selectively, not only by government authorities, but also by the HRDs themselves. This duality is a cause for confusion as each HRD has to negotiate its position vis-à-vis the local government.[134] Russian HRDs therefore balance between a constant pressure to reinvent their tactics to challenge the state within the boundaries of the domestic legal mechanisms and the hazards of using tactics that might further jeopardise the activist and his or her cause. The Russian NGO legislation has changed often and rapidly within the last decade; this has forced NGOs to find the legal resources to adapt to an ever-changing environment. In this changeable environment, HRDs need to continuously evaluate and develop their tactics to maintain their activities and avoid criminal prosecution or violence. Consequently, human rights protection programs could better aid HRDs to stay informed of their legal and practical opportunities and support their already existing ability to creatively reinvent their local tactics.

Acknowledgements

The authors wish to thank the editors Alice Nah, Karen Bennett, James Savage and Danna Ingleton for hosting the workshop on the protection of human rights defenders at the University of York (UK), for their support, and for their critical comments. We also wish to express our gratitude to the external reviewer (Lutz Oette) and the Associate Editor (Lars Waldorf) for their supportive comments on previous versions of this manuscript. Finally, we would like to thank Markku Lonkila, Lisa McIntosh Sundstrom, and the members of the Helsinki Political Sociology seminar for their suggestions to improve the article.

Disclosure statement

No potential conflict of interest was reported by the author.

Funding statement

This work was completed under the Finnish Distinguished Professorship (FiDiPro) project 'Regimes, Institutions and Change: Politics and Governance in Russia in a Comparative Perspective' at the Aleksanteri Institute, University of Helsinki. A part of this research was completed under the Finnish Graduate School for Social Sciences (SOVAKO), the Finnish Graduate School for Russian and East European Studies, and with the support of Academy of Finland mobility grants.

Notes

1. Tanya Lokshina, 'Russia's Civil Society Crackdown Continues', 25 September 2012, http://globalpublicsquare.blogs.cnn.com/2012/09/25/russias-civil-society-crackdown-continues/ (accessed 21 April 2015).
2. Human Rights Watch, 'Russia: Government against Rights Groups', 18 January 2015, http://www.hrw.org/news/2015/01/18/russia-government-against-rights-groups (accessed 20 April 2015).
3. Paul Gready and Brian Phillips, 'An Unfinished Enterprise: Visions, Reflections, and an Invitation', *Journal of Human Rights Practice* 1, no. 1 (2009): 1–13; Robin Redhead and Nick Turnbull, 'Towards a Study of Human Rights Practitioners', *Human Rights Review* 12, no. 2 (2011): 173–89.
4. Human Rights Watch, *An Uncivil Approach to Civil Society: Continuing State Curbs on Independent NGOs and Activists in Russia* (New York: Human Rights Watch, 2009), http://www.hrw.org/sites/default/files/reports/russia0609webwcover.pdf.
5. Debra Javeline and Sarah Lindemann-Komarova, 'How We Assess Civil Society Developments: The Russia Example', *PONARS Eurasia Policy Memo*, no. 34 (2008): 1–6.
6. Amnesty International, *Confronting the Circle of Injustice: Threats and Pressure Faced by Lawyers in the North Caucasus* (London: Amnesty International, 2013), http://amnesty.org/en/library/asset/EUR46/003/2013/en/6af890a1-d79f-487d-bd39-2af4020a5835/eur460032013en.pdf; Vanessa Kogan, 'Protecting Human Rights Defenders in the North Caucasus: Reflections on Developments from 2009 to the Present', *Journal of Human Rights Practice* 5, no. 3 (2013): 500–11.
7. Vladimir Gel'man, 'Subversive Institutions, Informal Governance, and Contemporary Russian Politics', *Communist and Post-Communist Studies* 45, no. 3–4 (2012): 295–303; Vladimir Gel'man, 'Cracks in the Wall: Challenges to Electoral Authoritarianism in Russia', *Problems of Post-Communism* 60, no. 2 (2013): 3–10.
8. Richard Sakwa, 'The Dual State in Russia', *Post-Soviet Affairs* 26, no. 3 (2010): 185–206; Alena Ledeneva, *Russia's Economy of Favours: Blat, Networking, and Informal Exchange* (Cambridge: Cambridge University Press, 1998).
9. Alfred B. Jr. Evans, 'Vladimir Putin's Design for Civil Society', in *Russian Civil Society: a Critical Assessment*, ed. Alfred B. Jr. Evans, Laura Henry, and Lisa McIntosh Sundstrom (London; New York: M.E. Sharpe, 2006), 147–158.
10. James Richter, 'The Ministry of Civil Society? The Public Chambers in the Regions', *Problems of Post-Communism* 56, no. 6 (2009): 7–20.
11. Robert Horvath, 'Putin's "Preventive Counter-Revolution": Post-Soviet Authoritarianism and the Spectre of Velvet Revolution', *Europe-Asia Studies* 63, no. 1 (2011): 1–25; Graeme B. Robertson, 'Managing Society: Protest, Civil Society, and Regime in Putin's Russia', *Slavic Review* 68, no. 3 (2009): 528–47.
12. Françoise Daucé, 'The Duality of Coercion in Russia: Cracking down on "Foreign Agents"', *Demokratizatsiya* 23, no. 1 (2015): 57–75.
13. F. Joseph Dresen, 'Anti-Extremism Policies in Russia and How They Work in Practice', *Wilson Center*, 2013, http://www.wilsoncenter.org/publication/anti-extremism-policies-russia-and-how-they-work-practice.
14. Federal Law #18-FZ, On Introducing Amendments to Certain Legislative Acts of the Russian Federation, 10 January 2006.
15. Richter, 'The Ministry of Civil Society?', 10.
16. Thomas Carothers, 'The Backlash against Democracy Promotion', *Foreign Affairs* 85, no. 2 (2006): 55–68.
17. Thomas Ambrosio, 'Insulating Russia from a Colour Revolution: How the Kremlin Resists Regional Democratic Trends', *Democratization* 14, no. 2 (2007): 232–52; Mark R. Beissinger, 'Structure and Example in Modular Political Phenomena: The Diffusion of Bulldozer/Rose/Orange/Tulip Revolutions', *Perspectives on Politics* 5 (2007): 259–76; Sidney

Tarrow, *The New Transnational Activism* (Cambridge; New York: Cambridge University Press, 2005), 107–13; Valerie J. Bunce and Sharon L. Wolchik, 'International Diffusion and Postcommunist Electoral Revolutions', *Communist and Post-Communist Studies* 39, no. 3 (2006): 283–304. These revolutions in Serbia, Georgia and Ukraine took place in the early 2000s and were seen to have started democratic 'transitions' in those countries.

18. Human Rights Watch, *Choking on Bureaucracy: State Curbs on Independent Civil Society Activism* (New York: Human Rights Watch, 2008), http://www.hrw.org/en/node/62400/section/1.
19. Ibid.
20. Ibid., 57–8.
21. Gel'man, 'Cracks in the Wall'.
22. Sean Roberts, *Russia's Pressure Politics: The Kremlin's Uncompromising Approach to Opponents Threatens Political Stability* (Helsinki: The Finnish Institute of International Affairs, 2012), 6, http://www.fiia.fi/en/publication/301/russia_s_pressure_politics/.
23. Human Rights Watch, *Laws of Attrition: Crackdown on Russia's Civil Society after Putin's Return to the Presidency* (New York: Human Rights Watch, 2013), http://www.hrw.org/node/115059.
24. Ibid.
25. Niklaus von Twinckel, 'NGOs Face 'Foreign Agent' Harassment', *The Moscow Times*, 21 November 2012, http://www.themoscowtimes.com/news/article/ngos-face-foreign-agent-harassment/471796.html.
26. Human Rights Watch, *Choking on Bureaucracy*; Human Rights Watch, *An Uncivil Approach to Civil Society*; Human Rights Watch, 'Russia: Reject Restrictions on Peaceful Assembly', 8 June 2012, http://www.hrw.org/news/2012/06/08/russia-reject-restrictions-peaceful-assembly.
27. Roberts, *Russia's Pressure Politics*, 7. Roberts finds, however, that targeted arrests were made. For instance, three members of the punk band Pussy Riot were arrested after they had staged a 'punk prayer' on 21 February 2012 in Moscow's Cathedral of Christ the Saviour.
28. Javeline and Lindemann-Komarova, 'How We Assess Civil Society Developments', 3.
29. Richter, 'The Ministry of Civil Society?', 11.
30. Ibid.
31. Ibid., 10.
32. Meri Kulmala, 'Russian State and Civil Society in Interaction: An Ethnographic Approach', *Laboratorium* 3, no. 1 (2011): 51–83.
33. Linda J. Cook and Elena Vinogradova, 'NGOs and Social Policy-Making in Russia's Regions', *Problems of Post-Communism* 53, no. 5 (2006): 28–41; Suvi Salmenniemi, *Democratization and Gender in Contemporary Russia* (New York: Routledge, 2008).
34. Daucé, 'The Duality of Coercion in Russia'.
35. Ibid.
36. Human Rights Watch, *Choking on Bureaucracy*, 4.
37. Human Rights Watch, *Laws of Attrition*.
38. Ibid.
39. Masha Gessen, 'Putin Shows His Iron-Fisted Hand', *Newsweek*, 24 February 2014, http://mag.newsweek.com/2014/02/28/putin-shows-iron-fisted-hand.html (accessed 19 April 2015).
40. Kathy Lally, 'Trial of Bolotnaya 12 Seen as a Warning against Challenging the Kremlin', *The Washington Post*, 2 November 2013, http://www.washingtonpost.com/world/trial-of-bolotnaya-12-seen-as-a-warning-against-challenging-the-kremlin/2013/10/29/5e1dec92-381f-11e3-89db-8002ba99b894_story.html (accessed 20 April 2015).
41. *The Moscow Times*, 'Judge Extends Bolotnaya Case Detentions Until February', *The Moscow Times*, http://www.themoscowtimes.com/news/article/judge-extends-bolotnaya-case-detentions-until-february/489946.html (accessed 22 November 2013).
42. Interfax, 'ECHR Requests Info from Russia on Bolotnaya Square Case, Expects Answer by Jan 17 – Lawyer', *Russia beyond the Headlines*, http://rbth.co.uk/news/2013/11/11/echr_requests_info_from_russia_on_bolotnaya_square_case_expects_answer_b_31640.html (accessed 22 November 2013).
43. Todd Landman, 'Holding the Line: Human Rights Defenders in the Age of Terror', *The British Journal of Politics & International Relations* 8, no. 2 (2006): 123–47.
44. Ibid., 141.
45. Charles Tilly, *From Mobilization to Revolution* (New York: Random House, 1978).

46. Mara Loveman, 'High-Risk Collective Action: Defending Human Rights in Chile, Uruguay, and Argentina', *American Journal of Sociology* 104, no. 2 (1998): 477–525; Doug McAdam, 'Recruitment to High Risk Activism: The Case of Freedom Summer', *the American Journal of Sociology* 92, no. 1 (1986): 64–90.
47. Rosanne Rutten, 'High-Cost Activism and the Worker Household: Interests, Commitment, and the Costs of Revolutionary Activism in a Philippine Plantation Region', *Theory and Society* 29, no. 2 (2000): 215–52.
48. McAdam, 'Recruitment to High Risk Activism', 67.
49. Jeff Goodwin, James M. Jasper, and Francesca Polletta, *Passionate Politics: Emotions and Social Movements* (Chicago: University of Chicago Press, 2001); Loveman, 'High-Risk Collective Action', 481.
50. Doug McAdam, *Freedom Summer* (Oxford: Oxford University Press, 1988).
51. James C. Scott, *Domination and the Art of Resistance: Hidden Transcripts* (New Haven, CT: Yale University Press, 1990).
52. Erving Goffman, *The Presentation of Self in Everyday Life* (New York: Anchor Books, 1959).
53. Jeff Goodwin and Steven Pfaff, 'Emotion Work in High-Risk Social Movements: Managing Fear in the U.S. and East German Civil Rights Movements', in *Passionate Politics: Emotions and Social Movements*, ed. Jeff Goodwin, James M. Jasper, and Francesca Polletta (Chicago: University of Chicago Press, 2001), 282–302.
54. Michael Lane Bruner, 'Carnivalesque Protest and the Humorless State', *Text and Performance Quarterly* 25, no. 2 (2005): 136–55.
55. Ron Dudai, 'Introduction – Rights Choices: Dilemmas of Human Rights Practice', *Journal of Human Rights Practice* 6, no. 3 (2014): 389–98.
56. Laura Lyytikäinen, *Performing Political Opposition in Russia : The Case of the Youth Movement Oborona* (Helsinki: University of Helsinki, 2014), https://helda.helsinki.fi/handle/10138/45024. Lyytikäinen collected the data among liberal youth movements in Moscow from 2009 to 2012. The data consist of 39 interviews, participant observations in five Strategy-31 demonstrations and in various other meetings, as well as activists' writings in online blogs and social media.
57. Graeme B. Robertson, 'Russian Protesters: Not Optimistic, But Here to Stay', *Russian Analytical Digest*, no. 115 (2012): 2–4; Denis Volkov, 'Protestnoe Dvizhenie v Rossii v Kontse 2011-2012 Gg.', *Scribd*, 2012, http://www.scribd.com/doc/108557232/Протестное-движение-в-России-в-конце-2011-2012-гг.
58. Data of this case were collected between 2009 and 2012. Van der Vet conducted 40 interviews with HRDs working for NGOs in Russia, the United Kingdom, Finland and the Netherlands. These associations primarily work on litigation projects before the ECtHR.
59. Amnesty International, *Confronting the Circle of Injustice*; Kogan, 'Protecting Human Rights Defenders in the North Caucasus'.
60. Emma Gilligan, *Terror in Chechnya: Russia and the Tragedy of Civilians in War* (Princeton, NJ: Princeton University Press, 2010). Although the end of the conflict is disputed, the year 2009 marks the end of the anti-terrorist campaign in Chechnya with the withdrawal of most of the Russian federal military forces.
61. Human Rights Watch, *'Who Will Tell Me What Happened to My Son?': Russia's Implementation of European Court of Human Rights Judgments on Chechnya'* (New York: Human Rights Watch, 2009), http://www.hrw.org/sites/default/files/reports/russia0909web_0.pdf.
62. Aleksander Cherkasov and Dmitry Grushkin, 'The Chechen Wars and the Struggle for Human Rights', in *Chechnya: From Past to Future*, ed. Richard Sakwa (London: Anthem Press, 2005).
63. SRJI: http://www.srji.org/en/, EHRAC-Memorial: http://ehracmos.memo.ru/.
64. Interview, activist 1, St Petersburg, May 2011.
65. Interview, activist 2, Moscow, April 2011.
66. Interview, activist 3, Moscow, March 2011.
67. Interview, activist 4, Moscow, October 2009.
68. Interview, activist 4, Moscow, October 2009.
69. Interview, activist 5, Moscow, May 2010.
70. Facebook account, Anonymous, September 2010.
71. *Russia Today*, 'Court Clears Rights Activist Orlov of Slandering Chechen Leader Kadyrov', 14 June 2011, http://rt.com/politics/clears-activist-libeling-chechen/ (accessed 20 April 2015).

72. Françoise Daucé, *Report: Russian Federation: Kadyrov vs. Orlov: The Defence of Human Rights on Trial* (The Observatory of the Protection of Human Rights Defenders, 2012), http://www.fidh.org/IMG/pdf/obsrapportru28022012eng.pdf.
73. Interview, HRD, Nizhny Novgorod, May 2011.
74. The Nizhny Novgorod *Oblast'*, the Republic of Bashkortostan, the Mari El Republic, the Chechen Republic and Orenburg *Oblast'*.
75. Interview, HRD, Nizhny Novgorod, May 2011.
76. Interview, HRD, Helsinki, March 2010.
77. Seth Mydans, 'Monitoring Rights in Chechen Region, a Month at a Time', *The New York Times*, 24 September 2011, http://www.nytimes.com/2011/09/25/world/europe/in-chechnya-human-rights-workers-from-afar-put-in-tours-of-duty.html (accessed 4 April 2015).
78. Ibid.
79. Interview, Lawyer, Nizhny Novgorod, May 2011.
80. Frontline Defenders, 'Russia: Members of Joint Mobile Group in Chechnya Subjected to Verbal Abuse and False Accusations by Chechen President and Local Authorities', *Frontline Defenders*, 7 June 2012, http://www.frontlinedefenders.org/node/18593.
81. Frontline Defenders, '2011 Joint Mobile Group Winner of the Seventh Front Line Award for Human Rights Defenders at Risk', 2011, http://www.frontlinedefenders.org/node/16876.
82. Human Rights Watch, 'Russia: Stop Efforts to Ban Human Rights Book: Local Authorities Go After Activist's Account of Chechnya Conflict', 3 July 2013, http://www.hrw.org/news/2012/12/03/russia-stop-efforts-ban-human-rights-book (accessed 20 April 2015).
83. Stanislav Dmitrijevski, Oksana Chelysheva and Bogdan Gvarely, *Mezhdunarodny Tribunal Dlya Chechni (Chast 1 & 2) (International Tribunal for Chechnya (Part 1 & 2))* (Nizhny Novgorod: Obshchestvo Rossisko-Chechenskoi Druzhby, 2009).
84. Interview, HRD, Nizhny Novgorod, May 2011.
85. Human Rights Watch, 'Russia'.
86. Michel de Certeau, *The Practice of Everyday Life*, 2nd edition (Berkeley: University of California Press, 2002).
87. Interview, HRD, Nizhny Novgorod, May 2011.
88. BBC, 'Chechnya Human Rights Office Set on Fire', *BBC News*, 14 December 2014, http://www.bbc.com/news/world-europe-30470085.
89. Interview, activist 6, Moscow, October 2010.
90. Interview, activist 4, Moscow, October 2009.
91. Goodwin and Pfaff, 'Emotion Work in High-Risk Social Movements', 285.
92. Interview, activist 7, Moscow, October 2009.
93. Interview, activist 2, Moscow, April 2010.
94. Interview, activist 8, Moscow, October 2009.
95. Majken Jul Sorensen, 'Humor as a Serious Strategy of Nonviolent Resistance to Oppression', *Peace & Change* 33, no. 2 (2008): 167–90.
96. Lyytikäinen, *Performing Political Opposition in Russia*; Bruner, 'Carnivalesque Protest and the Humorless State'.
97. Interview, activist 9, May 2009.
98. Gene Sharp, *The Role of Power in Nonviolent Struggle* (East Boston: Albert Einstein Institution, 1994), 13, http://www.aeinstein.org/organizationse4f0.html.
99. Freek van der Vet, 'Seeking Life, Finding Justice: Russian NGO Litigation and Chechen Disappearances before the European Court of Human Rights', *Human Rights Review* 13, no. 3 (2012): 303–25; Freek van der Vet, 'Holding on to Legalism: The Politics of Russian Litigation on Torture and Discrimination before the European Court of Human Rights', *Social & Legal Studies* 23, no. 3 (2014): 361–81.
100. Memorial reports that between 3000 and 5000 people have disappeared during the Chechen conflicts after their alleged unlawful detention by state agents. Memorial, 'Chechnya, 2004 God. Pokhishcheniia I Izcheznoveniia Liudei', 2005, http://www.memo.ru/hr/hotpoints/caucas1/msg/2005/02/m31404.htm.
101. Freek van der Vet, 'Transitional Justice in Chechnya: NGO Political Advocacy for Implementing Chechen Judgments of the European Court of Human Rights', *Review of Central and East European Law* 38, no. 3–4 (2013): 363–88.
102. Başak Çalı, 'The Logics of Supranational Human Rights Litigation, Official Acknowledgment, and Human Rights Reform: The Southeast Turkey Cases before the European Court

of Human Rights, 1996–2006', *Law & Social Inquiry* 35, no. 2 (2010): 311–37; Lisa McIntosh Sundstrom, 'Advocacy beyond Litigation: Examining Russian NGO Efforts on Implementation of European Court of Human Rights Judgments', *Communist and Post-Communist Studies* 45, no. 3–4 (2012): 255–68.

103. Van der Vet, 'Seeking Life, Finding Justice', 313; Roemer Lemaître, 'Can the European Court of Human Rights Provide Justice for Victims of Russian Human Rights Abuses in Chechnya?', in *Russia and the Council of Europe: 10 Years After*, ed. Katlijn Malfliet and Stephan Parmentier (Basingstoke; New York: Palgrave Macmillan, 2010), 165–85.
104. SRJI, *Russian Justice Initiative Annual Report 2002* (Moscow, SRJI: 2003), 9, http://www.srji.org/en/about/annual/.
105. http://www.srji.org/en/legal/security/ (accessed 1 March 2013).
106. Telephone interview, Lawyer, Ingushetia, May 2011.
107. Van der Vet, 'Seeking Life, Finding Justice'.
108. Loveday Hodson, *NGOs and the Struggle for Human Rights in Europe* (Oxford; Portland: Hart Publishing, 2011); Van der Vet, 'Seeking Life, Finding Justice'.
109. Van der Vet, 'Seeking Life, Finding Justice'.
110. Alice M. Nah et al., 'A Research Agenda for the Protection of Human Rights Defenders', *Journal of Human Rights Practice* 5, no. 3 (2013): 401–20.
111. Sean Chabot, 'Framing, Transnational Diffusion, and African-American Intellectuals in the Land of Gandhi', in *International Review of Social History Supplements (No. 12), Popular Intellectuals and Social Movements: Framing Protest in Asia, Africa, and Latin-America*, ed. Rosanne Rutten and Michiel Baud (Cambridge: Cambridge University Press, 2004), 19–40; Tarrow, *The New Transnational Activism*.
112. Gene Sharp, *From Dictatorship to Democracy: A Conceptual Framework for Liberation* (Boston, MA: Albert Einstein Institution, 2003).
113. See also Randall Collins, 'The Micro-Sociology of Violence', *The British Journal of Sociology* 60, no. 3 (2009): 566–76.
114. Ellen Barry, 'Russian Dissident's Passion Endures Despite Tests', *The New York Times*, 12 January 2010, http://www.nytimes.com/2010/01/12/world/europe/12dissident.html (accessed 23 April 2015).
115. Interview, activist 10, Moscow, April 2010.
116. Taras Kuzio 'Civil Society, Youth and Societal Mobilization in Democratic Revolutions', *Communist and Post-Communist Studies* 39, no. 3 (2006): 365–86.
117. Ibid.
118. See Anna Rotkirch, *The Man Question : Loves and Lives in Late 20th-Century Russia* (Helsinki: University of Helsinki, Department of Social Policy, 2000); Suvi Salmenniemi, 'Civic Activity–Feminine Activity? Gender, Civil Society and Citizenship in Post-Soviet Russia', *Sociology* 39, no. 4 (2005): 735–53; Laura Lyytikäinen, 'Gendered and Classed Activist Identity in the Russian Oppositional Youth Movement', *The Sociological Review* 61, no. 3 (2013): 499–524.
119. Interview, activist 4, Moscow, October 2009.
120. Human Rights Watch, *Choking on Bureaucracy*.
121. Human Rights Watch, 'Russia'.
122. Ibid.
123. Interview, Lawyer, Moscow, December 2010.
124. Interview, Lawyer, Moscow, June 2012.
125. Claire Bigg, 'NGO's Legal Woes Threaten Pursuit of Justice for Chechens', *RadioFreeEurope/RadioLiberty*, 10 April 2012, http://www.rferl.org/content/russian_justice_initiative_struck_off_chechen _atrocities/24543341.html (accessed 24 April 2015).
126. Interview, Lawyer, Moscow, June 2012.
127. Ibid.
128. Ibid.
129. Presentation, Human Rights Council of St Petersburg, December 2012.
130. HRRC, *Inostrannye Agenty': Mificheskie Vragi I Real'nye Poteri Rossiiskogo Obshchestva* (St Petersburg: Human Rights Resource Center, 2015), http://www.hrrcenter.ru/public/detail.php?ID=1763.
131. Memorial, 'My Ne Agenty!', *Pravozashchita*, 2013, http://www.memo.ru/d/145816.html.
132. Daucé, 'The Duality of Coercion in Russia'.
133. Dudai, 'Introduction – Rights Choices'.
134. Daucé, 'The Duality of Coercion in Russia'.

Index

For Product Safety Concerns and Information please contact our
EU representative GPSR@taylorandfrancis.com Taylor & Francis
Verlag GmbH, Kaufingerstraße 24, 80331 München, Germany